Human pain works its way out of our consciousness over time. There is a season of sadness. A season of anger. A season of tranquillity. A season of hope. But seasons do not follow one another in lockstep manner. At least not for those in crisis. One day we feel as though the dark clouds have lifted, the next day they return. One moment we can smile, a few hours later the tears emerge.

But people do survive their heartbreaks. We don't recover all at once. In fact, we recover slowly. Gradually. Sometimes in almost undetectable ways. But if we are patient, we begin to see the signs of healing. And the prospect of a new life starts to unfold.

Berean Community Church
3157 Kenosha Drive NW
Rochester, MN 55901
289-4179 www.bereancc.org

Also by Robert L. Veninga
Published by Ballantine Books:

THE WORK/STRESS CONNECTION:
  HOW TO COPE WITH JOB BURNOUT
  (with James P. Spradley)

A GIFT
OF HOPE

How We Survive Our Tragedies

Robert L. Veninga

BALLANTINE BOOKS • NEW YORK

Library of Congress Catalog Card Number: 85-18149

ISBN 0-345-33760-3

This edition published by arrangement with Little, Brown and Company, Inc.

Manufactured in the United States of America

First Ballantine Books Edition: November 1986
Eighth Printing: November 1991

This book is dedicated to my colleague and friend:

JAMES P. SPRADLEY, PH.D.
(1933–1982)

DeWitt Wallace Professor of Anthropology
MACALESTER COLLEGE

Contents

Acknowledgments

There are a number of people who deserve thanks for their contributions to this project. Barbara MacIntyre gave valuable assistance and enthusiastic encouragement when the book was but an idea. She introduced me to a group of wonderful people who helped me understand the complexity of human loss and the process by which people overcome their heartbreaks.

I am appreciative of colleagues who took the time to read portions of the manuscript and who made valuable suggestions. These include Richard Hey, James Kincannon, Barbara Leonard, Lois Lindbloom, and Barbara Spradley. I am particularly indebted to Barbara Spradley for her ideas, encouragement, and friendship.

I want to thank Frank Veninga for his careful editing of each typewritten page and for the helpful suggestions given by Otila Veninga.

I want to thank Susan Lescher of the Lescher and Lescher Literary Agency, who voiced enthusiasm and gave helpful advice.

And special thanks must be given to William D. Phillips, senior editor, Little, Brown and Company, whose insights, suggestions, and ideas are imprinted throughout the book.

In particular, I want to acknowledge my debt to the person to whom this book is dedicated. James P. Spradley was an acclaimed anthropologist and a prolific author. Through his writings he touched the lives of students, colleagues, and untold numbers of people who benefited from his wisdom. He lived life with a zest and zeal that is rarely encountered. He was my mentor. A coauthor. And a friend whose presence continues to be felt.

Finally, I want to express appreciation to Karen Veninga, who gave many hours to this project. Her insights contributed greatly to the final product. I specifically want to acknowledge her assistance on Chapter 5. But more than for the technical suggestions, I want to thank her and our son, Brent, for their never-ending love and support.

ROBERT L. VENINGA
ST. PAUL, MINNESOTA

Author's Note

I am indebted to one hundred and fifteen individuals who let me into their lives and into their hearts. They have entrusted me with their pain and joy, their sorrows as well as their hopes. I have made a covenant with each that I would not abuse their trust. Therefore all persons in the case studies have been disguised to protect their anonymity. Some have been fictionalized although the essential truths within their stories have been carefully preserved. Unless footnoted, all names and geographical locations are pseudonymous.

*Great ideas come into the world as gently as
doves. Perhaps, then, if we listen attentively, we
shall hear, amid the uproar of empires and na-
tions, a faint flutter of wings, the gentle stirrings
of life and hope. Some will say that this hope lies
in a nation; others in a man. I believe, rather, that
it is awakened, revived, nourished by millions of
solitary individuals whose deed and works every
day negate frontiers and the crudest implications
of history. . . . Each and every man, on the foundation of his own suffering and joys, builds for all.*

—ALBERT CAMUS

O N E

Straight from the Heart

> *In the midst of winter, I finally learned that there was in me an invincible summer.*
> —ALBERT CAMUS

My friendship with Jim Spradley was relatively brief. But in the span of five years we became like trusted brothers. We would meet for breakfast and talk about work and new projects. We would share dreams and sometimes disappointments. Frequently we would plan weekend vacations for our families. We kept few secrets from one another. I would trust him with my life. And he would trust me with his.

But he died after a fifteen-month illness.

The day after the funeral I met my students at the University of Minnesota. I started to lecture but suddenly felt overwhelmed with emotion. All the events of the past twenty-four hours flooded my mind. I couldn't continue. I told the students what had happened.

To my surprise at least half of them stayed after class to talk. Reassurances were given. Even a few hugs. Heartaches, I have learned, bring people together.

I sat down weary, exhausted by all that had happened.

But then I noticed a graduate student waiting for me in the back of the classroom. When our eyes met, he said, "It will take time, but you will recover."

I was a bit offended by the quick reassurance and the tone of certainty. After all, what did he know about my heartbreak? How did he know that I would recover? What were his credentials to speak so boldly?

I quickly learned. His wife had died in a car accident thirteen months earlier. They had been looking forward to the birth of their first child.

I asked how it happened. He said it was a head-on crash. The driver of the other car was drunk. "I thought my life was over," he commented. "I loved her. I still can't imagine living without her." He talked about the gentleness of his wife and the anticipation of being a father.

But then he vented his anger. Much of the anger was directed toward the drunk driver. But some was directed toward friends and relatives who kept telling him to cheer up and move on with life.

"But you can't move on," he commented. "There's no button to push that cheers you up. You have to absorb all that has happened." He paused, reflecting on every word. "Sometimes I think you need to feel hopeless before you feel a shred of optimism."

As I drove home, I recalled his parting words: "It will be difficult. But in time you will get over your heartbreak. And you may discover a beauty about life that you have never known."

Under any other circumstance I might have dismissed the reassurance. But not after hearing his experience. For everything he shared came straight from the heart.

The following weeks were not easy as I struggled with my feelings of aloneness. I missed my friend's telephone calls and the exchange of ideas. But most of all I missed the encouragement that he gave to me and so many other people.

Fortunately I had good colleagues who expressed kind thoughts. But I have to tell you this. Deep down inside I wondered whether anybody understood what I was going through. I frankly doubted that anyone could understand in their soul my sense of loss and estrangement.

Months passed and I found myself changing. I became more contemplative, less urgent. And I found myself thinking about other people facing similar heartbreaks.

One day I walked through a large hospital not too far from my home. I saw a man who had lost most of his hair standing by a nursing station. I knew that he had been on chemotherapy.

Then I went by the surgery suite and saw the apprehension in a young man's eyes as he was being led through the big green doors.

I went by the neonatal unit and saw a two-day-old youngster hooked up to a life-support system. The parents were looking at their child through a glass window. I overheard them talking and I sensed their bravery. But I also sensed that they knew that life could turn against itself.

As I walked through the hospital, I kept asking: How do we survive the injustices that life puts in our path? How do we survive the loss of precious people? How do we cope when a terrifying diagnosis is given? And how can we ever believe in God—or in the goodness of life—when that which makes life so rich and beautiful is suddenly taken from us?

I decided to find out. I visited physicians and psychologists, nurses and chaplains. I asked them what they had learned in helping people through difficult crises.

They were agreed on two points: First, most everyone is changed by a crisis. Second, most people do in fact survive. And often they survive with a new purpose and a new direction. As a psychologist said: "Sometimes the new life is better than the old."

I agreed with the first point, for I knew that I had already been changed by my friend's death. But I had some reservations about the optimism. I wasn't so sure that the new life would be better than the old. I knew it would be different. But better?

The only way to find out, I reasoned, was to interview people who had experienced tough times. I wanted to talk with cancer patients and parents who had lost a child. I wanted to interview women who had been abused and spouses who had been divorced. I wanted to understand farmers who were faced with financial problems and land foreclosures. Finally, I wanted to visit with people like myself. People who had lost their best friend.

I located one hundred and fifteen individuals, each of whom had suffered a severe loss. I asked them to write their stories, for sometimes it is easier to put feelings on paper than it is to discuss them.

Then I selected twenty-five individuals for in-depth oral interviews.

As I listened to their stories, I heard sadness. But I also heard stories of triumph. People rebuilding their lives. Individuals starting over.

I learned much in the two and a half years it took to complete this project. I learned that people can get very angry. But they can also become very tender. I learned that people feel very alone after a heartbreak. But they also find a strength that they never knew they had.

Most of all, I learned much about faith. Why people abandon their faith. Why they return to it. And how the substance of faith comforts and sustains when everything seems bleak and hopeless.

After completing the interviews, I decided that I wanted

to share with others what I had learned, and that led to the writing of this book. The book is organized as follows.

The first step in overcoming a heartbreak is to understand what it does to us. In Section One we will learn the characteristics of a crisis as well as the characteristics of those who survive difficult times.

Section Two focuses on practical strategies for overcoming a heartbreak. We will learn how to take care of our health in a period of much stress. We will learn how families react to a crisis and how to strengthen family relationships during trying times. We will discover the importance of friends and support groups and learn how to select competent professional help. And we will discover why faith is such a powerful force in mending a broken heart.

But we will also learn why it is so difficult to get over a crisis.

Some people do all the right things to recover from a heartbreak. They seek professional help. They join support groups. They pray. They think positive thoughts.

But the pain doesn't go away.

A surprisingly large number of people think suicidal thoughts after experiencing a heartbreak. In Section Three we will learn what you should do if you feel suicidal. And we will learn how to find comfort when a loved one prematurely ends his or her life.

Finally, we will examine the toughest crisis of them all—death. We will visit a hospice and discover people who die with regrets, bitter about their past and distraught over their future. But we will learn the secrets of those who die peacefully, even when the pain does not let up.

I want to make a promise at the outset of our journey. There will be few platitudes and few pious pronouncements. My own experience with grief suggests that there are few simple answers.

But I am convinced of one thing: People do survive their

heartbreaks. It doesn't happen all at once. In fact, it happens slowly. Gradually. Sometimes in almost undetectable ways.

But if one is patient, the signs of healing begin to be observed. And the prospect of new life starts to unfold.

The Anatomy of a Crisis

T W O

The Stages of
Heartbreak

Nobody knows the trouble I've seen.
Nobody knows my sorrows.
—NEGRO SPIRITUAL

Marie Fisher was brought to a hospice to die.[1] Seven thousand rads of high energy radiation could not stop the cancer from spreading throughout her body. The hospice seemed to be the last stop for this frail fifty-three-year-old woman, depleted after months of therapy.

Upon being escorted to her room Marie made the observation that, while everyone expected her to die, it wasn't exactly what she had in mind. With a hint of fire in her eyes she informed the head nurse that she was going to get well. What's more, she intended to leave the hospice not in a wheelchair, but on her own strength.

Two days later Marie's health was rapidly failing. A nurse speculated that her heart was simply giving out. Three days later she slipped into apnea, a condition that is a forerunner of death. One minute she would take in a deep breath. Then endless minutes would seemingly pass before another breath was drawn. There was a general recognition that she wouldn't last out the night.

Marie, however, would not cooperate with death. Deep in her being was a tenacious hold on life that was more powerful than the forces that were pushing her to die.

An oncologist who was monitoring her condition shook his head in disbelief as he listened to a heartbeat that grew steadily stronger. A nurse noted that the vital signs were beginning to stabilize. When it was announced that Marie's blood pressure had reached 110/80, a quiet cheer went up in her room. "She simply would not give up," said her physician.

In the weeks that followed Marie was determined to get out of bed and walk a few steps every day. She was equally determined to set new goals for herself, for, after all, there were people she wanted to see and a huge stack of paperback novels that needed to be read.

But then came the setback. The cancer had spread into her pancreas. Not even high doses of morphine could control the pain.

An oncologist indicated that a surgical procedure might alleviate some of the discomfort. "However," he cautioned, "you should know that you are not a good surgical risk. Just getting you through the anesthetic would be an accomplishment."

Along with her thoughts, Marie examined her options. An hour later she signed the forms permitting the surgery to take place. She reasoned that there was a pretty good chance that the surgery might bring relief. More important, it might give her added life. The next day she successfully completed a three-hour operation.

While there was no sign of remission, Marie's bodily

functions gradually returned to normal. "I'm feeling stronger every week," she confided to a roommate. Soon she was walking with little pain. Then she abandoned her hospital gown in favor of street clothes, for, as she told a nurse, "A hospital gown is a symbol of sickness." And then she asked the question that had been on her mind ever since she had entered the hospice: "When can I go home?"

"I'll never forget the day Marie left the hospice," said Catherine Holmberg, the chief nurse in the unit. "Marie was radiant. She put on a bright red dress accented with a white scarf. You could tell that she was proud of every step she was taking. If there was any pain she wasn't going to tell anybody about it.

"The word quickly spread that Marie was leaving. The patients came out of their rooms and the nurses stopped all their tasks as they watched her walk down the hall with her head held high. Then someone started to clap. Pretty soon we all joined in. A few tears ran down the cheeks of some of the nurses. All we could do was marvel at her courage. She had survived."

Of course not everyone is as fortunate as Marie Fisher.

To understand Jonathan Blakefield you need to realize that the single most important thing to him in life was his sixteen-year-old son, Mike. They hunted and fished together and were loyal Chicago Cubs fans. They had one of the best father-son relationships you will ever see.

On a fateful evening, Mike was playing in one of the most important basketball games of the year. During the first three quarters Mike dominated the play. He was blocking shots, tearing down rebounds, and was the second leading scorer.

Four minutes into the fourth quarter the unthinkable happened.

During a time-out, Mike clutched at his side and collapsed on the hardwood floor. On the way to the hospital he died—a sixteen-year-old victim of a myocardial infarction.

"How could a sixteen-year-old have a heart attack?" asked his father. "How could a body be healthy one minute and dead the next?"

One week later, in a moment of total despair, he committed suicide.

> *Crisis: Opportunity riding on dangerous winds.*
> —ANCIENT CHINESE DEFINITION

Marie Fisher and Jonathan Blakefield represent two different responses to a heartbreak.

Jonathan, overwhelmed by sorrow, couldn't see any way out. Words of encouragement from relatives and friends didn't help. The prospect of better days wasn't reassuring. Sensing no exit from despair, he ended life.

Marie's situation was equally troubling, for she knew that physical survival was a remote possibility. But that wasn't the issue. The issue for Marie was how to survive psychologically. How to create meaning in a difficult situation. How to restore hope, regardless of whether there be one day, one month, or one year to live.

Most people recover gradually. In stages. And while everyone's experience is different, the attitudes, emotions, and feelings you will be reading about are fairly typical of those who have survived a broken heart.

Stage One: The Bombshell

There was a torrent of activity in the birthing room of Haverton Community Hospital. An obstetrician listened in vain for the heartbeat of the infant who was yet to be born. He promptly ordered a nurse to induce labor. Pitocin, a powerful drug designed to speed up contractions, quickly made its way into the mother's bloodstream.

Julie Morrow was acutely aware that something was wrong. She looked at her husband, who was witnessing the birth of their first child. They said nothing, but each knew that a nightmare was unfolding before their eyes.

Twenty-five minutes later their daughter was stillborn. The umbilical cord could be seen wrapped around the child's head, suffocating the youngster before she could inhale her first breath of life.

The shock was almost unbearable. Julie was given Seconal and fell into a deep sleep. Jack sat in an uncomfortable chair next to his wife's bed for most of the night. At 1:00 A.M. he walked down the hospital corridor to the nursery. Four healthy youngsters could be seen. A father, not knowing Jack's plight, pointed with pride to his son, who was less than an hour old.

"I was absolutely numb," said Jack. "And I didn't know what to do. I thought about calling my parents, but I didn't know what I would say. How would I tell them that their first grandchild had just died? I thought I should eat, but I wasn't hungry. I just felt paralyzed."

Numbness is defined as "devoid of sensation, devoid of emotion." The exploding bombshell puts most victims in a daze. Some go to bed and sleep. Some slump in a chair, gazing toward an unknown destination. And others turn to the telephone, hoping that a familiar voice will diminish their worst fears.

In the darkness of the night, Jack decided to go for a walk. "I must have walked several miles," he recalled. "And all I could think about were the joyous rituals Julie and I had gone through anticipating our child's birth." Jack thought about his first purchases—a stuffed animal and a baseball bat. He pictured the child's bedroom, which had been decorated with bright, cheerful wallpaper. He could picture the dresser, which was filled with clothes that Julie had carefully arranged. A special quilt she had selected was neatly folded and was awaiting the trip home from the hospital. And then he thought about Julie and how she would react once the sedative had worn off.

Upon awakening, Julie's first reaction was disbelief. "This never happened, did it?" she repeatedly asked whoever happened to be in her room. But then reality broke through the fog. Jack tried to comfort her, but she turned her face toward the wall. As much as she wanted to, she couldn't cry.

The period of numbness usually lasts twenty-four to thirty-six hours. And while everyone's reactions are unique, most heartbreak victims share three characteristics during this first stage of healing.

First, most have an inability to make decisions. The mind is overloaded with so many emotions and thoughts and questions that it is nearly impossible to be analytical and objective. Nor is it possible to concentrate. Thoughts move from one topic to another, often without an awareness of what was previously said.

Second, it is difficult to carry on meaningful conversations, even with trusted friends. The attention span is short. Victims may suddenly stop talking and forget what they were saying. It is not uncommon for crisis victims even to forget the names of close relatives and friends.

Nonverbal messages signal that trouble lies beneath the surface. The tone of the victim's voice may be euphoric one moment as an old friend stops by to offer comfort. But the next moment there are tears. Fingers often dance nervously on the tabletop, while frequent yawns and sighs suggest that a crisis is deepening.

The day after their daughter's death, Jack and Julie Morrow had difficulty talking to each other. Fragmented thoughts were expressed, but it was too painful to carry on a conversation. At times long hours passed and all that could be heard was a deafening silence. "There just wasn't much to say," commented Jack. They held each other's hands and gave each other hugs. But the touching seemed mechanized. It was almost a ritual to be performed rather than the spontaneous sharing of grief.

Third, most people in this first stage of crisis are extremely anxious. Even those who appear calm. For some the anxiety is seen in intense chatter, a wringing of hands, hyperactivity, nausea and vomiting. Some turn stoic. Still others want aloneness and retreat to the quietness of a backyard or a bedroom.

It is difficult to stand idly by while a loved one suffers. Indeed, we want to help our loved one manage this crisis as we believe we would manage our own heartbreak.

Most victims, however, do not want advice. In fact they often resent it. For who, pray tell, could ever know what it is like to have lost a child? Dr. Elliot Luby's words reflect the agony: "When your parent dies you have lost your past. But when your child dies, you have lost your future."[2] And only a very few people who have walked the same path can understand what the pain is like.

Victims of tragedy do not want advice. And they may not even want your presence. It's not that they don't love you. But at this point it is simply easier to be alone.

Jack Morrow was deeply distressed that his wife didn't seem to want him around during her hospitalization. It wasn't that she was hostile or angry. Nor did she come right out and tell him to leave her room. Rather, he just sensed that she wanted to be alone.

Briefly Jack fantasized that perhaps his wife blamed him for the death of their infant. But upon later reflection he noted: "Julie was dealing with our crisis by being quiet. And I didn't have much to say either. We just could not reach one another."

The best way to assist those in the first stage of heartbreak is to let them know that you are near and that you will help in whatever way may be appropriate. But give them space— space to sort out their emotions and thoughts and fears. Stand by to help. But don't be surprised if they don't request it.

Stage Two: Deliberate Activity

The human spirit, once ravaged, has a remarkable ability to reestablish itself. When a storm rips through a community, most residents will survey the damage and then set out to clear the debris. Civil defense experts will tell you that the sound of power saws can be heard within minutes after a tornado has done its damage.

The act of locating a power saw is itself an act of affirmation. The individual in effect is saying, "I will not permit the storm to leave its legacy." And after the broken tree limbs and loose shingles have been cleared, the resident may lament the damage yet feel good that order has been restored.

At times the need to reestablish order is done out of sheer necessity. A single parent who has lost a job does not have the luxury to contemplate the meaning of the event when the cupboard is bare. Nor does a tornado victim when electrical wires hang menacingly over his home.

Fortunately most people are able to function competently in the weeks immediately following a heartbreak. They may even carry out their responsibilities with a measure of grace. When Lyndon Johnson died, a report marveled at his widow's ability to greet visitors with a smile. Mrs. Johnson explained: "Grief carries its own anesthesia. It gets you over a lot."[3]

Grief does carry its own anesthesia. It permits us to make

decisions, to meet our responsibilities, and to carry on with our lives.

After her hospitalization Julie Morrow returned home and began to reorganize the house. She went to the bedroom that was to have been their daughter's and in a matter-of-fact manner emptied the dresser drawers and stored the blankets. She folded the bassinet and placed it in the closet. She took down a mobile that was in the corner of the room. And she changed the curtains, making the room look more like a den.

Jack happened to walk by the bedroom and without Julie's awareness observed what she was doing. "I couldn't believe what I was seeing," he recalled. "She did all the rearranging without shedding a tear. She hides her feelings so well. It was like just another day in her life. I didn't say anything. But I sure resented how she was handling everything."

What Jack did not understand was that Julie was functioning with the benefit of what Lady Bird Johnson aptly called "anesthesia." Julie was bringing order into her life. And she was doing it in the only way that she knew how.

Sometimes those who do not understand how the human spirit responds to a crisis are mistakenly encouraged as they see someone reestablish a life. In contrast to Jack's reaction, Julie's colleagues were heartened by the way she was getting along. "Oh, she's doing well," said her boss. "Julie is such a strong person. When she came back to work, she asked us how we were doing and what all was happening in the company. She talked briefly about her hospitalization but she didn't dwell on it. I think she's just kind of accepted what has happened."

Nothing could be further from the truth. After the initial shock there is a relatively short period of time—often measured in weeks—in which heartbreak victims appear to have regained control over their lives. They make decisions. They seem in relatively good spirits. They manage their work lives. They greet friends and thank them for their help. And the tears abate.

But the "grief work," as Sigmund Freud called it, is only delayed. Several years ago a tragedy shocked Kansas City and the nation. A skywalk in the Hyatt Regency Hotel collapsed, killing one hundred and thirty-three people. In a study designed to determine the effects on survivors, a psychiatrist found that all but two individuals had suffered significant symptoms of distress, including repeated recollections of the tragedy, recurring dreams and nightmares, hypersensitivity to noise, anxiety about overhead objects, anger, and guilt.

Immediately after the tragedy survivors reported a loss of appetite, difficulty in concentrating, insomnia, and fatigue. For many these symptoms had disappeared one year later. But other, *delayed* signs of grief were now present. And they had a crippling effect on some of the survivors.

One woman, who lost a husband and two of her friends when the sixty-five-ton steel and concrete structure came crashing to the ground, stated that she was easily startled by noise. She was also filled with pent-up anger. Another person stated that she is wary of buildings that have high ceilings, exposed beams, and overhead structures. She now checks out every building she enters. Once, upon finding herself on a balcony, she ran back into the building in a panic.[4]

The fact that crisis victims can move through the initial phases of a crisis and remain in good mental health is a well-known phenomenon. The crew of a combat plane may function with perfect discipline. But once that crew is on the ground, the strain of what they have been through breaks into the open. Some become irritable and tense. Others become quiet and withdrawn.

Likewise, military personnel can survive long confinement in an enemy prison camp and in spite of wretched conditions maintain high morale. But once they return home the goodwill often vanishes. Charges of disloyalty and even treason are made against one another. Each in his own way is struggling to come to grips with what has happened— often at the expense of former buddies.[5]

In the hours, days, and even months following a heartbreak, most victims struggle to reorder their lives. In effect, they are seeking to rebuild the foundations to their psychological homes. They make decisions. They meet their responsibilities. They may even draw up plans for the future. But then, almost without warning, the bottom drops out.

Stage Three: Hitting Rock Bottom

The basic objective in stage two is to stabilize one's life. Much like a sea captain who strives to keep his ship upright in a storm, the individual struggles to keep a firm hand on the tiller. And one tends to do this by acting out hopes for the future.

Some people engage in shopping sprees, hoping that a new purchase might fill the nagging void. Others thrust themselves into work, putting in sixty or seventy hours per week. And still others become involved in civic and church groups, believing that if you help others you will also help yourself.

But the hustle and bustle comes to a crashing halt in stage three. The long work weeks only camouflage the pain. The new purchases bring but a momentary respite. And helping others does not erase one's own heartache.

Stage three represents the beginning of a wrenching pilgrimage into the darkest corners of life. Frequently it begins with a deep sense of anger. Listen to Jack Morrow describe his experience:

Three weeks after our daughter Jenny had died, I awoke from a fairly good sleep. I began the day in the usual way. I had breakfast, read the sports page, and went over my calendar for the day.

I got into my car and started to back out of the garage when I happened to see a fishing pole that my father had sent in anticipation of the birth of his grandchild.

Seeing that fishing pole really unbuttoned me. I slowly drove out of the driveway. But I stopped the car when I noticed a whole group of healthy, happy kids waiting for the school bus. Then I saw a neighbor working in her garden. Another neighbor was just finishing his jog.

Everything seemed so normal. That's what I couldn't get over. It was like everybody was happy and enjoying life. I felt like shouting: "For God's sake, don't you know what has happened? Don't you realize that I lost my child? Don't you realize that life just can't go on as if everything is O.K.?" I just wanted to explode.

Anger seems to blindside us at the most unexpected moments. As Virginia Woolf poignantly noted in *Jacob's Room*, we experience the death of someone we love not at the funeral, but when we come suddenly upon an old pair of his shoes.[6] And when we come unexpectedly upon a fishing pole or an old pair of shoes, there is a stabbing pain that reminds us that we lost something precious. Equally important, there is a terse reminder of the unfairness of life.

For some individuals the anger that erupts gives way to a burning resentment. Often the resentment is targeted on those whose actions seem so cruel and unfair. The farmer who cannot make his mortgage payments may vent his anger on a capricious and hard-nosed loan officer who wants to foreclose on his property. The young man who is denied admission to medical school may vent his anger on a faceless admissions committee that has just aborted his career. The woman who is raped is not only angry at the violence that was committed against her, but is revolted by a judicial system that lets her assailant walk the streets.

For some there is a need to counterattack. The farmer might fight the injunction in the courts. The medical school applicant might demand an explanation from the committee. The woman might work with police to help prevent a crime that happens to 81,000 women a year.

Such actions bring relief, particularly if the banker relents, the admissions committee reconsiders, or the assailant is put behind bars. But anger and fear simmer beneath the surface. The young woman finds it impossible to enjoy a quiet walk in the evening. The young man is paralyzed, thinking about his future. And the beleaguered farmer finds it difficult to trust anyone.

The anger eventually plays itself out. When the storm of anger has subsided, a new emotion quietly sinks into our consciousness. It is an emotion that is soft and sad, tender in its own way, yet terrifying. The most poignant feeling that heartbreak victims share in stage three is loneliness.

Why do we feel so lonely when we are struggling with a heartbreak? Freud long ago suggested that our lives are largely given to overcoming our fear of being separated from other human beings.

In infancy the child longs for affection and some visible sign that it is still connected to a human being. When investigators examined orphaned babies cared for in a Brazilian foundling home, they found that the physical care given to the children was excellent. Sanitation was good. The children's dietary needs were met. Unfortunately there wasn't enough staff to provide human warmth and affection. The children may have received ample food, but they were essentially alone. Most died during their first year of life.[7]

As children grow into maturity their need for affection continues to be felt. They often claim independence, but most want an interdependent link with at least one parent. If that link is not present, the child will retreat into a fantasy world in which affection and approval are lavishly given by an imaginary parent, teacher, or friend.

As we move into adulthood, we become cognizant of our separateness. We may live in suburban communities where we are in close proximity to hundreds of other adults, yet feel emotionally isolated.

We work in offices where the conversation frequently focuses on profits and losses as well as company politics. We attend social gatherings where the discussion drifts from one benign topic to another. And while we may long for some sense of closeness to one another, we also know that there is an invisible line drawn around those topics that we dare not discuss.

We can analyze why the Yankees are in a slump, but the personal slumps that we encounter are seldom shared. We can engage in endless hours of conversation about the condition of our schools and our communities, but we tend to be reluctant to share our deepest hopes and gravest fears. We therefore routinely carry on discussions that do not touch the nerve endings of life. We may leave the company picnic with our stomachs full but with empty souls.

Paul Tournier, the Swiss physician, made the observation that an individual can spend years in a factory, shop, or office without meeting anyone who takes the slightest interest in him as a person, in his intimate concerns, in his difficulties, or even in his secret aspirations. "The daily routines, together with the prevailing atmosphere of our times, make it possible for him to associate with companions whom he really does not know and who do not know him."[8]

The impersonality of modern life was symbolized for me by a for-sale sign that went up on a home within my community. The deeply etched furrows in the owner's brow signaled that not all was well. He explained that he had lost his job seven months earlier.

I asked why he hadn't informed anyone about what had happened. He said he didn't want to bother anybody. But then he added, as if to recapture a measure of self-respect, that he wondered whether anyone would care.

That evening as I thought about my neighbor's experience an image of thirty years ago flashed by. My family was living in central Iowa near some of the richest farmland in the world. On a cool October evening my father responded to a disturbing telephone call. A friend had lost an arm in a corn picker.

Within hours, neighbors gathered in the Baptist church to determine how they were going to pick Charley Braested's corn. Decisions were made as to who would feed the cattle and milk the herd. They decided how they would fill the family freezer. And they determined who would split the firewood. After all, the frigid Iowa winter was only a few months away.

We seem to be more estranged from one another than we were thirty years ago. Of course there are instances in which people today show genuine concern for one another, but dramatic sociological changes in our cities and towns have diminished the possibilities for community and togetherness. And as the opportunities for community have decreased, a sense of aloneness has increased.

In adulthood we often learn to tolerate and even accept our separation from neighbors, colleagues, and family members. Sometimes we encourage such separateness because it makes us less vulnerable to their demands and emotions.

But then a heartbreak hits and we sense our vulnerability. Indeed, we sense our aloneness. The fundamental fact of our existence—we are solitary human beings who must confront our tragedies by ourselves—comes crashing into our consciousness.

What makes a heartbreak so difficult is that we may have spent a lifetime convincing ourselves that we are not alone. We have valued acquaintances and friendships. We may have married, perhaps have had children. We have the telephone numbers of people handy just in case we ever find ourselves in a jam.

But when a tragedy occurs, we are brought face-to-face with the fact that our journey to recovery is a solitary experience. A spouse might give love, a friend might care, and acquaintances might call to give support. But when they leave and return to their own interests, we realize anew that our pilgrimage must be made alone.

There is, however, another threat. Not only do we become aware of our separateness from others at a time of crisis, but we are often thrust into impersonal institutions that take control of our lives.

During this year, there will be over 39 million admissions into American hospitals. For many, hospitalization epitomizes estrangement. We are hooked up to strange machines that send blips to nameless technicians. We are probed and stuck, tested and analyzed. And all too often we are treated as clinical parts rather than whole human beings. It's hardly a wonder that when patients leave the American hospital, their number-one complaint relates to the impersonal encounters they had with hospital personnel.

John McGivens was hospitalized for seven weeks with excruciating back pain after an accident on a loading dock. When I asked him what was the high point of his hospitalization, he replied without a moment's hesitation: "It was the very last day. My doctor *touched* me. It was the only time I felt any caring in that place."

The feeling that "I am alone" is one of the most poignant of all human emotions. And even if one is lucky enough to have a lot of friends, an existential aloneness often penetrates the core of our being.

In James Agee's novel *A Death in the Family*, the heroine's husband is killed in an automobile accident. Her father warns her that it will take time for the loss to sink in, and then it will get worse: "It'll be so much worse you'll think it's more than you can bear. Or any other human being. And worse than that, you'll have to go through it alone, because there isn't a thing on earth that any one of us can do to help, beyond blind animal sympathy."[9]

One of the perceptions that many victims of a tragedy share is a belief that things are going to get worse, rather than better. They find that their lives are governed by fears— a fear that they might not be strong enough to survive the crisis. Perhaps a fear that they can never again find happiness.

Four negative themes frequently appear in this third stage of heartbreak, as fear begins to govern the life of the crisis victim. The first theme is, *My life will never be the same*. Implicit is the belief that one's former life has been better than anything possible. No matter how good the future might be, the past represents the "golden years." Listen to Julie Morrow:

> There were times when I really doubted that Jack would recover. You have to understand him to realize what an awful event this was in his life.
>
> He came from a very large family. The one thing he wanted was to have children. Kids represented life. His work, his hobbies, not even his friends meant as much to him as the joy he felt when he knew I was pregnant.
>
> But after Jenny's death, I really began to worry. He would sleep ten, twelve hours a night. And then he would complain that he was tired. Instead of playing golf a couple of times a week, I would find him sitting alone.
>
> I told him that we would have another child. And I encouraged him to get back to his golf. I tried to get him to go out once in a while. But he lost his spark completely. I couldn't do anything to get him to think ahead. He was all wrapped up in the past. I tried to reach him, but he was locked into his own thoughts.

In this stage of recovery, the victim is "locked into his own thoughts." Jack later commented: "I got to the point where I didn't want to see anybody or be around anybody. And the more time I spent alone the more convinced I was that there wasn't anything to look forward to. Life had kind of ended."

There is of course truth in the belief that life will never be the same. Susan Henderson, a twenty-eight-year-old attorney, became pregnant in spite of practicing birth control. Her lover abandoned her despite what was once a strong commitment to each other. She decided to have an abortion although the very thought of it was against some of her deepest religious values.

Taking a vacation day from her law practice, she went to an outpatient clinic in a Baltimore suburb. Unfortunately there were complications. She bled profusely and was hospitalized. The anonymity she had hoped for quickly disappeared. She had no choice but to let her office know that she would be out of work for at least a week.

Susan's parents were devastated when they learned of her plight. They were deeply religious people who viewed abortion as murder. They felt betrayed. Not only was abortion morally reprehensible, but the thought that their daughter was having premarital sex was more than they could bear.

In the weeks after her release from the hospital, Susan counted her losses. "I lost a child, my best friend, and my parents. I don't think you can lose more than that."

Susan gradually recovered, but there is a melancholy about her that suggests that life will never be the same as before her heartbreak. One senses that if you scratched beneath the surface there would be a sadness, perhaps even a longing for an era in which life was less complex.

Once you have been beat up, you look at life through a different pair of lenses. The impeccably dressed executive may appear to be the picture of self-confidence. But you see a different person when a physician informs him that his angina is a forerunner to a heart attack, or when his wife informs him that she has taken a lover. Suddenly, the pillars that undergird life are shaken. Health is not assured and the covenants made at the altar change. And the carefully constructed structures that support human existence no longer seem quite so secure. It is then that we begin to believe that our lives will never again be quite as hopeful, quite as simple, or quite as good.

A second negative theme that frequently plagues heartbreak victims is, *I have let everybody down*. The essence of this theme is that "Somehow I am responsible for my heartbreak, and therefore any pain that is coming to others must be my fault."

There is a large element of irrationality in this theme. How can it be your fault when a drunk driver rams into your car, hurting a passenger? Or how can it be your fault when an economy spins out of control, costing you your job?

Nevertheless, many heartbreak victims attest to the fact that even when they intellectually know they are not responsible for what has happened, their gut tells them that they have somehow failed. Susan Henderson's situation is a case in point.

After the abortion, Susan visited her parents. She had always been amused by their attitudes toward sex and morality, but it had never been a big issue. Now, however, it threatened their relationship.

The minute she stepped into her home she knew that a wedge had been driven between them. The hugs were less than spontaneous. The conversation seemed stilted. She longed for the days in which she and her dad would sit by the oak kitchen table, drinking coffee together and talking about how things were going on their farm. But those days seemed to be gone forever. In the core of her being, Susan felt that she had let them down.

It is important to recognize that when we feel that we have not lived up to what we believe to be the expectations of others, we are in effect saying that we have let ourselves down. If only we were smarter, or if we had planned things differently, then we would not have had the car accident, or lost our job, or been forced to have an abortion. It may be irrational, but we tend to believe it.

Of course the higher the standards you set for yourself, the greater the sense of failure when the standards are not achieved. And if you believe that you should never make a mistake, when a problem develops you take a pretty hard fall.

Ricky Denton was only eleven years old when he had the biggest crisis of his young life. His basketball team was losing by one point in the final minute of overtime when he stepped up to the free throw line. He had to make only two shots and his team would win the game.

Carefully he studied the basket. The first shot went up, rolled along the rim, and fell to the side. The second shot was an "air ball"—it didn't even make it to the backboard.

The opposing team was jubilant, but Ricky could barely look his teammates in the eye. That night his father heard a few muffled sobs. "I let the entire team down. Why couldn't I make those darn free throws?" The boy paused as if to survey the damage. "You know, I never thought that I would be the one to blow a big game."

Ricky's father later reflected: "Ricky is just like me. You shouldn't make a mistake. It's O.K. if someone else blows the game. But you shouldn't be the one to do it."

No one wants to "blow the game." We set very high standards for ourselves. Our children should be born perfect. Our teenagers should excel. Our careers should ascend in a straight line.

Yet one of every ten children is born with some type of congenital defect. Our kids have ups and downs and sometimes we wonder whether they will ever make it. And nearly everyone reaches a career plateau.

The belief that we have betrayed the standards that we set for ourselves is terribly disruptive to our well-being. And every time we convince ourselves that somehow we could have handled our situation more effectively, we lay the groundwork for a third negative theme: *I will never be happy again.*

The bigger the crisis the greater the probability that we will come to believe that there is no hope. Unfortunately the belief that there is no hope can become a self-fulfilling prophecy.

In a remarkable study, fifty-five individuals were interviewed as they were being admitted into a nursing home. They were asked how much freedom they had in coming to the home, how many other options were available to them, and how much coercion relatives had applied to get them to enter.

Seventeen individuals indicated that they had no alternative but to reside in the nursing home. Of this group, sixteen were dead within ten weeks. But for the thirty-eight who saw an alternative to nursing-home care, there was only one death in that period.

In another sample, forty additional people were interviewed. Family members had made application in twenty-two instances. Nineteen in this group died within one month after application. But of the eighteen who made their own applications, only four had died by the end of the month.[10]

If you see options for yourself, you see hope. And if you see hope, you live.

And now we come to a crucial point, which if understood could save families a lot of grief. When you hit rock bottom, a fourth theme is frequently sounded: *My spouse does not understand me.*

Marriages frequently fall apart in the months following

a crisis. This may seem strange, for we have been led to believe that when our backs are against the wall, the family becomes cohesive.

Unfortunately the belief that hardships create strong marriages is largely a myth. Heartbreaks tend to test marriages and put a severe strain on family interaction. If the marriage was ailing before the crisis, it may not be able to withstand the pressure that must now be confronted.

In the months following their daughter's death, Julie Morrow became highly organized as she methodically put her life in order. She returned to work, thanked everyone for their understanding, and vigorously addressed work-related problems.

Work was Julie's therapy. She completed reports, chaired committees, and projected a major expansion for her department. Outwardly there was hardly a hint that she had been through a major crisis. On a few occasions when she allowed herself to think about what had happened, she would shut the door to her office and shed a tear. But she always regained her composure as well as her good spirits.

Jack was not so fortunate. He had recurring periods of illness. An asthmatic condition that he had not had for a decade suddenly returned. Frequently he called in to work sick. Alone at home, he constantly asked himself why misfortune had struck. He knew that he was in a deep state of depression but didn't know how to crawl out of the hole.

One night his frustration spilled forth in a hostile encounter. He was surprised when Julie indicated that she would not be home in the evening because of a company dinner. Jack's anger exploded.

"How can you go to a company dinner after all that we have been through?" he shouted. "How can you work night after night? What about me? Don't you care about my feelings? Don't you understand that we just lost a child?"

Julie was stung by the criticism. But her own frustrations

with Jack's moping around the house had been building for weeks. "I know that we lost a child. And it's as hard on me as it is on you. But I keep busy. I do things. I try to be productive even when I don't feel like it. I also live for the future. There is nothing you or I can do that will ever change what happened." She then paused as if to measure every word. "You've got to go on living. Or your self-pity will do you in."

The frustrations continued to build. Neither Jack nor Julie knew how to de-escalate the hostility.

When Julie returned from her company dinner, Jack resumed his verbal assault. "Someday," he admonished, "you are going to have to deal with what's happened."

Julie became stone silent, as she frequently did whenever there was an emotional outburst. That night they slept in separate beds for the first time in their marriage. Alone with her thoughts, Julie wondered whether their marriage might be over.

When a husband and wife share a heartbreak, each must plot a defense. You cannot plot the defense of your partner. Nor can you effectively plot a joint defense. Responding to a heartbreak is a solitary experience.

Some of us, like Julie, respond to a threat by becoming stoic. We tend to be silent and throw our energy into work. We do not rely on others to bail us out of our ordeal. Nor do we tend to be emotional, for we reason that emotions kind of clutter up rational thought.

But others engage in a defense that is similar to Jack's. We feel the hurt deeply and show it. We dwell on our loss, wondering why it happened and what we could have done to prevent it. We want the empathy of others; not to get it is a kind of torture.

These divergent coping mechanisms have been finely honed through childhood and adulthood. Some learn to be combative and strike back when a threat looms. Others learn to flee uncomfortable situations. And still others become immobilized, hoping that the pain will go away on its own.

The longer you have been married, the greater the probability that you have accepted the way your spouse responds to threatening situations. You may even have come to see that your spouse's method of dealing with the jagged edges of life has some merit, even if it is contrary to the way in which you confront your own losses. But when a crisis occurs, divergent ways of coping frequently create tension and produce additional stress.

Fortunately there are marriages in which a heartbreak strengthens the bonds of friendship rather than weakening them. In such marriages the partners gain strength and rely on one another. They respect the different way each responds to the crisis. They touch one another physically and psychologically. The heartache begins to heal.

At first the healing is slow and all but undetectable. It is as if you have an open wound, and day after day you look at it and wonder whether any rehabilitation is taking place. But physical healing always occurs from the inside where it cannot be observed, and then moves to the surface.

So it is with psychological pain. The signs of healing are initially small, even undetectable. Nevertheless, if one looks diligently, the signs are unmistakably present.

We might wake in the morning and discover that we are thinking about something other than our sorrow. We might venture to see a movie or a ball game. Or we might surprise ourselves when someone asks, "How are you doing today?" to find that we respond with an affirmative "I'm O.K."

Indeed, we might even begin to make peace with those awful moments of loneliness. And if we can do that, we will then begin to understand what author Clark Moustakas meant when he said:

Loneliness leaves its traces in man but these are marks of pathos, of weathering, which enhance dignity and maturity and love. . . . Loneliness is as much a reality of life as night and rain and thunder and it can be lived creatively. So I say let there be loneliness, for where there is loneliness, there is also sensitivity, there is awareness and recognition to promise.[11]

Stage Four: The Awakening

I frequently asked victims of a tragedy whether there was a particular event that gave them hope. It was amazing to see their reactions. Those in stage three would get a quizzical look and in effect say: "Of course not! Nothing could make me feel better."

But those who had rediscovered a meaning within their lives would smile. And then they would share an event that had kindled a sense of anticipation and even hope.

A sixty-six-year-old widower with a twinkle in his eye recalled how he had met a new friend at church: "She smiled at me from across the aisle. It sure surprised me. She looked beautiful and I reckoned that she was about my age. I took a shine to her immediately!"

A thirty-three-year-old woman who was not able to bear children recalled a telephone call from an adoption agency informing her that she was about to be a mother to a three-year-old Asian-American. "I was so excited I couldn't remember my husband's telephone number at work. But I got a hold of him and told him that he was a father. He was so choked up that he couldn't talk."

A thirty-one-year-old graduate student who flunked the final oral examination for his doctorate found his self-defeating thoughts vanished when he was offered a job that paid him twice what he could ever earn as a full professor.

Such incidents have a way of altering dramatically our perceptions of ourselves and our heartbreak. Sometimes they are mind-blowing events, which firmly convince us that we can in fact pick up the pieces of our lives and move into the future. But usually they are small happenings that in and of themselves do not appear important, but that give a sense of hope.

Before achieving his notable success, author Alex Haley spent four years without generating any sales, receiving nothing but form rejections from various publishers. Rejection after rejection created discouragement. But one day an editor scribbled across a rejection slip two little words: "Nice try." "I almost cried," said Haley. "I was just moved beyond words. There really was someone out there who reads these things [manuscripts]. It was not just some machine sending out rejections."[12]

Donald Westfall, the sixty-six-year-old widower, mustered all his courage to meet the attractive woman with the kind smile. He introduced himself, and they went to the narthex of the church where people were visiting and drinking coffee.

Ten minutes passed and then twenty. People started to leave the room, but Donald and his new friend were so deep in conversation that they scarcely noticed the passing time. Finally when it was apparent that they were the only two people remaining, Donald became self-conscious, fumbled his coffee cup, quickly thanked her for her time and said how much he enjoyed meeting her. As she was leaving, she gave him a firm handshake and said that she hoped she would see him again.

"When I got into my car, I had a lump in my throat that was the size of an apple! I felt like a teenager! The whole week I thought about her. I could hardly get her out of my mind. Sunday couldn't come around soon enough. And sure enough, she was at the church and we talked for another half hour!"

Fortunate coincidences that powerfully reorient our thinking take a thousand different forms. One man down in the dumps from a recurring illness received an unexpected financial bonus, permitting him to make a down payment on a small piece of lakeshore property. A new dream was born. More important, a sense of hope was restored.

A woman whose personal problems were of such magnitude that she contemplated suicide was sent a Christmas card by her boss, who had no idea that anything was amiss. Inside the card he had scribbled a note: "I don't know what we would do without you. Thanks for being so competent, so helpful." Later she commented: "I framed that card and put it up in my kitchen. It's like a sign that says, 'You're going to make it!'"

All such events have one powerful denominator: They force us to restructure our view of ourselves and the world in which we live. And they make us aware that there might be something for which to hope.

Hope is the one ingredient missing in stage three. But a fortunate happening, such as meeting a stranger who gives an approving smile, reverses the gloom. Instead of tripping over ourselves in the darkness, a light is switched on. The shadows begin to recede. The threats we thought were lurking behind closed doors begin to vanish. In brief, the acuity of our vision is restored.

Victor Frankl, the famed Viennese psychiatrist, who was imprisoned in a German concentration camp, relates a particularly touching moment in the life of the camp when all hope seemed dashed to bits. There were 2,500 prisoners on the edge of starvation. Cold and hungry, irritable and tired, sitting in the dark, Frankl was asked to speak a few words of comfort and hope.

Frankl began his remarks by saying that their situation was not hopeless. By so doing he was striving to help the prisoners change their perceptions. He suggested that much of what they had lost could be restored, including health, happiness, professional abilities, fortune, and position within society. He referred to Friedrich Nietzsche's remark, "That which does not kill me, makes me stronger."

Then Frankl focused on the meaning of life.

> I told my comrades (who lay motionless, although occasionally a sigh could be heard) that human life, under any circumstance, never ceases to have a meaning, and that this infinite meaning of life includes suffering and dying, privation and death. I asked the poor creatures who listened to me attentively in the darkness of the hut to face up to the seriousness of our position. They must not lose hope but should keep their courage in the certainty that the hopelessness of our struggle did not detract from its dignity and its meaning. I said that someone looks down on each of us in different hours—a wife, somebody alive or dead, or a God—and he would not expect us to disappoint him. He would hope to find us suffering proudly—not miserable—knowing how to die.
>
> And finally I spoke of our sacrifice which had meaning in every case. It was in the nature of this sacrifice that it would appear to be pointless in the normal world, the world of material success. But in reality our sacrifice did have meaning. Those of us who had any religious faith, I said frankly, could understand without difficulty. I told them of a comrade who on his arrival in camp tried to make a pact with Heaven that his suffering and death should save the human being he loved from painful end. For this man, suffering and death were meaningful; his was a sacrifice of the deepest significance. He did not want to die for nothing. None of us wanted that.[13]

The desire to imbue one's life with meaning is a sure sign that healing is taking place. The executive who is transferred to a remote city against his will imbues his life with meaning as he seeks to discover the beauty of his new community. The battered wife who divorces her husband and with determination builds a new life is imbuing her existence with meaning. The vice president who receives the distressing news that his subordinate has been promoted to the presidency imbues his life with meaning when he writes a note congratulating his colleague.

Webster defines the word *imbue* "to tinge or dye deeply." A merchant who takes a bland piece of cloth and then transforms that blandness into rich colors has imbued that cloth with life. Likewise individuals who can see good in each day have imbued their lives with riches.

When Jack Morrow was in the pit of his hell, any suggestion that he imbue his life with meaning would have been put down as sheer nonsense. Indeed, he had worked himself into such a state of bitterness that there was no joy to be found anywhere. But years later, after he had fully recovered, he discussed an event that altered his view of himself, his marriage, and the death of his baby.

I can put a date on the beginning of my recovery. It was August 11. That was the day my boss called me into his office and chewed me out.

He opened our "conference" by saying: "We have all been patient with you. We know that it was a terrible blow when you lost your kid. But that was eleven months ago. Your sales figures are depressed and they keep going down every month. You walk around the office like you are carrying a one-hundred-pound bag of cement. I'm going to put it to you straight: You've got to shape up your sales figures. We like you. We know you're a good salesman. And we want to keep you. But enough is enough."

At first I was madder than hell. What did he know about losing a child? Not one damn thing. But then it struck me that if I lost my job it really would be a disaster.

I went home and started to think about what my boss told me. And although I hated to admit it, everything he said was true. And then I thought about my job and how much I really did like it.

Then the doorbell rang. Three members of my staff were at the door. I could tell they were a bit nervous. They told me that the word had gotten around the office about my conference with the old man, and they just wanted to assure me that they would support me no matter what might happen. They gave me a bottle of champagne and left.

I sat down and thought about how lucky I was to have friends like that. Then I thought about all the things I had going for me. I could see Julie reading in the den and I thought about how much I loved her, even if I hadn't shown it much lately. And I looked at our living room and thought how much I enjoy our house. I got up and looked at our backyard and got a good feeling as I saw the neatly stacked firewood sitting by the fence. And then I said to myself: "By God, I'm going to make it. I don't know how, but I am going to make it."

Stage Five: Acceptance

Those who transcend their heartbreak come to accept the fact that they have experienced a major loss. But let us be clear as to what acceptance means. Acceptance does not mean forgetting—as if to deny the significance of the heartbreak. Acceptance does not imply that one glosses over the hurt. Nor is acceptance shrugging one's shoulder and saying, "But what else can I do but accept the situation?"

Acceptance of a tragedy is predicated upon understanding two concepts found in Indian philosophy. The first is *duragraha*; the second is *satyagraha*.[14]

Duragraha is stubbornness. It implies that you must learn to live with your suffering. It is, Mohandas K. Gandhi suggested, a "hardness of heart." Individuals who govern life by *duragraha* distance themselves from human suffer-

ing. The outward stance is: "I can handle my problem."
"Difficult experiences happen to everyone." "You just got
to move forward."

But if *satyagraha* is your guiding focus, you enter fully
into whatever life offers. When the bad times come, you
shed tears and at times feel overwhelmed. You sense the
magnitude of that which has been lost. And you resist those
who want you to forget the past and move into the future.

But *satyagraha* also means capturing joys that surround
us. *Satyagraha* implies being grateful for the love of friends
and taking comfort in the kindness of strangers. It suggests
celebrating anything that brings hope. Perhaps more than
anything else, *satyagraha* means forgiving the injustice as
well as any person who may have been responsible for it.

Forgiveness is an ancient concept. In fact, you can examine the writings of many who have shaped human thought
and find that the theme of forgiveness is at the heart of their
philosophies. And if you dig deeply into psychoanalytical
thought you will find that the act of forgiving others as well
as oneself is often the prototypical sign that healing is taking
place.

Gandhi suggested that the path to inner healing is forgiveness. In the movie of his life there is a poignant scene
in which a Hindu father whose child has been killed by a
Muslim comes to Gandhi's home. The Hindu father is tormented by grief. But he is also filled with hate toward the
Muslim people. Out of a sense of retribution he has killed
a Muslim child. He now kneels before Gandhi asking how
he can get over his remorse and his guilt.

Gandhi, who is gravely ill, tells the man that he must
go and adopt a boy and raise him as his very own son. That
request seems reasonable but then comes a requirement: In
order to find inner peace, the Hindu man must raise the boy
to be a Muslim.

Overwhelmed at the inconceivable thought of raising a son as a Muslim, the man leaves Gandhi's room in total disarray.

Later, however, he returns and again kneels beside Gandhi's bed. He now understands *satyagraha*: He must take the hostility from his heart and replace it with love.

It was difficult for Julie Morrow to forgive that which happened. On the surface she appeared to be coping quite well. But as the months passed, she found herself thinking more and more about her daughter. And as the one-year anniversary of Jenny's death approached, Julie found herself terribly troubled. She had tried to become pregnant again, but couldn't. She saw her daughter in the eyes of other children and each time felt like cursing God for never giving their child a chance at life.

One year to the day that Jenny had died Julie awoke with a splitting migraine headache. She went to work but, truth be known, she could barely focus her thoughts. She hoped that the tasks awaiting her would somehow keep her mind off her sorrow.

She hung up her coat and went into her office. To her surprise the papers and reports that usually cluttered her desk were neatly stacked to the side. In the middle of the desk was a single white carnation and a handwritten verse taken from the writings of Kahlil Gibran. Her secretary had remembered.

Slowly Julie began to read words that reached deep into her soul:

>   Your children are not your children.
>
>   They are the sons and daughters of Life's longing for itself.
>
>   They come through you but not from you,
>   And though they are with you yet they belong not to you.

You may give them your love but not your thoughts,
For they have their own thoughts.

You may house their bodies but not their souls,
For their souls dwell in the house of tomorrow, which
you cannot visit, not even in your dreams.

You may strive to be like them, but seek not to make
them like you.

For life goes not backward nor tarries with yesterday.[15]

Julie's eyes filled with tears as she reread the words. "I can't explain it," she said. "But for the first time since Jenny's death I let go of my regrets. She will always be with me and I will always miss her. And I will always wonder what she would have been like. But she had her own life that I could not control." Julie paused as if to measure the significance of every word. "I had to let her go."

In her own way and after twelve months of heartbreak, Julie Morrow released the hurt. She did it with difficulty and with pain that only a parent who has lost a child can comprehend. But by so doing she moved into the house of tomorrow.

T H R E E

Characteristics of a Crisis

Sedula curavi, humanas actiones non ridere, non
lugere, neque detestare, sed intelligere.
*(I have striven not to laugh at human actions, not
to weep at them, not to hate them, but to understand them.)*

—SPINOZA

In the last chapter we learned that healing after a crisis takes place in stages, each of which has its own emotions, its own challenges.

But what actually is a crisis? And why can it have such a devastating impact on our self-confidence and our hopes for the future?

To answer these questions we need to understand the nature of a crisis. We need to discover why a crisis generates anxiety and frustration. But we also have to learn a difficult lesson: Heartbreaks have a redemptive quality that often goes unnoticed.

There are six characteristics of a crisis.

First, a crisis hits suddenly, without warning. And it

often strikes at a point in life in which everything is going well.

Several years ago an airplane crashed in the North Carolina woods, killing all sixty-eight passengers and crew members. When the aircraft took off, there was not a hint of trouble. There was ample fuel. The pilots were in good health. The plane had been mechanically checked and deemed airworthy. It was to be a routine flight from Charleston to Charlotte—a flight that had been completed thousands of times without mishap.

After the airplane crashed, officials from the Federal Aviation Administration examined the wreckage, seeking to discover the cause of the accident. They poked and sifted through the ashes. They examined the engines and the black box that recorded the pilot's last words.

Then they came to a startling conclusion: The pilot and crew had not been paying attention to their altitude. The aircraft simply drifted down to earth. And everyone perished.[1]

Heartbreaks often strike when skies are clear. The day starts in a normal fashion. The kids go off to school. The parents leave for work. The plane takes off smoothly.

But then an alarm sounds and the safety of our routines is shattered. Intuitively we know that life will never be the same.

Within a few minutes, perhaps seconds, the crisis for those aboard Flight 212 was over. But the heartbreak was only beginning for relatives, as each contemplated what life would be like without a loved one or a friend.

In the moments after a crisis we are stunned as we seek to comprehend what has happened. The very first words that are spoken are usually "I can't believe it." As Jack Morrow said after their baby was stillborn: "I was in a daze. I walked around for hours. I simply could not comprehend that this had actually happened."

Tragedies hit us when we least expect them. It is this element of unpredictability that makes a crisis different from all other challenges that life presents.

For example, if you know that you will lose a job in six months, it may be upsetting but you can rationally plan for the future. If you know that your company will transfer you to another part of the country within a year, there is ample opportunity for the family to absorb the news. And if you know that you will retire at a certain age, you can begin to do things that will ease the transition.

But a crisis comes on suddenly. And when it arrives, you don't have the luxury of sitting back in a detached manner to analyze options. Your whole being becomes absorbed in the event. And you wonder whether life will ever return to a normal state of affairs.

The second characteristic of a crisis is that it threatens security. Crisis situations cause us to panic because we might lose something very precious—something that has given structure, meaning, and purpose to life.

After a devastating automobile accident Warren Jenkins lay pinned behind the steering wheel.

> I smelled the gasoline and I knew the car could blow any minute. Suddenly I realized that I might never see my five-year-old daughter again.
> I was terrified and just about went crazy. I pushed like hell against the twisted wheel, getting one leg free, then the other. I crawled away from the car and as I lay by the side of the road, I thought about how I almost lost everything that mattered.

For Warren Jenkins the crisis was the car accident. But the upsetting aspect of that situation was the realization that a relationship about which he cared deeply might be destroyed.

Sometimes the most troubling aspect of a heartbreak is the fears that begin to surface. When the stock market crashed in the 1930s, the crisis was not the loss of a business or a farm or a bank account, as serious as those events were in people's lives.

The crisis was the realization that there wasn't enough food for the family. It was the realization that there wouldn't be enough money to send a son or a daughter to college. For those who saw their farms turned into dust bowls, the crisis was the fear that they would never again be economically secure.

The characteristic that unifies all human beings is the strong desire to protect against threats to security. The Vietnamese peasant wants to be able to tend to his rice paddies without worry that an explosive mine might still be hidden beneath a random rock. The Polish worker wants to be able to go to his factory, to participate in union activities, without the constant fear that the authorities might yank him off the line and send him to a detention facility. The American wants to have a job that is secure and not subject to the whims of recessions and economic recoveries. The drive for inner security is very powerful, which is why any loss that shatters security is so difficult to take.

We want to see our children go happily off to school with the knowledge that they have teachers who care about them. We want to have decent jobs and periodic raises so that we can enjoy the good things in life. We want houses that protect us from the elements and friends who will bolster our spirit.

We therefore send our kids to what we hope are good schools. We take on new jobs that promise greater security. We build houses with tighter insulation and we select friends who seem warm and friendly. And in the process we build bridges to what we hope will be even firmer ground.

But then something totally out of our control happens and we feel deeply threatened. The school is a playground of drugs. A punitive boss threatens our livelihood. The home becomes a place to do our worrying. Our friends get caught up in their own struggles. Our pillars of security are shaken and we feel vulnerable.

When we lose something that has given life meaning, purpose, and structure, we become melancholy. But we may also become bitter.

When Marilyn Crandall lost her secretarial job, she was at first philosophical. "Losing your job happens to everyone nowadays. But I've got skills. Companies always need secretaries."

Two weeks later, after a dozen job interviews and no offers, her anger surfaced.

> I felt very discouraged. I found myself thinking a lot about my old job. I thought about my friends at work and how much I would miss them.
>
> But the more I thought about the impersonal way I was treated, the angrier I became. There were no warnings. There were no thank-yous. Not even a statement that they would help me find a new job. Nothing. They didn't even say good-bye.
>
> Now I ask you . . . who wouldn't be angry?

In one sense Marilyn Crandall is fortunate. She had someone to blame for her hurt. As Thomas Mann noted in *Royal Highness*, a story about a prince born with a withered arm, the worst kind of misfortune is one for which no one is to blame. For whom do you blame if your child is born with a withered arm? Whom do you vent your anger toward if you receive a diagnosis of uterine cancer?

There is no one. As the father of a nine-week-old son who died unexpectedly in his crib said, "You can't sue God."

Indeed, you can't sue God. And even if there is somebody from whom you can legally collect damages, the money only cushions the sorrow. No life insurance check can take the place of a loved one with whom you have shared your most intimate hopes, fears, and dreams.

A third characteristic of a crisis is that its resolution is unpredictable. There is an element of uncertainty in all heartbreaks. We simply do not know how things are going to turn out. We like to believe that we can weather the storm. But in our quiet moments we wonder whether it can be done.

The element of unpredictability is the most unsettling component of a crisis. If you could predict with 100 percent certainty that open-heart surgery will be successful, there would be little cause to worry. But as most coronary bypass patients know, there are individuals who never leave the operating room alive. The odds for recovery are certainly in the patient's favor. But there is an unpredictable aspect that leaves most patients unsettled and somewhat fearful.

Fortunately there are crises that end quickly. Suppose you have a sharp pain in your abdomen. You consult a physician who informs you that you have an inflamed appendix. Surgery is scheduled. A week later you're back on the job. The crisis came and the crisis abated.

Unfortunately most heartbreaks are not resolved so efficiently. There is no cure for a child born with Down's syndrome. There are no surgical treatments that neatly resolve the problem. And there is no way to predict how the child will eventually cope with life.

This does not mean that the parents cannot cope with their challenge. And it certainly does not imply that the child cannot have a meaningful life. But it does mean that the parents will have to live for years without any certainty as to how their child will be able to succeed in a competitive world. It is this element of unpredictability that makes their problem so acute, so difficult to accept, and so worthy of compassion.

A fourth characteristic of a crisis is that it presents dilemmas. For example, "My husband has announced that he wants a divorce. Do I try to change his mind or let him go?" "I've just been fired unfairly. Do I protest or look for a new job?" "I've been told I have a serious form of cancer. Do I take the radiation treatments as my physician suggests or make the best out of whatever time I have left?"

A dilemma arises because there are no clear-cut solutions to difficult problems. A decision to discontinue radiation therapy for cancer will spare one from the nasty short-term side effects. But then the cancer may never be arrested. A decision to leave a difficult job might give one a sense of freedom. But it might not allow one to pay the bills.

Dilemmas usually follow in the wake of most crisis experiences. Heartbreaks simply don't have tidy solutions. And sometimes we are forced to make decisions on issues about which we have little knowledge and little experience.

Dick and Ruth Carlson's teenage son was critically injured in a motorcycle accident. After their son was stabilized, a physician outlined a year-long plan involving multiple plastic surgeries. The prognosis was guarded. The accident was severe and the outcome unknown.

The surgeon pressed the Carlsons for a decision, for he wanted to operate within three days. Said Dick:

> I was filled with questions. Would this plan work? Does he need all those surgeries? And who should do the surgeries? Should it be a plastic surgeon? An orthopedic surgeon? Who is best qualified? And how do we go about finding out who is qualified?

The Carlsons had never been faced with a crisis of this magnitude. They talked to the surgeon, who seemed to be offended by their inquiries. Dick talked to his buddies at work and Ruth visited with her friends at church. Everyone was sympathetic. But no one could give much help.

The Carlsons discussed the situation backward and forward, inside and out, for two solid days. Should they go ahead with the surgery? Should they go to a major medical center in another town to see what other surgeons might have to say? Should they rely totally on the judgment of this one physician? Just what should they do?

On the second night after the accident they went to bed physically exhausted and emotionally drained. But Ruth's frustration burst into the open. She was a trusting person and from the moment the surgeon outlined what needed to be done she had mentally agreed to do it.

She resented Dick's reservations. She saw him as someone who saw dark clouds even when they didn't exist. His questioning and indecision created additional anxiety. Finally she said: "I can't talk about it anymore. You decide."

Dick sat up alone with his thoughts. He felt an estrangement from his wife. But worse than that, he realized that the decision was now on his shoulders. The next day he told the surgeon to operate. They agreed to the surgical schedule that had been outlined.

But neither Dick nor Ruth felt good about the situation. Ruth sensed new frictions in their marriage. And Dick felt anxious because he simply didn't know whether they were doing the right thing.

The following year was difficult for the Carlsons. The surgeries were not as successful as had been anticipated. And the outcome looked less and less promising.

Frequently Dick second-guessed the original decision. While neither talked about it, both Ruth and Dick wondered whether there weren't better ways to have handled their problems.

A crisis experience produces dilemmas. Sometimes you will be forced to make decisions with little information. Sometimes you will be forced to choose between unattractive options. And sometimes, even after consulting with informed people and learning all you can about your situation, you still will not know what is the best approach to take.

If this happens, remember: Time is the greatest healer of a heartbreak. Anxiety lessens. Perspectives sharpen. And decisions can be made more sanely.

If you are faced with a dilemma, consult with friends, loved ones, family members, and anyone else who can help. But if the decision can be delayed without harming yourself or anybody else, your best path is to put off till tomorrow what you are asked to do today.

A fifth characteristic of a crisis is that it erodes self-confidence. Ruth Carlson was a very trusting person. Nothing had happened to her in life to make her suspicious. She had never experienced a problem that couldn't be solved.

But the motorcycle accident shook the ground underneath her feet. The accident was bad enough, but she realized that she had been changed by it. And she didn't like what she was seeing, for she was becoming more cynical and less trusting.

> I think about the accident all the time. I find myself crying sometimes at the strangest times. I feel unsure of myself, more withdrawn.
>
> I can't understand these feelings, for I used to be such an optimistic person. I used to get up in the morning full of energy. But now I sleep in—sometimes until ten or eleven o'clock. I don't seem to have the energy to do my work. And I would rather be alone than with my friends.
>
> I don't know what has happened to me. But I just seem unsure of myself. It's kind of like you don't know whether anything is worthwhile any more.
>
> I keep telling myself it is going to get better and it probably will. But right now I sure have lost my confidence.

It is not uncommon for heartbreak victims to lose self-confidence. Consequently they approach life with apprehension, a reservation that was never present before.

When Harry Livingston returned to his office after a two-month absence, his subordinates noticed a subtle but definite change in his outlook. Said one:

> Harry's heart attack was real serious. All of us wondered what he would be like.
>
> At first everything was just the same. He seemed to be his old self.
>
> But you can tell that he has lost some confidence. He doesn't seem to be so eager to get into new projects. He hesitates before making decisions. He is reticent about giving advice. I guess he's just more cautious. Is that what a heart attack does to people?

The answer is a qualified yes. And it doesn't happen just with a heart attack. It can happen with any crisis.

Why do we feel less confident?

Everything we have talked about in this chapter takes a cumulative toll on a person's outlook. The sudden impact of a negative event reminds us that life is fragile. The unpredictability of the outcome leaves us unsettled. Dilemmas create anxiety. The net result is that there may be an apprehension about life that wasn't present before the crisis.

Does that old self-confidence ever return? Does the apprehension subside? I don't think your confidence ever returns in quite the same form as it was once expressed.

This does not imply that you are sentenced to a life of morbidity and downcast expressions. And it certainly doesn't imply that you can't regain happiness.

But once you have been emotionally hurt, you look at life differently. You feel the pain of others. You understand that life can be terribly unfair. And you know life takes unexpected turns.

Fortunately a crisis also leaves hopeful legacies. This brings us to the sixth characteristic of a crisis.

A difficult experience helps us redefine our values.

As we have learned, most people go through a period in which they are angry about their misfortune, and usually they have every reason to feel the way they do.

When Jack and Julie Morrow, for example, were told by the obstetrician that they had lost a child even before it was born, they had every right to be angry. The child who learns that the only way the nodules in his arm can be treated is through massive doses of chemotherapy that will leave him bald and depleted does have reason to ask, "Why the hell did this happen to me?"

Bitterness is often the logical conclusion of a crisis event. It doesn't have to be that way, but it often is.

Yet for every individual who loses something precious and becomes bitter, there are others who vow that their tragedy will not destroy them.

Crisis events in their most ugly form compel us to address the only question that matters: "Why should I continue to live?"

When Janice Hastings was told that she would have to have a radical mastectomy, which would leave her with two large scars, she thought about doing away with herself. "It was impossible to comprehend what was about to happen. I cried hysterically. I could not imagine what it would be like. It was so inconceivable that I was actually living this nightmare."

A week before her surgery she began to have suicidal thoughts. What kept her from doing it? Later she reflected on one important thing that helped:

> One night I thumbed through the day's mail. I noticed a postcard sent by my best friend. He had written one word on the postcard, scrawled in big letters: LIVE. Whenever I was tempted to harm myself I would look at that word and repeat it again and again and again: Live! Live! Live! I began to believe that I was not my body—*I was me*.

The French philosopher Jean Paul Sartre states that you

cannot understand "being" (life) until you comprehend "non-being" (death). For when one stares death squarely in the face, then one begins to comprehend the profound gifts of life. Non-being is nothingness; being is potential. Non-being implies blowing oneself away because it is impossible to live with our loss. Being implies that self-destruction is the ultimate insult, for we have snuffed out hope that is buried deep within our psyches.

A crisis event explodes the illusions that often anchor our lives. When you wake up in the coronary care unit, it matters little whether you meet your production goals. When your teenager lies critically ill in some sanitized hospital, it makes little difference whether he or she has made the scholastic honor roll or has missed last night's curfew.

In the midst of tragedy, we learn what is important, and that is the redemptive legacy of any crisis experience. Listen to Judy Carter as she talks about her experience:

> I was only twenty-seven years old when I learned that I had MS. Multiple sclerosis is a progressive disease that can leave you confined to a wheelchair. When I received the diagnosis, I was vice president of a large savings and loan company. I also was the mother of two children ages two and five.
>
> The news that I had MS hit me like a thunderbolt. For weeks my husband and I walked around our home asking the question: "Why us?" We both knew about MS and how it can leave people almost helpless.
>
> I did well the first several years and continued at my job, which I loved. But then my symptoms became acute. I started to go downhill. I had to quit my job and then the bills really began to pile up. As the symptoms of my disease became more and more acute, the stress must have taken a toll on our children, for they started to do poorly in school. Of course, I blamed myself for the problems they were having. My husband didn't know how to respond, partly because one day I would be angry and depressed and on another day I would be cheerful. He never knew what kind of a roller coaster I was going

to be on when he came home from work.

I saw the medical bills coming in. I knew the kids weren't doing well and I thought our marriage was shaky. I also had tremendous guilt. I would have killed myself but I just didn't have the nerve, especially when I looked at the kids.

But one day I realized that while there might not be a whole lot I could do about my illness, there was a lot I could do about my attitude. That was my first breakthrough. I made an appointment with a psychiatrist who just happened to be a longtime friend of our family. I cried uncontrollably in his office. All the grief that I had bottled up for years came flowing out.

After I had brushed away my tears the psychiatrist took out a big yellow pad of notebook paper and we started outlining what I really cared about in life. We jotted down major headings such as "family," "money," "travel," and "friendships." Under each heading we wrote goals that would enable me to enjoy that which I really cared about. We decided that my kids needed some counseling about the problems they were facing at school and at home. He told me about community health nursing services and how they could keep me in optimal physical health. Suddenly travel seemed like an option, for I learned that airlines serve special food for people such as myself and have all kinds of services in the event you need a wheelchair. Then he had me work on changing my goals from that of a professional woman to that of a homemaker. That really was a challenge. But slowly I came to understand the important joys that one can find in one's home.

The real breakthrough came with my husband. One night when the kids had gone to sleep he came to me and held me close. He said he had been doing a lot of thinking, and the more he thought about it the more determined he was to help me through this situation. His support was almost overwhelming. He took me by the hand and said, "When we took our wedding vows we said, 'For better or for worse.' Well, this might be the worst part, but we will stick together as close as we can." We both felt a tremendous new sense of inner peace. Suddenly I didn't think everything was hopeless. Rather,

I saw us changing the exterior parts of our lives to accommodate the illness. But I saw the interior parts growing stronger and stronger. I might not lick this thing, but I am convinced that I can live.

There is a good side about a crisis experience. Admittedly no one would ever choose to have a heartbreak just to discover positive outcomes.

But years later most people, as they look back on that difficult period of life, will readily admit that some good came out of it. And in spite of the anger, the bitterness, even the self-doubts, they were able to move into a new era in their lives.

A number of years ago tragedy struck the Flying Wallenda family. They were performing for a circus audience in a midwestern community. While undertaking a difficult formation on the high wire, two members of their family were killed, while two others were injured for life.

For a brief period of time the Wallendas did not perform. As we noted, heartbreaks have reason to make us cautious, to pull back, to withdraw.

But then they announced that they would get back up on the wire. They would attempt to do the very same act that had killed their loved ones.

There was excitement and trepidation in the air as the Wallendas went up the wire to perform their human pyramid tightrope exercise. With difficulty, but with exacting precision, they completed the feat that had caused them so much suffering.

After the performance reporters gathered and asked the senior Wallenda a penetrating question. "What made you come back to the act after the tragic fall a few days ago?"

Without hesitation the senior Wallenda commented: "To be on the wire is life. All else is waiting."[2]

The question is: *How do you get back on the wire after you have taken a tragic fall?* How does one dare love again when that which you have loved most in life has been taken from you? How does one gather courage to once again face life with confidence?

To answer these questions we must turn to those special people who have successfully navigated through their personal storms. In the experiences of people like ourselves— executives, assembly-line workers, housewives, nurses, public service employees, teachers—we can obtain practical clues as to how to manage our own heartbreaks.

FOUR

How People Survive Adversity

> *It's not what happens that matters
> but how you take it.*
> —HANS SELYE

It is difficult to fathom, but small miracles occurred in the Nazi concentration camps. Jewish prisoners would give bread to one another even when they themselves were hungry. They would share clothing in order to protect themselves from freezing temperatures. When there was no hope, the Jewish people sang to one another, wept with one another, and prayed for one another. Because of such support an estimated two million Jews survived a man-made hell.

Today others are surviving tragic experiences. Consider the seventh floor of the University of Minnesota Hospital, where patients with spinal-cord injuries come for help. You are immediately struck by the fact that many of the para- and quadriplegics are teenagers. Most have been cut down in the prime of life by a random automobile accident or by a sporting event.

You would expect to see depression in the eyes of these young people, and at times you do see despondency. But mainly what you hear is a lot of good-natured bantering. They challenge one another to accomplish simple tasks. Their partially paralyzed fingers struggle to grasp elusive objects placed in front of them by therapists. As your eyes gaze across the room, you see a young man attempting to get behind the wheel of a simulated automobile. Eagerly he listens as the therapist explains the car's special control mechanisms, which will permit him to drive and regain a measure of freedom.

How can there be laughter in such a room, given all that these young people have lost? A physical therapist puts it this way:

> Shortly after their accidents almost all go through a period where life is not worth living. They may lie around and mope for weeks, sometimes months.
>
> But one day you come to their room and you sense that something is different. Nothing about their medical condition has changed but you sense that their spirit has changed.
>
> Sometimes a simple question gives you a clue that they are starting to think they can make it. Yesterday one sixteen-year-old who had just obtained his driver's license before he severed his spine in a gymnastics drill said, "You really think I can drive a car again?"
>
> When I told him he could, I saw his eyes glisten. He saw a flicker of hope. A few minutes later I saw him struggle from his bed and into his wheelchair. He then wheeled over to the car. He must have stared at it for twenty minutes. I sensed a great debate going on in his mind as to whether he could ever drive again. Then he came by my desk and said, "I want to start learning to drive as soon as possible." At that point I knew he would make it.

The list of awful things that happen to good people is truly imposing. Yet within any aggregate population that has suffered a tragedy, there will be a high percentage who will not only survive but will move on and live productive lives. Here are their characteristics.

Characteristic One:

Almost without exception those who survive a tragedy give credit to one person who stood by them, supported them, and gave a sense of hope.

If you want to survive a tragedy, you need a friend. At least that is the experience of most individuals who have withstood some of the stiffest challenges that life can bring.

Michelle King is a sixteen-year-old Michigan girl who survived months of punishing chemotherapy. Each time she was injected her best high school friend would be with her. "I would lie on my back after those treatments and be emotionally and physically exhausted. But my friend would hold my hand and softly repeat: 'You're going to make it. I know you're going to make it.'"

Kahlil Gibran once remarked that we can forget those with whom we have laughed, but we can never forget those with whom we have cried. Most friendships worth their salt are those nourished in human struggle. Once you have suffered together, there is a bond that is not severed by the passage of time.

What is there about a friendship that is so powerful? Why do we turn to others for comfort when unwanted news lands on our doorstep? And why is it that we feel better after we have confided our worst fears to someone who cares?

The answer in part is that a good friendship helps us

cope with our most terrifying fears. When a crisis occurs, we feel vulnerable to shifting forces of life. It is not uncommon for crisis victims to worry about the next bad event that might be lurking in the shadows, for after all, "If one bad thing happened, you know that other bad things might occur." Like a boxer repeatedly hit with blow after blow, we cannot plot our defenses. Being stunned, we struggle just to conclude our daily tasks.

The feeling of being vulnerable masks a more basic fear. Psychologists have long known that the most primal fear is the threat of abandonment. When an infant monkey is left alone, it seeks to cope with the disappearance of its mother by frantically running back and forth in the cage. The infant gives off one distress call after another, hoping that its mother will return. Within hours the infant learns that all the frenzy will not bring its mother back. The infant is overwhelmed. Soon it curls into a ball and quietly whines, feeling totally abandoned.

The fear of abandonment is learned at birth. The infant quickly discovers that survival is dependent upon the caring of others, for without such care it will die. As the child grows older, it becomes more independent. In adulthood self-sufficiency is often rewarded. Yet intuitively most of us know that survival is dependent upon an employer who provides a paycheck, a trucker who brings groceries to a neighborhood store, a mechanic who checks the safety of our automobile, the physician who gets us on our feet once we have been ill. While we comfort ourselves by our self-sufficiency, at the core of our psyches is an understanding that we are all deeply interdependent.

A crisis threatens at least one interdependent link with other people. For example, when there is the first hint of divorce, a child will panic. "But who is going to take care of me?" "With whom will I live?" The fear of abandonment is acutely apparent.

The same fear may be reflected in the parents as they contemplate their impending aloneness. "I knew that I wanted out of the marriage," said Ralph Brunner, "but I wondered what it was going to be like living in an empty apartment." The fear of abandonment, even when one wants to be abandoned, seems to be a peculiar but a much-understood paradox.

Stripped of all its other definitions, a friendship affirms that we will not be abandoned. Robert Stephan, a forty-six-year-old bachelor, described his feelings of vulnerability as he registered in the admissions department at St. Francis Hospital:

> When they clipped the identification band on my wrist, I felt momentarily out of control. It was like I was no longer in charge of my life—somebody else was now calling the shots.
>
> Then they took me to my room and I had to put on a white gown that must have been made for a man a foot shorter than me. I looked at myself in the mirror. I didn't know whether to laugh or to cry but I sure felt alone.
>
> As I lay in my bed I knew that I needed somebody. I thought about all the people with whom I worked and the person who I knew would understand is a fellow by the name of Jerry Creider. We aren't really close but we had worked together for nine years. So I called him and asked whether he would come to the hospital while I was having surgery.

The next morning Jerry Creider arrived at the hospital just before Robert was transferred to the surgery suite. After surgery the nurses allowed Jerry to enter the recovery room for a brief moment. Jerry firmly squeezed Robert's hand and told him that he was doing fine.

Months later Jerry commented on the experience: "Robert is such a self-confident guy. You would think that he could get through anything by himself. But I guess that on that day he just needed someone to give him a little boost."

Out of the simple request to have a colleague sitting in the hospital coffee shop while one was undergoing surgery, a genuine friendship was born. A friendship that will probably last as long as each one draws a breath.

The first gift of friendship is companionship, which is the knowledge that one will not be abandoned. The second is a gift of hope. A good friendship affirms that good things can still take place no matter what the magnitude of the loss.

The most frequent perception after a tragedy is a sense of helplessness. The perception that one is helpless is rooted in a belief that it is not possible to control the negative forces impinging on one's life.

The middle-level manager who senses that he might lose his job feels particularly helpless when the executives are meeting in the next room determining how to make budget reductions. The helplessness felt by cancer patients stems from the belief that the events rushing over their lives cannot be reversed and hence cannot be controlled.

After helplessness, a sense of hopelessness appears. We feel hopeless when we believe that we have been so ravaged by a tragedy that it is impossible to recover a sense of joy, purpose, or vitality.

The major threat posed by hopelessness is that such feelings can take a toll on one's health. Over the years investigators have built a powerful case for how our thoughts influence our psychological state. One of the earliest accounts of this phenomenon came from R. J. W. Burnell, a South African physician, who had witnessed six middle-aged Bantu men cursed with the admonition, "You will die at sunset." At sunset each had died and when an autopsy was performed no cause of death could be found.[1]

In a study that has important implications for a possible

connection between stress and cancer, investigators interviewed fifty-one women who had regular Pap smears. Each of the women had suspicious-looking cells in her cervix, although none was diagnosed as having cancer. Eighteen of the women had experienced a significant loss in the last six months and each had feelings of hopelessness. The researchers predicted that those patients who felt hopeless would be predisposed to develop cancer, even though everyone in the group appeared to be equally healthy. Of the eighteen individuals who felt hopeless, eleven subsequently developed cancer. But of the other thirty-three women, only eight developed cancer.[2]

In a study of twenty-six Eastman Kodak workers who died unexpectedly, investigators found that depression seemed to be the predominating premorbid state. When depressed individuals were provoked to anger or hostility, cardiac arrest followed.[3]

Even the possibility of catching the flu seems to be influenced by the state of our minds. Six hundred employees of the military were given a battery of personality inventories. Several months later an influenza epidemic swept the area and twenty-six people came down with the flu. Three weeks later twelve individuals still had the flu symptoms. A trait was common among those who were still ill: Each had been significantly depressed during the previous six months.[4]

Now, you may ask, what has all this to do with friendship? The answer is as simple as it is profound: *A friend has the power to break the gloom*. Good friends, by their presence and sometimes with their words, help us to see that we are not helpless and that while our loss is horrible it can be managed.

When crisis victims have told me about a friend who helped them, I often inquire as to what it was about their friend that they found comforting. Most reported that their friend was nonjudgmental, a good listener, and usually slow to give advice. I was surprised, however, at how many indicated that they had received something in writing that they cherish.

Joyce Friestad, a beautiful twenty-six-year-old graduate student, was overwhelmed when told by her obstetrician that she would give birth to a stillborn child. In the months following her loss Joyce struggled to regain control over her life and to find glimpses of hope. A letter written by her aunt came to have special meaning:

Dear Joyce and Andy:
Thank you for calling and telling me about the death of your baby. Nothing that I can say will take the pain away. But we all know that your child is an angel in heaven. It's likely that she is happier than she ever would have been here on earth. Yet even that knowledge doesn't always seem to help. For some reason we feel the pain of our children more deeply than we feel our own pain. But I have learned through the years that God does not give us more than we can bear. And I have learned that children have their own futures that we cannot control. I really believe that children are only loaned to us for a short time. They just kind of pass through.
I cannot say I know how you are feeling. I have never had the type of disappointment that you are now going through. But each night when I go to bed I pray for you and hope that you both have the courage and strength to work this through. I know it is not an easy task.
I love you.

A good friend pulls us away from our self-defeating and often hopeless attitudes. A good friend gives advice, but as Samuel Taylor Coleridge stated, the advice is like snow. The softer it falls, the longer it dwells and the deeper it sinks into the mind.

A good friend affirms our fundamental goodness and

shows us that our misfortune is understood in a profound way. We receive from friends the courage to continue our journey.

Dr. Elton Mayo perceptively and correctly noted, "One friend, one person who is truly understanding, who takes the trouble to listen to us as we consider our problem, can change our whole outlook on the world."[5]

Characteristic Two:

Those who survive a tragedy understand the magnitude of that which they have lost.

If you want to recover from a crisis, you need to enter fully into your tragedy. You need to feel in the depth of your being what it is that you have lost. You should talk about your losses over and over again with a sympathetic friend. And you need to let the tears flow when your world is spinning out of control. In short, you need to acknowledge the enormity of that which has happened.

Some people have a natural ability to understand in the depths of their soul what it is that they have lost. Perhaps they had previously acknowledged that life's random events could strike close to home. If so, they usually have some knowledge as to what they would do if an unwelcome intrusion occurred.

But many of us are not so fortunate. It is not uncommon for people to deny that tragedy will ever appear on their doorstep. Sigmund Freud once remarked that in the unconscious, every one of us is convinced of his own immortality. Perhaps that is the way it should be. Far better it is to enjoy life to its fullest than to brood over the plagues that could dwell on our house.

Yet when we have spent a lifetime denying what Thomas Mann once described as a "sympathy for the abyss," we are overwhelmed when tragedy occurs. In fact, to deny that a tragedy can happen is almost a guarantee that once it occurs our spirit will be ravaged.

Some not only deny that a tragedy could occur, but they deny the magnitude of the tragedy once it happens. There are a hundred and one ways of negating a loss.

Some keep themselves busy by running from one social event to another. Others may throw themselves with renewed vigor into their work. Still others intellectualize the difficulty by saying: "These things happen to all of us. We'll get over it."

Cliff Kranston was forced by his company to take an early retirement. He attempted to escape his regrets by keeping busy.

> I'd play golf. I'd go to movies. We would eat out. We attended concerts.
>
> But I wasn't enjoying any of those things. In fact, I was miserable. When I couldn't shake my depression I went to see a counselor.
>
> There I learned all that I had been denying. I learned how much I missed my job, the satisfaction of getting up in the morning and doing something which you really want to do. I missed making money. I missed joking with my friends.
>
> I thought about all the things that I had lost in retirement.
>
> I then realized that all my activity was simply a way of covering up my losses.

Affirming what one has lost is an important part of the healing process. Perhaps that is why the Vietnam Veterans Memorial in Washington, D.C., is visited by thousands of people every week.

The memorial is not visible from the street. It is shaped

like a wide V and is placed in the grounds of Constitutional Gardens. There is a narrow, winding stone pathway that follows along the two granite wings, each of which spans 247 feet.[6]

The first piece of polished black granite to emerge from the ground is a sliver that contains but one name. Then, as you move into the crux of the V, the granite grows taller and taller with row upon row of names of servicemen who had died. In the middle on either side the black granite towers over everything.

"It's like walking into the war," said a veteran. "You can feel us getting deeper and deeper into it, more and more death."

At first people don't know how to respond when they see the memorial with the names of 58,022 servicemen. Some veterans refuse to get close enough to touch it. Others blot out an entire name with a hand—almost as if they wish they could blot the entire experience from memory.

But some, like Ronald Townsend from Queens, New York, understand its importance.

> The fellow I came to visit, I was his burial escort. He was from Chelmsford, Massachusetts. I was 18 at the time, and he was 20. And his family really left an impression on me. They helped me out a lot in terms of setting my own values in life. And so perhaps . . . in some way or another, he is living through me, I feel that. So that's why I came today.
>
> I didn't think the wall was going to have an impact. I just thought that people overdramatized it. But it does have an impact. It makes you . . . it stops time. It makes you feel that you're back there, all over again.[7]

What does the black wall do?

It helps us to remember what we have lost. It helps us

focus on that which is important: friendship, loyalty, sacrifice, bravery.

But it also helps heal our spirit.

One of the most important steps in recovering from any tragedy—whether it be the death of a buddy in Vietnam, the loss of a job, the erosion of health—is to understand that something profound has been taken from us. For to deny that something serious has happened is to put grief on hold. Years later we may need to relive that experience, trying to sort out a problem that was earlier denied.

Why do we deny the significance of our disappointments?

In American culture there is a strong drive to get life back in order after an unwanted event has intruded. That need, which is sometimes referred to as the "technofix ethic," is a belief that most problems can be efficiently and effectively resolved.

The technofix ethic suggests that, if the car breaks down, it can be repaired. If profits lag, there are new markets to pursue. If the football team is losing, a new coach will resolve the problem.

There is something seductive in the technofix ethic. We want to believe that it is possible to manage our losses much as we manage our careers and our investments. A father might pat his son on the back after he has been cut from the high school basketball team and say, "Don't take it so hard . . . you're young . . . you have lots of potential."

The son may go off by himself and recite the father's well-intended admonitions. But in his aloneness he can feel only the pain of knowing that his buddies made the team and he didn't. It would be far better for the father to meet his child in his aloneness and acknowledge the magnitude of what the son has lost.

At the heart of the technofix ethic is a belief that we can lay out a plan of action that will neatly resolve our problems.

Much like a doctor who prescribes a medication that enables us to feel better each succeeding day, we hope that our formula will have predictable results.

Unfortunately few who have lost something of value are able to move from sadness to happiness in a straight line. For most there are many detours, dead ends, and wrong turns. You have good days, not-so-good days, and just plain awful days. Said Martha Strakowski, who was getting over a difficult divorce:

> One week I would feel great and have an enormous sense of freedom. But on another day I would feel discouraged and even depressed. Over time, though, I thought I was getting better.
>
> Then one day eight months after the divorce I had to meet my former husband because of some legal matters related to the settlement. I was with him barely an hour but all the old feelings came over me. I felt resentful, angry, and even fearful. It was then that I realized that I still had a ways to go.

Human pain does not let go of its grip at one point in time. Rather, it works its way out of our consciousness over time. There is a season of sadness. A season of anger. A season of tranquillity. A season of hope. But seasons do not follow one another in a lockstep manner. At least not for those in crisis. The winters and springs of one's life are all jumbled together in a puzzling array. One day we feel as though the dark clouds have lifted, but the next day they have returned. One moment we can smile, but a few hours later the tears emerge.

When all optimism lies dormant, there will be those who will actively encourage you to "get over" your grief and to regain control over your life. Some will encourage you to make a fast adjustment to what has happened because they genuinely care about you and do not want to see you suffer.

Others may give advice rooted in their own discomfort with sadness. A few might callously put their own interests before yours.

Manuel Hernandez encountered all of these reactions when his wife died unexpectedly of cerebral aneurysm while vacationing in Phoenix, Arizona.

> There were many people who tried to help me get my life back to normal after Juanita's death. My friends invited me out to their home for dinner and to ball games and even to some social occasions at their churches. My boss called and expressed his sympathy but also gently inquired as to when I would be back on the line. My kids called every night to see how I was doing. My insurance agent nudged me to get the death certificates filed because I only had sixty days to get the forms in. My work buddies kidded me about being the most eligible guy in the plant.
>
> But all I wanted to do was sit and think about my wife. I didn't want to go to ball games and I didn't want to go out for dinner. I just wanted to be alone.
>
> I guess the best advice I got was from someone who works on my shift and who had lost a child in a car accident. She told me to cry as often as I could and to keep all the pictures of my wife and to sit in her favorite chair as often as I could. Night after night, that's what I did. It took a full year to get my life put back together. But if I had gone to all those backyard barbecues and ball games and all those social gatherings, it would have taken me an eternity to get over this thing.

There is one marvelously redeeming motive for entering fully into one's sorrow: Once you have experienced the seriousness of your loss, you will be able to experience the wonder of being alive. It is a fact that once you experience pain, it sensitizes you to joy. Jurgen Moltman, the German philosopher, accurately noted: "The more passionately we love life, the more intensely we experience the joy of life.

The more passionately we love life, the more we also experience the pain of life and the deadliness of death. We experience joy and pain and we become alive and mortal at one and the same time."[8]

Becoming "alive and mortal at one and the same time" is perhaps a peculiar paradox when first examined. But the more we become comfortable with the paradox, the more we recognize the importance of affirming that the good and bad seasons are often mysteriously jumbled together as we journey toward recovery.

It is true that as we take two steps forward in our journey, we may take one or more steps backward. But when one affirms that the spring thaw will arrive, the winter winds seem to lose some of their punch.

Characteristic Three:

Those who survive a tragedy have learned to transcend their guilt.

If you have experienced a major loss, the probability is high that you will have a large measure of regret. Few of us, for example, can go to a grave site without experiencing some gnawing feeling that we should have done more for our loved one or our friend. Perhaps we could have been more understanding. Perhaps we could have related in a more compassionate way. Whatever the reason, we have regrets. It is as if there is unfinished business awaiting us, yet the situation precludes us from completing it.

About what do we feel guilty? In *maturational crises* we tend to feel guilty for not living up to the high expectations we have for ourselves. The well-known middle-age crisis is at its core a feeling that we have let ourselves down. We have not achieved that which we set out to do. Or if we have met our expectations, we begin to doubt the merits of what has been accomplished.

In *situational crises* guilt is usually riveted on a belief that we could have done something to prevent the crisis from happening. There are few spouses of the 500,000 people who die annually from heart attacks who don't carry a measure of regret. As Rebecca Kurswalter said after her husband's heart attack left him permanently incapacitated:

> In my *head* I knew I wasn't responsible. But in my *heart* I blamed myself for how hard he had worked, for not showing more affection, for not being more sensitive to the pressures at work, and, well, you name it, I felt guilty about everything related to the problems he had before his heart attack.

Behind guilt exists a stream of "if" statements. "If only I had buckled my baby into her car seat, she might have survived the accident." "If I had not taken DES [diethylstilbestrol] twenty years ago to prevent a miscarriage, my daughter would not have vaginal cancer." "If I had shown my husband more affection, then maybe he wouldn't have had an affair."

A hospital chaplain who works in oncology stated that the most frequent reaction he receives from a newly diagnosed cancer patient is, "What have I done to deserve this?" Patients frequently say such things as, "I always thought I was a pretty good person. I am involved in my community. I am a good mother (or father). I provide well for my kids. What did I do wrong?"

Guilt can tear an individual's psychological support structure to shreds. In so doing guilt delays recovery more than any other factor.

One summer evening Corinne Meyer played with her

three-month-old daughter before putting her to bed. She felt so good about the child. Her daughter's eyes twinkled with life. She was healthy and alert. The bond between mother and child could not have been stronger.

The next morning Corinne's baby was dead, and no amount of frantic activity could bring her to life. "My reaction was that I had killed her. The only thing that came to mind when we found her face down was that I must have let her smother herself."

For months Corinne blamed herself for what happened. "If only I had kept the crib in our bedroom, this wouldn't have happened. . . . If I wasn't such a sound sleeper, I would have heard her cry. . . . If I hadn't delayed her monthly checkup with the pediatrician, maybe this could have been prevented."

Corinne's reactions are understandable. Nevertheless, for her to recover it was imperative that she quit blaming herself for the tragedy. How did she let go of her self-condemnation?

Our pediatrician suggested we get involved in the Los Angeles chapter of the Sudden Infant Death Syndrome [SIDS] Foundation. There we met parents who had also lost their baby.

We talked a lot about our feelings. I mentioned that I felt responsible for my baby's death. That I could have done something to have prevented it.

Everyone understood. All of us felt we must have done something wrong.

Then a physician talked to us. He said that our feelings were understandable. In fact, he did not know of any parent of a SIDS child who did not feel responsible.

But he assured us that there was nothing that we did that caused the child's death. Nor could we have prevented the death.

Slowly I began to realize that it was not my fault and, as I looked around the room, I could tell that other parents were coming to the same conclusion.

After the meeting we hugged one another. For the first time most of us realized that we did not harm our child. And for the first time, some of the guilt started to leave.

Of course there are people in crisis because their actions did result in misfortune to other people. Allen Comstock did not see his four-year-old son as he backed up the family station wagon. He heard a scream, got out of the car, and realized that he had run over the child's leg. His boy survived, but he walks with a limp.

How do you forgive yourself when such an event takes place? It took Allen Comstock thirteen years to make peace with what happened. Year after year he lived with the guilt of knowing he was responsible for his child's problem:

> I would go to hockey games with my boy and I would look at my son and feel horrible because I knew that my accident had kept him forever from skating and doing all the normal things kids do. Or we would go to the beach and I would see the ugly scars on his leg and I would turn my head away from him and cry. When he started dating, I could see how hesitant he was and I just knew it was because of his mid-leg.
>
> But as he got into his mid-teens, I started to see that he was going to make it. He's got a girlfriend who is the envy of all his buddies. He received a scholarship to the University of Kentucky. As I saw him doing so well I had to ask myself why I was so depressed. He obviously had learned to cope with the situation, and I hadn't.
>
> Then one day, we were driving to a repair shop to pick up our TV. For the first time, he asked me to explain *in detail* what had happened on the day of the accident. It was the one question that I had feared him asking all these years.
>
> I started to recall the events and broke down. I told him everything that occurred and even how the passing years had not taken away feelings of being responsible.

And you know what my kid did? He put his hand on my shoulder and said: "I never blamed you for what happened. I never thought of it as your fault. And I never will think of it as your fault."

That night I wept. But they were tears of relief. For the first time in thirteen years, I went to bed without blaming myself for what happened.

Sometimes other people need to give us permission to rid ourselves of guilt. But most of the time we need to forgive ourselves. How do you diminish guilt? Unfortunately there is no easy formula, no sure guarantee. Guilt is one of the strongest and most difficult emotions to conquer.

But there is one suggestion that seems to work for many people: *You diminish guilt by consciously defining your good qualities.* You remind yourself that you are a person of worth; a person who has strengths and qualities that are valuable and admirable.

How is this done?

I have known children who after a parent's death felt guilty for not being better sons or daughters. But I have seen the guilt diminish as they recalled meaningful conversations and expressions of tenderness that had been forgotten.

I have seen managers unfairly fired for incompetence who subsequently were plagued with guilt. But then they located a new company that recognized their abilities and rewarded them for who they were and what they could do. Quickly the guilt receded.

And I remember an uptight boss who had a bitter argument with a trusted subordinate. Later he recalled his hot words and his cutting remarks and was overwhelmed with remorse. He drove to his subordinate's home and offered a handshake. No words were spoken for the longest time. Yet everything important was said.

Paul Tillich once remarked that the first duty of love is to listen.[9] That comment not only is true of our relationships with other people but should be true of our relationship with ourselves.

The best way to reaffirm self-worth is to listen to ourselves talk. And when the talk is negative or when the talk reflects self-reproach, we need to remind ourselves that we do not have to be perfect. For to be human is to fail. And to make mistakes.

But we also have to remind ourselves that we have qualities others admire. Qualities that permit us to love others. Attributes that permit us to be loved.

Finally, we need to act, for in doing something for others we put regrets behind us.

If you have done someone wrong, make amends. But get back to work, do the things you enjoy, try to make the load of others a bit lighter.

And if you lost someone you loved, do not list all the things you failed to do. Rather, list all the things you tried to do.

Making peace with ourselves isn't easy. But those who survive a tragedy have discovered an important lesson: It does little good to punish ourselves. As Alexander Graham Bell once observed, "When one door closes, another opens, but we often look so long and so regretfully upon the closed door that we do not see the one that has opened for us."[10]

Characteristic Four:

If you want to survive a crisis, you need a reason to live.

To put the issue bluntly: If you live your life in the past, you will be overwhelmed with guilt. You not only will regret what has happened but will probably convince yourself that it is impossible to recover.

It is admittedly difficult to think about the future when you are overwhelmed by past events. Indeed, no one can prescribe for another the appropriate time to chart new directions.

Some find it possible to redefine a purpose in life within a few weeks after a tragic incident. Others take longer—months and even years may pass before they feel any sense of hope.

Nevertheless those who have successfully moved through a crisis experience are usually able to pinpoint a period of time in which their thinking switched from past losses to future gain.

Ed Northam's daughter was born with a congenital deformity called a cleft palate. When the child was two years old, the palate was repaired. But the surgeon said the defect was so severe that it was unlikely that the child would ever speak normally.

Ed had pinned all his hopes on a successful repair. When it didn't turn out as anticipated, he went into a deep depression. In the weeks following surgery, Ed re-experienced the grief he felt at the time of her birth. He couldn't imagine why his child had an impairment when all the other kids in his neighborhood seemed so healthy and so well adjusted. And when he thought about the future he became very depressed, for he had difficulty seeing how his daughter could ever live a normal life.

But then there was a breakthrough.

I talked to a speech therapist who invited us to attend a speech clinic. There we heard kids talk before and after they had therapy. I couldn't believe the difference. For the first time since the surgery, I started to feel some optimism. At least there was something we could do that might help.

But the real breakthrough came that evening. My daughter sat in my lap and I thought about how fortunate we were to have her.

Then I thought about how negative I had become. A thought crossed my mind: Why do I have so little confidence in her? What makes me think that she is going to have trouble in her life?

Since birth I had seen her as frail, weak—less normal than other kids. But why take that point of view? Why not see her as a strong person, a person who will not only be able to manage her handicap, but who can be successful as well? Right then, I decided to put pretty scary thoughts behind me.

Philosophers have long suggested that there exists within each of us a reservoir of hope. Ralph Waldo Emerson once noted that in our core we are prepared to recreate the whole world out of ourselves even if no one else existed. What is it that creates this kind of optimism?

In *The Revolution of Hope*, Erich Fromm presents a straightforward thesis: Hope is basic to man's existence. "Does the infant not hope to stand erect and to walk? Does the sick man not hope to get well, the prisoner to be free, the hungry to eat? Do we not hope to wake up to another day when we fall asleep?"[11]

Within the essence of our being there is, to use a Hegelian concept, a real possibility that life can change for the better. The word *possible* as it is used here does not signify abstract possibility, nor does it mean projecting dreams that do not have a basis in fact.

Rather, a real possibility means that others facing equally troubling situations have been able to transcend their loss. Nowhere is this more clearly demonstrated than in observing diabetic children.

Most children are stunned when they learn that they have a disease, for, after all, diseases happen to old people. But now they are the ones who are ill and they must come to grips with the fact that their bodies have failed them.

In the weeks following the diagnosis most diabetic children are overwhelmed by the unwanted intrusion that has swept into their lives. They are bewildered by the many new changes that must be made in their diet and in their exercise patterns. They must learn how to monitor something called blood sugar. They must give themselves daily injections of insulin, which seems to be a particularly cruel injustice. Many, however, will tell you that the worst part of the whole experience was thinking about death for the very first time.

Nevertheless, hope slowly begins to crowd out fear. Through Diabetes Education Centers the children learn that it is possible to backpack, play football, be fully involved in school activities. They learn that prominent personalities, such as Mary Tyler Moore and former New York Yankee star Jim ("Catfish") Hunter, are diabetics who live full and exciting lives. Soon the children begin to think, "If they can do it, why can't I?" Six months after the initial diagnosis most of the children will have moved from past threats to present joys. Not only have they learned to cope with a serious problem but they are usually living full and active lives.

Even when a "normal" life cannot be anticipated, individuals have an uncanny way of projecting hope. Consider Doris Nelson, who lived in a paralyzed state for thirty-six years before her death. Doris was a victim of a polio epidemic that swept the United States from the 1930s to the 1950s. She was placed in a huge metal cocoon, an "iron lung," as it was aptly named. The machine kept her alive as its motor-driven bellows contracted and expanded her chest, forcing air in and out of her lungs.

When Doris learned that she would never regain her health, she became so despondent that she tried to persuade others to give her pills to end it all. But, not unlike the experiences of diabetic children, hope began to replace depression.

While Doris Nelson's body was paralyzed, her mind was alert. She recognized that it was possible to expand her interests into the areas of religion, gardening, and crafts. She ordered seed catalogs and various kinds of plants and flowers, which with the help of relatives were planted and observed.

Using a jerry-rigged typewriter, Doris wrote an eloquent autobiography entitled *Through a Looking Glass*. Holding a rubber-tipped stick in her mouth, bending the few inches forward that her head could reach, she painstakingly typed letter by letter.

> My life, in many ways, is better now than at any time since I contracted polio. The accomplishments I've achieved, the closeness to God I've found, have given me a fuller life, but in spite of this I sometimes have a deep longing, *an expectancy to something more*.[12]

An "expectancy to something more" seems to be at the heart of the recovery process. It is a feeling that while we can't always see into the future, there is the possibility that something good might be awaiting us.

To repeat: Within the essence of our being there is hope. But is this a mere metaphysical speculation? Is this philosophical gibberish? I think not. During this year more than 800,000 people will be told by a physician that they have cancer. While some will lose hope, the vast majority will not. As Fromm states: "If you have cancer you know in your soul that the issue is not one of statistical probability.

It does not matter whether the chance for cure is 51 percent or 5 percent. Life is precarious and unpredictable, and the only way to live is to make every effort to save it as long as there is the possibility of doing so."[13]

To see man at his worst one need only focus on Auschwitz. Yet even there one can see man as a hopeful and courageous being. Gisella Perl, a seventy-two-year-old Jewish physician, takes us back to the concentration camp:

> The greatest crime in Auschwitz was to be pregnant. The so-called doctor of death [Joseph Mengele] of Auschwitz performed savage medical experiments on prisoners, in particular women, the physically handicapped and twins and was in charge of deciding who would go to the gas chamber.
>
> Dr. Mengele told me that it was my duty to report every pregnant woman to him. He said they would go to another camp for better nutrition, even for milk. So women began to run directly to him, telling him: "I am pregnant." I learned that they were all taken to the search block to be used as guinea pigs, and then two lives would be thrown into the crematorium. I decided that never again would there be pregnant women in Auschwitz.[14]

Dr. Perl interrupted the pregnancies "in the night, on a dirty floor, using only my dirty hands. . . . If I had not done it, both mother and child would have been cruelly murdered."

Perl had no beds, no bandages, no drugs, no instruments. She saw every disease brought about by torture, starvation, filth, lice, and rats, as well as broken bones and heads cracked open by savage beatings. But she did have one palliative, the spoken word:

> I treated patients with my voice, telling them beautiful stories, telling them that one day we would have birthdays again, that one day we would sing again. I didn't

know when it was Rosh Hashanah, but I had a sense of it when the weather turned cool. So I made a party with the bread, margarine and dirty pieces of sausage we received for meals. I said tonight will be the new year, tomorrow a better year will come.[15]

Imagine—a party held in Auschwitz. A party with "bread, margarine and dirty pieces of sausage." If a party can be held in Auschwitz, it can be held anywhere. At any time. At any place. This is the most difficult, yet the most powerful lesson that a crisis experience can teach us.

Survival Strategies

Preserving Your Health in Tough Times

Suffice it to say that after about an hour of solitary pillow-hugging, I began to realize that for two years of my life I had been drawing on resources that I did not possess, that I had been mortgaging myself physically and spiritually up to the hilt.

—F. SCOTT FITZGERALD

There are many challenges in the months following a crisis. Decisions will have to be made and complex problems will need to be solved. You will be redefining your future goals and adapting to a new way of life.

You cannot accomplish these tasks if you are fatigued and emotionally strung out. Nor will you be able to make good decisions if your perceptions and emotions are altered by tension and sleepless nights.

Therefore an important goal should be to stay in good

mental and physical health. But how do you do it? How do you stay healthy in a period in which you are under so much stress?

In the following pages we will learn how to cope with physical exhaustion and mental fatigue. We will learn what to do when sleep doesn't come and how to fortify ourselves through nutrition and exercise. And we will learn how to take care of our spirit when we are vulnerable to depression and despondency.

It should be emphasized that there is no one way to maintain health. Nor is what follows a complete guide to fitness. But if you follow these suggestions, you will probably feel better. And you may discover answers to perplexing problems.

Panic First Aid

Everyone has experienced panic. I remember as a child blindly driving my bicycle onto a busy street. There was a blast of the horn, the screech of tires, and the driver's angry look. An accident was averted by the driver's quick thinking. But I tingled all over. I am sure that my complexion was knuckle-white.

I retreated to the security of my home and tried to explain to my mother what had happened. But I couldn't remember anything. My mind was a blank.

The same dynamics appear in most heartbreaks. When Carol Stanford, a single parent, was informed that she was being laid off work, she panicked.

> I couldn't think right. My mind was a blur. I went home and my child said, "Are you all right, Mom?" And I said, "Sure."

But I wasn't all right. My mind was a jumble. How would I find a new job? How would I afford food for next week's meals?

I couldn't take it. It was too much. I just lay down in bed and cried.

Any crisis can cause panic. But there is one type of crisis that seems to generate panic faster than any other, and that is an unfavorable medical diagnosis. Said Rochelle Thiesen:

I went in for a routine physical examination. The doctor said he found an "irregularity." I knew it was cancer.

The night before entering the hospital I couldn't sleep. Finally I dozed off, but then I woke in a cold sweat.

I had a dream that I was being taken into surgery. The doctor made a long incision. I thought to myself, "I'll never again be able to wear a bathing suit." There were doctors everywhere all peering into my stomach. Finally the tallest surgeon said: "There is nothing we can do. Close her up."

I rolled over in bed and woke my husband. I said, "I'm only thirty-five. I can't die. I got three kids to raise."

I cried my eyes out. I was so anxious I could hardly breathe.

How do you control the panic?

You do it by reminding yourself that you have not lost everything. You have your loved ones and your friends. You have physicians who care. And you have a faith that is probably a lot stronger than you ever realized.

Specifically, if you have received a diagnosis of cancer, you need to remind yourself that many cancer patients are not only surviving but living useful lives. In some instances the advances in treatment were unavailable—or even unheard of—a decade ago. As Frank Rauscher, Jr., vice president for research of the American Cancer Society, says: "The years of 1983–1984 will be looked back upon as the golden age of cancer research. It's all coming together."[1]

It is all coming together. And if you doubt the medical advances, hospitals and research centers can give you examples of former patients who are now living life to the fullest. Among them is Phillip L. Karr, sixty-seven, a retired Santa Barbara engineer.

Phillip had lymph-node cancer that did not respond to three years of standard drug therapy. But in only four weeks after treatment with monoclonal antibodies—which destroy only cancer cells—his fatigue and fever vanished. Twenty-two months later he swims and hikes, the first human to be saved by the technique.

Or you might consider Sean Kelley, a seventeen-year-old Houston High School junior. He had a 70 percent chance of not surviving when told he had acute lymphoid leukemia at age ten. His physician, Dr. Donald J. Fernbach, pediatrics professor at Baylor College of Medicine, said, "If he'd been diagnosed three years earlier, there's nothing we could have done." But new drugs have spelled success.[2]

You stop panic by reversing negative thoughts. You stop panic by ceasing to dwell on your fears or dreary prognoses or feelings that you can never again be happy or well. And in their place you find reasons for hope.

For the cancer patient it is the realization that there is a whole arsenal of therapies that can be used to assist you. For the unemployed it is an affirmation that there is a company somewhere that needs your skills. For the rejected lover it is understanding that there are others who want you as a friend.

Panic feelings usually subside rapidly. Particularly if you reorient your thinking. But anxiety can linger for days, weeks, and even months.

Anxiety might be defined as a sense of apprehension and doubt concerning one's capacity to cope with a situation. It's the perception that you may never get well or may never again be happy. It's sensing that life is out of control. It's the knot in the stomach that doesn't go away.

But most of all, anxiety is the fear of the unknown.

Suppose you find yourself in a strange city. You have to walk to the hotel. You hear footsteps. They become louder and louder. The person seems to be gaining on you.

Is it a mugger? Could it be a jogger? Is someone going to harm you? Anxiously you look around. You are reassured. The individual crosses the street.

But suppose the person didn't cross the street. Suppose the individual looks like a thug. And suppose he has a weapon. Now what would you do?

Most of us would run if we had the chance. Or we might fight if attacked. That's how we tend to manage our crises: fleeing the situation or fighting it.

The problem with a heartbreak is that usually you can neither run nor fight. If your child has to have complicated and possibly life-threatening surgery, you can't run from it. You need to go through it.

But as you sit outside of the operating room, you have a knot in your stomach. For the outcome is unknown.

Anxiety is the fear of the unknown. If you knew with absolute certainty that you would find another job, there would be no anxiety. If you knew beyond a shadow of a doubt that you could fall in love again, there would be less need to worry.

But heartbreaks aren't that simple. If you can't run from them or fight them, the only recourse for many is to worry. And to be anxious.

How can anxiety be diminished?

There are several strategies that seem to work. Each one

in its own way calms the body, soothes the mind, and diminishes the fear.

A BREATHING EXERCISE

"I just can't get my breath" is a common complaint of someone who is anxious. Others note their rapid pulse rates and sense that their hearts are "pounding." This frequently happens at bedtime, thus making sleep difficult to obtain. Here is a way to resume normal patterns of breathing:

> Lie comfortably on the floor or in your bed. Or if you prefer, sit on a firm chair.
>
> Close your eyes. Relax.
>
> Inhale slowly and deeply through your nose. Breathe so that your stomach pushes out.
>
> Exhale slowly through your mouth.
>
> While breathing, count slowly to about six or eight while inhaling and about eight or ten while exhaling (a longer count for exhaling).
>
> Repeat this exercise eight times or as long as it is comfortable.
>
> Breathe normally and rest quietly for a few minutes.[3]

When should you use a breathing exercise? Whenever you feel uptight. Find a quiet place. Close your eyes. Breathe deeply. The anxiety will soon diminish.

A RELAXATION TECHNIQUE

Have you ever noticed how your muscles stiffen when you are tense? The muscles that seem to tighten the fastest are located in the back of the neck, through the shoulder blades, and into the lower back. Some people feel tension in the muscles of the jaw and/or in the muscles of the legs.

A technique that both reduces muscle tension and decreases anxiety is described by psychologist Dr. Eugene C. Walker:

First sit on a comfortable chair or lie on a couch or bed. Then say something like the following to yourself: "I am going to relax completely. First I will relax my forehead and scalp. I will let all the muscles on my forehead and scalp relax and become completely at rest. All of the wrinkles will smooth out of my forehead and that part of my body will relax completely. Now I will relax the muscles on my face. I will just let them relax and go limp. There will be no tension in my jaw. Next, I will relax my neck muscles. Just let them become tranquil and allow all the pressure to leave them. My neck muscles are relaxing completely. Now I will relax the muscles of my shoulders. That relaxation will spread down my arms to the elbows, down the forearm to my hands and fingers. My arms will just dangle from the frame of my body. I will take a deep breath and relax, letting all of the tightness and tenseness leave. My breathing will now be normal and relaxed, and I will relax the muscles of my stomach. Now I will relax all the muscles up and down both sides of my spine; now the waist, buttocks, and thighs down to my knees. Now the relaxation will spread to the calves of my legs, my ankles, feet, and toes. I will just lie here and continue to let all of my muscles go completely limp. I will become completely relaxed from the top of my head to the tip of my toes."[4]

A TECHNIQUE TO VISUALIZE POSITIVE IMAGES

This technique will help you to focus on affirmations. It's a good technique to use when life feels out of control.

First, find a quiet place where you will not be distracted. Sit or lie down in a comfortable position. Remove uncomfortable clothing, eyeglasses, or contact lenses. If you are in a hospital, ask the nurse if you can be alone for ten or fifteen minutes in order to meditate. Shut the door to the room or pull the curtain around the bed.

Now give yourself permission to think creatively. Decide on one image that has a great deal of meaning and has brought you much joy.

For example, you might see yourself skiing, swimming, or walking. You might remember a scene at the ocean or in the mountains. Or you might focus on the warmth of the sun; the sensation of sitting by a fireplace on a cold winter night. Some hospitalized patients find contentment in simply focusing on their home and all the joys that it provides.

Think about that image for as long as it gives you pleasure. Enter into it fully. Remind yourself of the many things which bring you happiness.

Second, become fully relaxed. Close your eyes slowly. Relax the muscles in the eyelids to the point where they are so relaxed and comfortable that you feel you are unable to pull your eyelids open.

Now transfer your relaxed, comfortable feeling to other parts of the body one by one, from top to bottom—head, chest, arms, hands, back, stomach, legs, and feet.

Try to imagine yourself floating on a white cloud bathed in warm sunlight. Everything that you see, touch, or hear is peaceful. Quiet. Become fully aware of how relaxed you feel.

Third, focus on positive images. If you are ill, envision healing. Remind yourself that you are surrounded with the best technology and the best therapies this world has ever seen.

If your crisis is the death of a loved one, remind yourself of all the good times you had together. But remind yourself that your loved one would want the best for you, and that would mean moving on with your life.

And if your problem is unemployment or a financial reversal, remember that you have talents that you have not yet explored. Remind yourself that you will eventually find employment. And that your financial affairs will improve.

For any other problem you might have, think about a positive response. Chase away any negative thoughts.

Now gradually return to your present reality. But continue to rest comfortably. Let your mind focus on that which is good.[5]

There is one other exercise that is often helpful in reducing anxiety.

Take out a sheet of paper and under the heading labeled *losses* write down everything you have lost or feel that you might lose because of your heartbreak. Then under the heading labeled *assets* write down all the resources that are available. For example, you probably have supportive loved ones and friends. A job. A hobby. A realization that you have made it through difficult times in the past and you probably can do it again in the future.

Here is what Rochelle Thiesen reported when she completed this exercise:

I started to write down all the losses associated with cancer. Going to the hospital. Losing my hair from the treatments. Maybe not being cured. Not seeing my kids grow up. . . . When I thought about my kids, I just broke down and sobbed.

A couple of days later I decided to complete the exercise. I thought about a little booklet written by the American Cancer Society called *The Hopeful Side of Cancer*. Half of all cancer patients are now being cured. Deaths from seven of the ten major forms of cancer are down. There are powerful new drugs. So under assets I wrote, "I'll be treated in a good hospital with good physicians."

Then I thought about my mom. She too had cancer. But she survived for seventeen years and she lived a full and wonderful life. So I wrote down, "Others have survived, why can't I?"

The doctor said that after the treatments were over

we could take a vacation, so I wrote down "Vermont—the place where we want to go."

Then I thought about my faith. For some reason a verse from the Bible jumped into my head: "They that wait upon the Lord shall renew their strength; they shall mount up with wings as eagles; they shall run and not be weary, and they shall walk and not faint."

I wrote down the word "faith." I knew that it was going to be tested. But at least I had some.

After I was done writing I looked over my list. Everything under the loss column was so foreboding. But then it struck me that many of the things that I put down were fears. It wasn't reality. I erased those things. Nevertheless that which remained frightened me.

Then I looked at the positive things. What impressed me was all the many things that I had going for me: good care, good friends, my mom's legacy, my loved ones, my faith.

Every day I go back to that sheet and study it. Whenever my faith gets weak or I am overwhelmed with doubts, I reread my assets. It pushes the clouds away.

How to Obtain a Good Night's Rest

Sometimes the anxiety is so great that it is difficult to get a good night's rest. Many people have difficulty falling and staying asleep. Consequently they get up tired and irritable and may have a difficult time coping with their emotions throughout the day.

One man said that not getting sleep was bad enough. But what made it worse were all the people at work who kept telling him that he ought to get some sleep! "Oh, if they only knew how hard I try," he commented.

Sleep problems represent a kind of vicious cycle. On the one hand we know that we need the sleep. But on the other hand sleep simply doesn't come. The more frustrated we get the more difficult it is to relax and to drift off into a sound sleep. Why can't we sleep, especially if we are tired?

It's because our minds are working overtime. While the body might be shutting down for rest, the mind continues to operate. In fact the mind often shifts into high gear— cruising away, dreaming up new concerns, replaying old conversations, and making plans for tomorrow. Fortunately there are practical and proven ways of slowing the mind down and getting the sleep we need.

First, don't sleep during the day. Some people can catnap and not have it affect nighttime sleep. But many are not so fortunate. The reason is simple: Most people have natural periods of being awake and being asleep. When these become interchanged, as by taking afternoon naps, the body is confused. It may respond by not letting you sleep at night.

Second, do some mild exercise before going to bed. A short walk will diminish anxiety. But it will also create a sense of fatigue, signaling the body that it is time to rest.

Third, avoid eating so much food before going to bed that you feel bloated. But don't go to bed on an empty stomach. Sometimes a cup of warm milk will coat the stomach and soothe the nerves.

All stimulants should be avoided in the five hours prior to bedtime, including coffee, tea, and hot chocolate. You should also be aware that certain medications contain caffeine, including a wide number of aspirin products. Consult the instructions that come with the medications and determine if they contain stimulants. If so, avoid using at bedtime.

Fourth, relax. Use the deep-breathing exercise and/or the relaxation technique mentioned earlier. Follow up with a warm (but not hot) bath.

Fifth, don't stay in bed if you can't sleep. Get up. Pour yourself a hot drink and read a magazine. When you begin to feel drowsy, go back to bed. If sleep doesn't come, get up and repeat the process.

What usually happens is that we go to bed and think: "I feel tired, but I know I won't sleep. I'll toss and turn all night." Not surprisingly, we do toss and turn. We look at the clock. First it is 1:00 A.M., then 2:00 A.M., and then 4:00 A.M.! And as every hour goes by, we get madder and madder because we can't sleep.

Far better to do something you enjoy. Get up—and don't go back to bed until you feel tired.

Sixth, remember that the greatest single cause of sleeplessness is the fear that you will not get to sleep. Tell yourself that you are going to have a good, sound, restful sleep.

But if your hopeful words do not come true, remind yourself that there is healing in rest. If you cannot sleep, move to another bed or to the living-room couch. Lie down and this time simply relax. Don't even try to sleep. Enjoy the quiet of the moment. It's good therapy. And you will probably fall asleep.

The Benefits of Exercise

One of the most frequent complaints of heartbreak victims is that they don't have any energy. Why do we feel so weary and exhausted after a heartbreak?

Because we are using an immense amount of energy coping with our problems. We struggle to comprehend what has happened and why it happened. We struggle with important decisions. And we often form new relationships.

Many people have little understanding of how these demands influence health. In fact, many deny that they are under stress. One hospitalized patient said that he wasn't under any stress because all he was doing was lying in bed.

Nothing could be further from the truth. While in the hospital he was thinking about his illness and his family. He was concerned about the amount of time he was away from work and what his colleagues might be thinking. Most of all he was worried about the outcome of the diagnostic tests.

It's not uncommon for people to be unaware of their stress. They push hard, but then they collapse. That's what happened to Molly Anderson five months after her husband had a heart attack.

Her husband's heart attack resulted in partial paralysis. But nine weeks later he was told he could leave the hospital and return home.

> I was so happy. But I was totally unprepared for what was to happen.
>
> He became very demanding. He was scared of having another heart attack and wanted me to be by his side twenty-four hours a day. He would call just to be sure that I was nearby. He would want me to stay in his room.
>
> At times he was incontinent. I would have to wash his bedding several times a day. I would even have to help him dress.
>
> I didn't realize what this was taking out of me. One night I almost collapsed in the living room. And then I realized for the first time how tired I was. I was bone tired. I could barely lift myself to bed.

How do you keep from feeling "bone tired"? What can you do so that you don't collapse?

You need to exercise. The president of the American Medical Association put it this way: "It begins to appear that exercise is the master conditioner for the healthy and the major therapy for the ill."[6]

What are the benefits of exercise? First, if you exercise

on a regular basis, you will have more energy.

Frank Launder complained of feeling tired all the time. Actually he was angry after being demoted at work. Experiencing some chest pains, he went to the doctor.

The physician examined him and reported that his physical condition was excellent. "But the mental report," said the doctor, "isn't quite so optimistic. You're depressed." The physician prescribed eight hours of rest a night and a regular program of exercise. Here is what happened:

> I was told to jog one block and then walk two. I was to do this three times a week for a month.
>
> Well, I tried it. And I felt better. The same thing happened the next time I jogged. And the next.
>
> Finally I had to admit that what the doctor said was true: You *really* do feel better after working out.
>
> I kept up the jogging routine. Before I knew it I could go a full city block. Then two. I was up to a quarter of a mile. Then a half-mile.
>
> I couldn't believe it. I use to make fun of all those joggers going by my house. But you know what, now I am out there too. Even in the rain. I just feel so much better.

Why does regular exercise make you feel better? And why do you have new energy and a renewed sense of vitality?

Within a matter of weeks after starting an exercise program, there are positive changes in health. Your muscles will have a more extensive network of blood vessels, enabling your blood to be transported more efficiently. Additional red blood cells will be produced, carrying more oxygen throughout the body. Furthermore, a greater volume of blood will be transported and your lungs will be able to consume a greater volume of air. All of this contributes to an increased sense of stamina and strength.

Your heart in particular benefits from exercise. It will be

able to pump an increased amount of blood with every beat and will slow down and rest more efficiently between beats.

Sedentary people have a heartbeat rate of approximately eighty to ninety beats per minute. But if you are in good physical shape, your resting pulse rate will be approximately seventy beats per minute. Consequently the heart makes thousands fewer beats per day, which in turn reduces wear and tear on the heart valves and blood vessels.

It is not only the heart that benefits. Calories are burned, thus contributing to weight control. Hypertension may be reduced. And muscles become firm.[7]

But most of all—you have more energy.

A second reason for exercising is that it beats back the blues.

At the University of Wisconsin researchers wanted to compare the benefits of running and long-term psychotherapy. Individuals who were depressed were placed in one of two groups. Some were assigned to ten weeks of running therapy and ten weeks of psychotherapy. This group met with their therapist and exercised three times a week. They were not permitted to discuss their depression during the run. The other group was strictly in psychotherapy.

When the experiment was concluded, the running patients showed the most improvement. More important, a year later most of the joggers were still running and were free of depression.[8]

I have known individuals who felt better after a single walk. And after a couple of weeks of playing tennis or volleyball they no longer feel quite so tired. Nor so blue.

Not only does exercise lift depression, it also dissipates anger. Robert Hawkins works for a punitive boss in a high-pressure environment. He is angry a good share of the time. I asked him how he managed to stay well. A smile came to his face and he said: "I play raquetball. When things get so bad at work, I go to the gym and swat the ball. Sometimes I am so mad that I figuratively name the ball————[the name of his boss]. Then I hit it. I always feel better."

You may not need to swat a ball to get over your anger. But exercise will dissipate it.

There is one other advantage of regular exercise. Most people discover that their creativity is enhanced after a workout. In fact, many find that a new idea or a mental breakthrough comes while exercising. One executive, for example, takes a little pad of paper with him on his jog, because he knows that some idea will surface that he won't want to forget.

I have known individuals going through extremely trying times who have largely survived by doing one thing: physical exercise. More than one person has told me that it was their morning jog or their nightly walk that made it possible for them to function at work and at home.

What kind of exercise is best?

Walking seems to be the ideal therapy for a heartbreak. Why walking? Because it has both physical and psychological benefits. Almost anyone can do it. And there is no expense outside of a good pair of shoes.

How do you walk so that it improves both mental and physical health? Walk slowly at first. But gradually build up speed. Now bend your arms to a ninety-degree angle at the elbows and start to pump back and forth, as though you wanted to hit an imaginary punching bag. Keep your arms close to the side. As the arm goes backward vigorously your foot will be thrust forward on each stride. Take long strides. Move at a comfortable clip, but not so fast that you feel dizzy.[9]

Here are some practical guidelines for beginning a brisk walking program:

- Time of day: before a meal or one hour after.

- Frequency: at least five times a week. Try not to skip two days in a row. A 1980 study demonstrated that exercise done four and five times a week is three times as effective as exercise done three times a week.

- Amount: start at ten minutes and gradually work toward thirty minutes. Your eventual target will be fifty minutes with a ten-minute warm-up (stretching exercises, slow walking), thirty minutes of brisk walking, and a "cool-down" period of ten minutes (slow walking).

- Goal: to achieve a pulse rate that is 70 percent of your maximum rate. The easiest way to find your maximum pulse rate is to subtract your age from the number 220. For example, if you're forty, your maximum rate is 180 ($220 - 40 = 180$). Multiply that by 70 percent and you will know that your goal should be a pulse rate of approximately 126 beats per minute ($180 \times .70 = 126$).[10]

Brisk walking has many of the benefits of other types of vigorous exercise activities. Muscles are toned, excess weight is lost, and the heart beats more efficiently. Personal problems don't go away, but they are put in perspective. And psychological energy is restored.*

In spite of the many benefits of exercise many people resist the idea. Why? They don't have the time. Or if they are depressed, they may feel so tired that they can't imagine jogging or playing tennis or swimming.

I understand such feelings. But you need to exercise. There will be new energy and vitality. And there will be pride in knowing that you are doing something to improve

---

* If you have been physically inactive, it is important to have a physical examination before initiating an exercise program. Additional information on how to establish a safe exercise program can be found in Ernst L. Wynder, ed., *The Book of Health: A Complete Guide to Making Health Last a Lifetime* (New York: Franklin Watts, 1981).

your physical health and emotional well-being. For assistance in establishing a sound exercise program, consult your physician or organizations such as the YWCA and YMCA.

Eating to Stay Well

When a heartbreak occurs, the last thing we tend to think about is food. A young woman whose fiancé was killed in a car accident said: "I lost twenty-three pounds in five months. I just didn't feel like eating." A middle-aged man struggling with a career change commented: "I just skipped meals. Nothing tasted good; nothing looked good."

But the opposite can happen. Some people consume whatever is in sight, including candy, soda, chocolates, pastries, cakes and pies. Mary Filensted told what it was like to binge: "I put on forty-three pounds in the year following my divorce. I would bring home bags of potato chips. I would eat frozen dinners. Sometimes I would pick up a dozen fried doughnuts. And when I went to a restaurant, I would eat whatever looked good."

Health problems related to nutritional deficiencies tend to surface in the months following a heartbreak. There is tiredness and a general feeling of being run down. There are stomach pains and abdominal cramps. And then there are headaches, which can often be traced to poor nutrition.

If you have had a heartbreak, this is not the time to go on a diet. Nor is this the time to select your foods haphazardly. Rather, this is a time in life in which you will want to pay close attention to what you eat and drink. Here are some practical steps to ensure sound nutritional health.

First, do not skip any meals. Because if you do you probably will feel tired. You may feel listless. There will be an increase in gastric acidity, which produces canker sores and can eventually lead to stomach ulcers.

If you stop eating or eat indiscriminately over a period of weeks, the results can be quite serious. For when there is a calcium deficiency, bone strength degenerates. When there is a protein deficiency, muscle strength is lost. And if life-sustaining vitamins are not ingested, there will be an increased susceptibility to illness.

It is particularly important to enjoy a hearty breakfast. Breakfast prepares your body for the day's work. It provides the energy that you will need to meet the challenges that are ahead.

What should you be eating for breakfast?

The type of breakfast you want is one that is high in protein but low in sugar content. Foods and beverages that are particularly nutritious are milk, yogurt, whole-grain cereals, breads, and lean meat products.

Researchers compared children who ate high protein breakfasts with those who ate sugary cereals. The differences were startling: In the high protein group the students gained an average of 7 months in reading achievement in a 4-month period, while the group eating sugary cereals gained only 5.25 months. Similar results were found in another study: The high protein group gained 4.25 months in reading achievement compared with 1.82 in the other group.[11]

Second, eat foods that will preserve and enhance your strength throughout the day. Here are some helpful guidelines produced by the American Health Foundation:

1. Limit all sources of calories (including alcohol) to reach and maintain your ideal weight. A nutritionist employed in a hospital or health department can inform you about your ideal weight as well as the number of calories you need to keep at that ideal weight.

2. Use fish, chicken and very lean meat in place of fatty meats. Have occasional meatless meals. In its place obtain protein from skim milk, low-fat cheese, lentils, peas and soy products.

3. Use skim milk or two percent fat milk instead of whole milk. Minimize cream and butter in your diet.

4. Use soft margarine, polyunsaturated oils; limit butter and solid shortening.

5. Egg whites may be used freely, but limit yolks to three per week.

6. Use low-fat cooking methods (steaming, broiling, etc.).

7. Eat more vegetables, fruit, whole-grain bread; fewer baked goods, candies, sugar.[12]

Third, prepare your own meals. Don't rely on restaurant food or prepackaged products.

Convenience foods and mass-produced products often have poor nutrient content. For example, food in most vending machines is high in fats and starch and loaded with sugar. And while "just a spoonful of sugar" is needed for the replenishment of our energy reserves, we consume approximately twenty teaspoons a day, or over 100 pounds per year, per person. We don't need that much sugar. In fact, it is potentially harmful.

Perhaps a more important reason for preparing your own meals is that when you cook, you are caring for yourself. In effect you are saying: My health is important. Furthermore, if you invite friends and neighbors to your home for dinner, you are reestablishing ties to other people. Cooking for others is one of the easiest ways to overcome loneliness.

"But," you might say, "I have never learned to cook." If that is the case, this might be the time to learn. There are cooking schools in most communities. Or you might ask a friend to teach you. Cooking nutritionally sound meals isn't that difficult. And it might bring you considerable joy.

Now we come to a very important suggestion: Be aware of the harmful effects of stimulants and depressants, which we often use as a substitute for a balanced diet.

Let's first look at caffeine, since it is one of the world's most widely used drugs.

Caffeine is found in coffee, tea, cola drinks, cocoa, and over-the-counter cold remedies as well as in various aspirin products. If you recall what you have consumed during a day, you might be surprised to learn that you have had the equivalent of six to eight cups of coffee.

What happens when you drink coffee? Within five minutes caffeine has raced to every part of your body. It increases the flow of urine and stomach acid, and it steps up the intake of oxygen. It speeds up your basic metabolic rate by 10 percent. The heart pumps faster.

But three to five hours later you will feel "let down"—tired and listless. It is then that you may again turn to coffee, tea, or a cola drink for an additional lift.

Can caffeine harm you? A typical cup of coffee contains at least 100 milligrams of caffeine. Only 250 milligrams of caffeine can cause you to exhibit the same symptoms as those who are suffering from clinically detected anxiety.[13]

Four hundred milligrams of caffeine—or approximately four cups of coffee—can bring on irritability, headaches, tremors, and nervousness. If that dose is doubled, a jittery coffee drinker may suffer hallucinations, even convulsions.

Five cups of coffee a day can cause you to be dependent upon it. And if you decide to quit, you may experience withdrawal symptoms, including nausea, headaches, irritability, and depression.[14]

Individuals who are anxious, tense, and uptight should

stay away from products with caffeine. Particularly if their hearts are racing or pounding.

Stay away as well from "pep pills" or "uppers," all of which stimulate the nervous system. These drugs, called amphetamines, were first made available to the public in the 1940s. Benzedrine was sold over the counter in an aromatic form to clear stuffy noses. But it was taken off the market when it was discovered that college students were breaking the containers and dissolving the contents in soft drinks.

Today you can buy amphetamine-like drugs in most every pharmacy. Dieters use them to lose weight. Students use them to stay awake in marathon study sessions. Truck drivers take them on long overnight hauls.

But heartbreak victims also take them to find relief from their depression. One worker who was going through a difficult divorce said:

> I don't sleep well at night. And therefore I am tired during the day. So I take an "upper" at least twice a day. In fact, I don't think I could get through the day without it.
>
> Do I worry about what I'm taking? Not too often, although lately I've noticed that I have to take a couple extra pills in order to get the same effect.

What are the risks in taking amphetamines? There can be nervousness, elevated blood pressure, and headaches, all from a single dose. And if used repeatedly there can be insomnia, dizziness, agitation, confusion, malnutrition— even delirium.[15]

Unfortunately people become dependent upon the drug, even if it is not addictive in a physiological sense. Tolerance develops. As the worker noted, he had to take a "couple extra pills" in order to get the same kick.

Now, some might say: "I don't take stimulants. But my doctor has prescribed a tranquilizer. Is there any danger in that?" Generally not—providing you take them as prescribed and for only a limited period of time. But it is possible to abuse sedatives just like any other drug.

You can become intoxicated if you take more than what is prescribed. Or you can fall into a deep sleep, followed by coma. If you mix them with alcohol in order to get a double effect, you might die.

It's tragic, but people do die from taking sedatives. How does this occur? They take the prescribed dose, but then fall half-asleep. Forgetting that they have taken the pills, they consume additional ones.[16]

It has been estimated that three to four billion doses of phenobarbital and Seconal (sleeping medication) are prescribed annually in this country. There is nothing wrong with taking a tranquilizer or sedative to help you fall asleep. And there is nothing to be ashamed of in taking a product that calms your nerves and enables you to function effectively at home and at work. But you do not want to become dependent on any medication. And you want to take them *exactly* as prescribed.

Here are some questions that you should ask about any medication. They are particularly relevant for sedatives:

1. What is the name of the drug?

2. Why am I taking this drug?

3. How should this drug be taken?

4. How many pills should I take at one time?

5. How frequently should it be taken?

6. What is the length of time that I ought to continue to take this medication?

7. What are the side effects?

8. Does taking the drug require me to change my diet or activities? (Should I avoid driving or working with dangerous equipment?)

9. What will happen if I miss a dose? (Be very reluctant to double a dose of any medication.)[17]

There is one other drug that must be mentioned in any discussion about heartbreak: alcohol. It is not uncommon for individuals to drink more heavily after a tragedy than at any other period in their life. Wanting to "get away from it all," they drink whatever happens to be around, whether it be wine, beer, or hard liquor.

Be very reluctant to use alcoholic beverages during this period in life. Alcohol can be a villain under the best of circumstances. But when you are in grief, it compounds the difficulties.

Here is what happens when you drink: The alcohol rushes to the brain. The central nervous system becomes depressed. Soon there is a soft glow, but if the drinking continues, that glow can quickly turn to excitement, restlessness—even agitation.

As drinking continues, there is a general depression not only of physical functions but of mental capabilities. It is a fact that many crimes, accidents, and violent deaths have been recorded as a result of a single, isolated incident of heavy drinking. It adds to a general feeling of depression and a feeling that "life isn't worth living."[18]

One of the biggest problems is that alcohol becomes a substitute for food. When this occurs, nutrients essential for living are omitted, thus jeopardizing health.

If you have had a heartbreak, don't use alcohol. Or use it sparingly. I state this with some feeling. On a number of occasions individuals I interviewed would say, "I think I could have managed my original problems, but alcohol made things worse."

There is one last suggestion that will improve nutritional health: Keep high-energy snacks in your kitchen. As we noted, some people don't eat when under stress. But some eat all the time. They search the cupboards and consume whatever happens to be handy. If you snack, keep nutritious foods at hand, foods that will provide energy and promote your nutritional health.

Here is a short list of some of the very best snacks: raisins, dried fruits, popcorn, orange juice, fresh fruits, hot chocolate, fig newtons, graham crackers, and granola. All of these products are high in carbohydrates and are excellent energy-producing foods.

Hippocrates left us much wisdom when he said, "Your foods shall be your remedies and your remedies shall be your foods." Eat well. Stay away from foods and beverages that will hurt you. Prepare your own food. And eat high energy snacks. You will feel better. And you will keep yourself in optimal nutritional health.

Mental Workouts

It's important to stay well physically. But it is also important to stay well emotionally. One of the best ways of preserving mental health is to enjoy hobbies, avocations, and the small delights that nurture the spirit.

Researchers in human development have emphasized the importance of doing things that keep you active and mentally alert. At the UCLA School of Medicine 134 sets of twins have been followed since 1946. Some of the subjects are now eighty years old.

Those twins who kept active mentally not only retained their cognitive ability better than those who didn't, but they were also healthier physically. Says one of the researchers:

> The mental activity seemed to be just as important as the physical activity. I think the important thing is to keep your mind working, which means making new connections in your brain rather than just doing the same old things over and over again. [Do] anything that's involving and challenging—and that you enjoy. I think the brain is like a muscle: If you don't exercise it, it wastes away.[19]

You need to exercise the brain. And pursuing an avocation is one of the best ways to do it. Furthermore, a hobby is sometimes the only thing that is powerful enough to break through gloom and despair. A depressed widow talked with enthusiasm about the coming of spring and the prospect of getting into her garden. A teenager fighting a difficult illness came to life as he talked about his favorite football team and the scores of recent games. A displaced worker said he knew he was over his bitterness when he cleaned his rod and reel and started to think about his favorite trout stream.

Unfortunately hobbies are often forgotten. In fact, we may even feel guilty about enjoying them.

Mark Seltzman missed the opening of hunting season, for the first time in twenty-three years. "I just couldn't go," he said. "My wife has been gone only a couple of months. I don't think I would enjoy myself."

Such feelings are understandable. We can't quite see ourselves enjoying life when we are struggling with a broken heart. Therefore hobbies, avocations, even relationships, tend to be put to the side.

Nevertheless it is important to enter into anything that brings joy. And you need to do it with determination. If you were in the middle of a project when your heartbreak occurred, finish it and move to another one. If you are a hiker, plan your next challenge. If you are an avid reader, keep going to the bookstore and visiting the library.

Your goal is straightforward: You want to stay mentally alert and creative. But you might say: "Maybe that's what I should be doing, but I'm not up to it. I can't concentrate. I can't take on new tasks."

Perhaps you should wait a while before pursuing a new goal or a former hobby. But don't wait too long. Because the longer you procrastinate, the harder it is to return to it.

What if you don't have a hobby? Now is the time to discover one. Look upon it as a new challenge. Find one much as you would approach an assignment at work: Read, talk to people, try out new ideas, and then decide on something into which you can put your mind and your heart.

It's never too late to find a hobby. Hilda Crooks lives in northwest Wisconsin. She climbed the highest mountain in the contiguous United States when she was sixty-six years old. When she was eighty-five, she climbed it for the twentieth time. Listen to her words, for she has something important to teach us:

> Many, many older people are depressed. They think there's nothing left in life for them anymore. The largest age groups for suicide are college age and older people. They're depressed, grim, unhappy, and disdainful. Young people see that and think that's what is ahead for them. It's a poor example.
>
> I once lived next door to an older single man, and every morning I'd go out into the garden in the back yard where there was just a fence between us. He'd be out there and I'd say: "Good morning, neighbor. How are you today?"
>
> He'd always say, "I'm just waiting for the Grim Reaper." That was his reply, every morning. "I'm just waiting for the Grim Reaper."

At the same time, I knew another man who I often met on the street. He was 101 years old. I'd see him on the street going to the library to read. He died before he was 102, but he never stopped trying to increase his knowledge, to improve himself.

No matter where you are, keep moving. There are always higher areas. When I can't walk anymore, then I'll crawl. It's the way we started and not a bad way to finish. I'd rather die on a mountain than in a nursing home.[20]

D. H. Lawrence in *Lady Chatterley's Lover* remarked, "You cannot insure against the future except by really believing in the best bit of you."[21]

What does "believing in the best bit of you" mean? For those who have had a heartbreak it means affirming every morning and evening that you are strong and that you will survive your loss.

But it also means taking care of your physical and emotional health. It means entering into your hobbies and quiet routines with optimism and enthusiasm. And it suggests being thankful for all the small joys that guide us through tough times.

What Happens to the Family in a Crisis

Even if I dropped one hundred balls and missed every block, my family and friends back home would say, "Good game."
— JOE SENSER, MINNESOTA VIKING
FOOTBALL PLAYER

If there is one thing that is known about a heartbreak it is this: Crises change families.

Sometimes families become more loving and more compassionate. They talk about their fears and converse about their hopes. When loved ones become discouraged, there are hugs and expressions of tenderness.

But other families cannot cope with the pressure. Frustrations build. Tempers become short. Accusatory statements are made. And if the frustrations are not resolved, relationships begin to fracture.

How do families cope with a crisis? Why do some become more loving while others splinter? Perhaps the starting point is to examine how a crisis influenced one family.

A Case Study: The Disintegration of a Family

Sam and Marjorie Christopherson lived in a fashionable San Francisco community. Sam was vice president of a large manufacturing firm. His yearly salary was $165,000, not counting his yearly bonus. Marjorie spent much of her time working in a small neighborhood boutique. They had one child, Eric, who was fifteen years old.

The signs of affluence could be seen everywhere. They owned an expensive home with a beautiful ocean view. There were expensive cars in the driveway. Several evenings each week were spent dining in fashionable restaurants.

Yet there was an uneasy truce within this family. It wasn't that Marjorie and Sam disliked one another. But after eighteen years of marriage the spark that had once lit evenings of torrid lovemaking had dimmed into a distant memory.

The first hint that their carefully planned life was about to shatter was seen in violent arguments that Sam had with their teenage son. Sometimes they were about Eric's low grades at school. And sometimes they were criticisms of Eric's friends and how he was spending his money.

Although the run-ins with Eric were disquieting, they were nothing compared with the total devastation that Sam felt when his own subordinate was appointed president of the company.

Sam could not comprehend the shifting fortunes of his career. For years he had been tacitly assured that the top position would be his. Indeed, he had spent many evenings drawing up plans as to how he would make the company more profitable once he was promoted. But his dream turned into a nightmare. His wife describes what took place during the following year:

I'll never forget the day that Sam learned that he wasn't going to be the president of the company. He came home very late, half drunk.

His appearance gave everything away. I knew something was terribly wrong. His tie was cocked to one side. His shirt was filled with perspiration. His speech was slurred. Then he told me that Fred Baines would be his new boss. Not only did he feel rotten about not getting the promotion, but he detested Fred Baines.

During the next six months he retreated into his own thoughts. He hardly ever conversed with me. I tried to reach him and help him. But whenever I tried, he would say, "You wouldn't understand."

Then he started to take out his frustrations on Eric. I would hear them argue for what seemed like hours at a time. I could see that Eric was coming to despise his father.

The whole year was hell. I heard through a friend that he wasn't doing well at work. I felt that maybe his job was in jeopardy. We never had been great talkers but now we hardly conversed. Not even at the end of the day.

I tried to keep busy during those difficult months, but I had trouble focusing on anything. I really worried about Sam's health. He put on forty pounds. He would not come home until late at night and I had no idea where he was.

In truth I wasn't doing very well either. I felt irritable and tense. I found myself yelling at Eric for not cleaning his room or doing his homework.

The problems with our son seemed insurmountable. One week after his fifteenth birthday he came home drunk. His teacher called and told us we better find out what was going on because he was flunking out of school.

I was slowly going mad. Sam didn't talk to me and Eric was disobedient. I couldn't sleep at night. My mind was a whirlwind.

Then two things happened that almost destroyed me. First Eric got mixed up with a bunch of thugs. He started to look mean and tough.

I pleaded with Eric to straighten out his life but he treated me like a nobody. At one point he grabbed me and told me I was a "stupid broad." He was barely fifteen but he weighed over two hundred pounds. His sheer size frightened me.

The second thing that really shook me up—I cannot describe this to you without having my heart pound so that it feels that it is coming out of my chest—is that I learned that my husband was having an affair. An affair with a girl half his age.

And you know how I found out about it? I was coming home one night from a school conference concerning Eric. I stopped at the corner grocery store for some milk, which took me by a motel. And there sitting in front of one of the rooms was my husband's car.

I was shocked. I drove up to the motel and just stared at the car. I thought maybe I was going crazy. Was it really his sports car? I looked inside the car but it was so dark that I couldn't tell much. So I wrote down the license plate number: LCD 811.

I went home and waited for him. I still had some doubts. Maybe I was imagining this whole thing. I was so nervous that I could hardly contain myself.

At 1:15 A.M., I heard the car. He told me that he had to work late. He immediately went to bed. After I knew he was asleep I went out to the garage. My worst fears were confirmed: the license plate read LCD 811.

I was absolutely beside myself. The only possible explanation was that he was having an affair.

I crawled into bed and didn't say a word. He was snoring. And then it dawned on me that Sam kept a gun tucked in a drawer next to the bed.

I froze as I thought the inconceivable. I got up and went to the drawer and pulled out the revolver. I thought about how much better everyone would be if I shot him.

And, as my mind was racing, I thought about killing Eric too. And then I would turn the gun on myself. Everybody would finally be at peace.

I pulled the gun out of the drawer. It shook in my hand. I looked over at the bed and thought about how easy it would be to shoot him. And then he would never again have to worry about his job or me or his son. Our whole insanity would be forever over.

I must have stood there for three or four minutes. But I just couldn't do it.

The next day I went to the drawer and once again got the gun out. But this time I carefully took it down the steps and put it on a shelf in the garage. I had to get that thing out of the house. I was terrified that I would fall asleep and do that gruesome act in my sleep.

The Christopherson family never recovered from this period in their lives. Sam eventually lost his job, not because he didn't have the talent, but because he lost the will to work. Without any salary coming in and having spent so much of their savings, they lost their home. Three years later, after having been turned down for a middle-management position that would have paid him about a fourth of what he once earned, he became an invalid—crippled with psychological depression.

Eric's life script was not much better than his father's. He became incorrigible not only at home but at school. He dropped out in his senior year and today, between hangovers, works at odd jobs.

But perhaps the saddest ending to the story centers on Marjorie, for she was a decent human being victimized by a whole series of dreadful events. She married a man who was married to his job. She mothered a child who seldom reciprocated love. And she was left with nothing but bitter memories.

After divorcing her husband, Marjorie moved to a one-bedroom efficiency apartment. Rarely does she leave the confines of her building. Rarely does she talk with anybody. With regret and bitterness she reflects on her life:

> Everything went to pieces. By most measures we were enjoying a good life. My husband was successful. We had plenty of money. And we had a healthy son.
>
> But in less than three years we went from having everything to having nothing. How did it all happen? How did I end up this way? What went wrong? How do you go from having everything . . . to having nothing?

The silence is deafening. No words can comfort.

How Families Hurt One Another

The Christopherson family disintegrated. Instead of finding solutions to their problems they began to fight one another. Instead of supporting each other they hurt one another. No matter how many good times they enjoyed in the past—and Sam and Marjorie had many—their tragedy forever fractured their home. Indeed, everything precious in life was taken from them.

It is a fact that families often hurt one another in the days and months following a crisis. Disputes that have been dormant for years erupt to the surface. Battle lines between opposing family factions are formed. Arguments break out over relatively insignificant issues such as how much should be spent on a casket or who should sing at the funeral. Suddenly the family has to deal not only with the crisis event, but with the conflicts left in its wake.

Families who do not cope well with a heartbreak share a number of qualities. *First, most are totally unprepared for the unexpected.*

Sam and Marjorie Christopherson never believed that life could turn against them. Sam's career was always ascending, never descending. The family had never had any serious health problems. And their future looked as bright as their investment portfolio.

Over the years the Christophersons had developed a number of skills that helped them survive in style when things were going good. They worked hard. They found work associates who helped them pursue their interests and their careers. They knew the value of ambition.

But the skills that help you on the upside of life are often not transferable to the downside. One week after Sam had been fired he walked around in a daze: "What should I do? Do I look for another job? Should I have taken an early retirement? I mean, what the hell do I do now?" Sam felt paralyzed. Everything he had learned in fifty-one years of living did not seem to be of much comfort at this juncture in his life.

Some individuals, buoyed by success, deny the possibility of failure. While they theoretically know that they could be ambushed by an unfavorable event, they don't fundamentally believe that anything could go wrong.

They therefore can live next door to a family going through a divorce, or can share an office with a colleague whose spouse has a chronic illness, but seldom feel the pain that the family or the colleague is experiencing. They may learn that someone their own age has had a heart attack, and while it may be a bit unsettling, it does not faze them.

There are other families who have blocked out the possibility of harm, not because life has been so extraordinarily good to them but simply because they cannot stand thinking about the possibility that life can turn against itself.

In November 1983 the ABC television program "20/20" showed a documentary of Kansas City made by photographers from the Soviet Union. The documentary focused on the harsh side of life in the city, including the high rate of unemployment and the blighted conditions in which some people reside.

The documentary was shown to a group of Kansas City citizens, most of whom appeared to be white and middle class. Upon seeing the film they were angry and upset. Why hadn't the Soviet photographers focused on their thriving businesses, the affluent neighborhoods, their beautiful homes and schools and churches? Why hadn't the Soviets high-lighted the thriving aspects of their community?

But then a young man who was also from Kansas City suggested that perhaps the Soviet documentary *was* an accu-rate portrayal of life in Kansas City—at least for some people. After all, unemployment was hovering around 12 percent. He was hooted at, even scorned. In fact, one man was so upset that he appeared ready to grab the young man by the throat and toss him out of the room.

Few enjoy looking at the blighted side of life. Unfor-tunately those who do not cope well with a heartbreak are often those who have divorced themselves from that which is uncomfortable. It's as if their minds have been split into two parts. On the one side is life as they enjoy and wish to view it. It's a picture of happy children and vibrant schools and ascending careers. On the other side are the dark shad-ows, the unhappy moments, and the realization that life can go out of control. This side of the mind, however, is blanked out.

But then the unexpected happens. And the victim can't understand it. As Sam Christopherson kept repeating, "I don't believe that this is happening to *me*."

Those who have denied the possibility that a tragedy could strike close to home often seek comfort in slogans and philosophical expressions. Often these phrases come right out of childhood and reflect the comments made by members of another generation. "God has a plan in all this," said Marjorie Christopherson. Upon receiving a call from a concerned brother, Sam kept a stiff upper lip: "It's not so bad. A lot of people have it worse than we do." He concluded the conversation by noting that every cloud has a silver lining.

Such phrases are not always empty. Indeed, when they are supported with a meaningful philosophy of living, they may reflect strength rather than weakness.

However, for many people such phrases are hollow. And then an interesting thing happens: When people maintain that they are "doing just fine" when all evidence suggests that they are doing poorly, we pull back our support. As Sam's brother put it: "He didn't give me a chance to help. He just kept saying that everything's O.K."

Most people do not respond positively unless they are given a chance to help. We simply do not respond to plastic saints who seek to convince us through clenched teeth of their inner toughness.

Rather, our hearts go out to families with flesh and blood. We respond to families who are alone and afraid and who are willing to share their hurt. And we respond most to those who honestly say, "I need your friendship; I need your support."

Marjorie Christopherson relied on glib phrases for the better part of a year following her husband's crisis. "This is all going to work out," she kept saying. "I just have to trust the Lord." The words, however, rolled off her lips without conviction.

Marjorie could not bring herself to confide in anyone. Even when neighbors encouraged her to talk, she would smile and put on the "I've got it all together" look. Consequently her friends stopped calling. And the members of

her extended family ceased to write. She was truly alone.
Marjorie later commented:

> As I look back I now realize that our family simply
> didn't know how to handle our problems. It would have
> been far better if Sam and I had faced up to the seri-
> ousness of our situation, found good professional help,
> and relied more on our friends.
>
> But I had never been through anything like this. And
> neither had Sam. I didn't even realize that my family
> was disintegrating before my eyes. I just thought that
> this was a difficult time and that this too would pass.
> Little did I know.

If your family is unprepared for what you are now experiencing, do not be unduly alarmed. Survival skills can be
learned. But on the other hand you need to be keenly aware
of how your family is relating to one another. Families who
have denied the possibility of a heartbreak are often families
who have a number of destructive communication patterns.

And that brings us to a second characteristic of families
who do not cope well with a heartbreak: *They often hurt
one another by being silent*.

The year following Sam Christopherson's crisis, the family barely talked to one another. Listen to Marjorie describe
what happened when the family came together for their
evening meal:

> I used to dread our dinners. Eric would come home
> from school and I would ask him how it was going and
> he would give me a one-word response, "Fine." "Could
> you tell me something about school?" I would ask.
> "There's nothing to tell."
>
> Sam was gone most every day. God knows where he
> was. I would say, "What did you do today, Sam?" And
> he would reply: "I did what I do every day. I look for a
> job." And I would reply, "Can you tell me how it's

going?" And he would say, "I'll tell you something when I got something to say."

One night I fixed a special dinner, thinking it might cheer everybody up. But my husband brought the newspaper with him and started to read it while we ate. My son was reading a magazine. I looked at them buried in their own thoughts. Finally I just broke down and took my dinner into the other room.

But did my family do anything? They didn't even follow me to find out what was wrong. It was as if what happened to me didn't matter. And in truth, I guess that for them what I was feeling really didn't matter.

When a family faces a crisis, one of the most difficult challenges is to interact with one another. Family members often retreat into their private world. They do not share their thoughts. They do not ask questions. Nor are they particularly interested in finding out how another is coping. Consequently the family drifts apart.

Unfortunately there is usually one member of the family who finds silence almost impossible to bear. Sometimes it is the wife who hurts over the silence, particularly when her husband unilaterally decides to shoulder the family's plight. Sometimes it is the husband who feels the neglect, particularly if his wife keeps her thoughts locked into herself. And in some instances it is the children who feel alienated, especially when their parents do not permit them to share in the struggle that the family is confronting.

At times parents deny children the opportunity to understand their struggles because they don't want to burden the children unnecessarily. In other instances it is because they do not feel that the children could possibly understand or even help. When Marjorie suggested that Eric be informed about their family's difficulties, Sam ridiculed the idea: "Why would I tell him my problems? He can't solve his own."

Unfortunately Eric needed to learn what was tearing the family apart. If Sam had confided in his son, the boy might have been able to understand his father's plight. Indeed, he might have been able to give his dad a bit of much-needed compassion.

Children intuitively know when something is not right in their home. It is as if they have a sixth sense that tells them that the family is in trouble. It is therefore usually better to keep children informed about what is going on, because when they are forced to guess they frequently exaggerate the magnitude of the problem. Or they may unfairly blame themselves.

Sometimes families refrain from talking with one another at the time of a misfortune because they have never learned to communicate with one another when everything is tranquil. In large measure this was the central problem in the Christopherson marriage.

For twenty-nine years Sam had been wrapped up in his career. Seldom did he stop to observe the stream of occurrences in his own life or in the life of his wife. He just didn't have the time.

Nor did Sam take the time to enter into his son's world. To be sure, he would pat the child on the back when he brought home a good report card. But when it wasn't good, he was just as likely to use a firm hand to show his lack of approval. "I doubt that Sam had a dozen really good conversations with Eric in his entire life," said Marjorie.

Until faced with a crisis, Marjorie had never given much thought about how their family interacted with one another. She lamented the long hours that Sam put in on the job and she often wished that her son would confide in her. But she didn't believe that her family was all that unusual. "After all, most families don't do a lot of talking, do they?"

Marjorie's father was strong but silent—a good provider

but a very private person. There was little love overtly expressed. Nor were opinions solicited from the children.

Marjorie's adult family relationships turned out to be nearly a carbon copy of her own childhood experiences. She and Sam rarely shared ideas. There was little love expressed, although it was assumed that everyone loved everybody else. But no one took the time to really understand what each was experiencing.

One of the unfortunate by-products of not sharing is that power shifts to the silent member of the family. Silence is one way of exerting control over others. Out of desperation Marjorie blurted: "For God's sake, why don't you tell me what you're thinking about? Why don't you let me know what is going on inside your head?"

> Sam simply said that he didn't have anything to say and that the minute he did I would be the first to know. That was a put-down. He just would not talk. I felt very angry, but the more angry I got the quieter he became. It was like he was saying: "I don't need you. I can get through this without you."
>
> I felt powerless. And of course I was hurting too. Who was going to help *me*? His silence almost killed me.

Silence can kill families. Frustrations build. Misconceptions occur. Finally there is an explosion. And when the explosion occurs *the family blames one another for the problems they are having*. This is the third, perhaps one of the most important, characteristic of families who hurt one another at the time of a heartbreak.

When families have a problem, there is an almost irresistible need to pinpoint the cause of the difficulty. "If you had studied in high school, you wouldn't have such a hard time getting into college." "If you had wisely invested your inheritance, we wouldn't have such financial problems." "If you hadn't been driving so fast, you wouldn't have had the accident."

The need to pinpoint the cause of a problem is rooted in our desire to see a rational world. If we can explain something, then we will be able to understand it. And if we can understand it, then perhaps we will be able to accept it. The more troubling the crisis, the greater the need to figure out the cause of the problem and to determine who was responsible for it.

Consider what happened to Chuck Linder:

> Our three-year-old son will have permanent brain damage because he rode into the street while riding his tricycle. A man hit him as he was driving home from work.
>
> Several months after the accident I couldn't resist asking my wife what she was doing when Matthew rode his bike into the street. She became flustered and said that she was cooking supper. Nothing more was said until about a month later.
>
> Then suddenly she wanted to know why I asked her that question. "Are you blaming me?" she asked. "Was it my fault that I was fixing dinner instead of being outside?"
>
> I had to admit that in some ways I did blame her. And it was probably unfair. But she was watching over our son on that day. And if she had kept her eye on him, this would never have happened.
>
> We had very few conversations during the next couple of months. Then one day she said: "I know that you're blaming me for what happened. But if you remember, you were going to build a fence around the yard." She added, "If you are going to blame anybody, you better start with yourself."

Once family members begin to blame one another, intra-family warfare dramatically escalates. It escalates because once family members are attacked, they retaliate. As Chuck's wife said:

> When Chuck blamed me for not keeping a closer eye on Matthew, it really hurt. Unfortunately I knew that in some ways he was right. In my haste to get supper on the table I forgot about him playing in the front yard.
>
> But making this all my responsibility was simply too much to bear. And so I reminded him about that fence. I told him that the problem was at least 50 percent his fault.

The reason family fights are often vicious is because members know one another's vulnerable points. And we know how to press the knife skillfully against the most sensitive nerves.

Under normal circumstances families will never betray a trust. We will not, for example, tease someone about a weight problem when that person has confided in us about a poor self-concept. Nor will we chide someone for a lack of drive and ambition after being told what it is like to stand in an unemployment line.

But a crisis means that a family is no longer living under "normal circumstances." Information that was shared when trust was high suddenly can be used against one another when trust is low. All it takes is *one little comment* that rubs somebody the wrong way. The battle begins.

Unfortunately there is a lot of ammunition lying around when family members begin to fight. There are past grievances and present misunderstandings. Problems that were talked about years ago now surface. Since each member of the family knows one another's vulnerability, sharp comments quickly penetrate all defenses.

One of the more disquieting aspects of a crisis is that family members may blame one another *even when logic and good sense suggest that no one is responsible.* They will deliberately make one another feel guilty. I think, for example, of Marilyn and Ken Saunders, who had put off having children until they were in their late thirties. Finally, at age thirty-eight, Marilyn bore a daughter. Unfortunately she was born with severe Down's syndrome, a congenital problem associated with having children later in life.

The last thing Ken wanted to do was blame his wife for their daughter's problem. After all, he loved her dearly. And he also was aware of research studies that suggest the age of the father might have as much to do with a child's congenital problems as does the age of the mother.

Nevertheless he couldn't resist holding his wife responsible for what happened:

> In my head I knew that our daughter's problems weren't anybody's fault. But over and over again I said to myself: "Why didn't we start our family earlier? Why couldn't Marilyn have listened to me?" I showed her the statistics about what happens when women have children in their late thirties or forties. And she is smart. She knew all along that by waiting as long as we did the chances of having Down's syndrome really increase. I told her these things again and again. But she never seemed to care.

If conflict breaks out in your home at the point at which you feel most vulnerable, don't be surprised. Tensions are high. Emotions crowd out rational thought. Simple kindnesses toward one another are forgotten.

Long after the crisis has abated, comments made in anger will be remembered. After life returns to a more normal pace, problems that were churned up in the heat of battle will again surface. Regrettably, heatbreaks often give birth to lingering heartaches.

Three years later Ken recalled the way in which he unfairly indicted his wife:

I'll never know why I was so critical of Marilyn. I hurt all over thinking about what I did to her. To be sure, she ultimately made the decision to put off having our family. But I agreed to it. Not only did I agree to it, but I enjoyed a darn good life due to the money that she made during those years.

But when our daughter was born, I saw all of our happiness fly out of the window. I know how wrong it was to blame her. But I was so frustrated that it just spilled out. I did in fact blame her for our problems.

I have apologized to Marilyn again and again. Unfortunately she still has a lot of guilt about what happened.

Words spoken in anger can nibble away at the strength of even the best of families.

A fourth way that families hurt one another is by magnifying the seriousness of their problems.

Some families may have a relatively minor problem, but by the time they get through discussing it they have convinced themselves that the world is about to end. The seriousness of the problem becomes totally out of proportion to the nature of the threat.

Becky and Herb Walker are both in the helping professions. Becky is a social worker, while Herb's career is in welfare counseling. Every day they spend at least eight hours talking with clients, helping them sort out their problems and encouraging them to be analytical about life's difficulties.

But the talk doesn't stop when the workday is over. They return home, pour themselves a drink, and begin discussing the day's events. Becky usually begins by replaying a conversation that she had with an incompetent boss. Or she may discuss her frustrations with clients. Sometimes she muses about getting into a line of work where she could make a lot of money. Soon it is Herb's turn, and he too talks about how bad things are at work. His agency is threat-

ened with budget cuts, so he frequently complains about
how his organization is mismanaged. Sometimes he grum-
bles about the "horrendous" work load as well as the idiosyncrasies of a fellow employee.

Discussions of these irritants generally extend over the
supper hour. After the last dish has been wiped dry, the
Walkers retreat into the den to continue their work-related
conversation. By the end of the evening they have engaged
in twelve to sixteen hours of "therapy talk."

It's hardly a wonder that they go to bed feeling tense. If
you had listened to their conversation, you would have heard
nothing but "attack thoughts"—thoughts in which each projects the worst kind of scenario about whatever it is that
they happen to be discussing. Being critical of their colleagues and clients, they reinforced each other's biases. By
nightfall they are fully convinced that the people with whom
they work are slightly nuts, or at least peculiar.

Some people enjoy analyzing their difficulties. They can
do it hour after hour after hour. Solutions are seldom found
and hardly ever acted upon. And at the end of the day they
have convinced themselves that the world is a pretty bad
place in which to live.

It is possible to magnify an irritant until it becomes a
huge problem. But if there is a family member who is
sensitive to the harmful side of negative conversation, it is
possible to change both the content of the discussion as well
as the pessimistic feelings that underlie it.

After one particularly depressing conversation Becky
decided to alter the nature of their "therapy talk":

    I went to bed and realized that I felt rotten. I couldn't
figure out why I was so discouraged.

    But then I thought of our conversation and all the
negative things we talked about. By the time we went

to bed we had convinced ourselves that our lives were pretty dull and bad.

The next morning I told Herb that I needed to get off all this self-analysis stuff. To my surprise he agreed.

The next night we walked over to a high school baseball game. The hot dogs were cold and our team lost— but we had a good time. That night for the first time in a long while I slept soundly. And things went a bit better at work the next day.

It is an interesting paradox that some family members hurt one another by not talking at all, while others hurt one another by talking too much, about too many negative things. But such is the nature of family dynamics.

How do we avoid hurting one another when our family is having a crisis? How do we *avoid blaming* one another? How do we *avoid withdrawing* from each other, particularly when our energy is so dissipated that we feel that we have nothing to give? And how do we know when we are *talking too much, about too many negative issues*?

To answer such questions we want to turn our attention to healthy families and learn how they manage their losses. In this context *health* does not mean physiological well-being. Nor does health imply that these families are able to breeze through their difficulties.

Rather, these families are termed *healthy* because they make the best of very difficult situations. Healthy families pull together, assess the damage, and plan for their future. Healthy families recognize that each member has something to contribute in overcoming a disappointment. Although there are discouraging days and sometimes family quarrels, in the core of these families there is a quiet understanding that they must pull together if they are going to survive.

Cohesive Families: How They Survive Their Losses

Families have an enormous capacity for resilience when a crisis threatens. As one mother stated: "My kids were my Achilles' heel. I'd kill for them. I told my son if he were ever beaten on Hennepin Avenue, I'd go down there in my tennis shoes and find those guys."[1] What made this woman so remarkable was the discovery that her son was a homosexual, whose lifestyle was not easy for her to accept.

It is true that heartbreaks splinter families. But often a crisis mobilizes a family's dormant emotional and intellectual resources. Even when there has been a long history of family conflict, the petty squabbles often recede: "My father and I have never gotten along. But when he heard that my husband was in a car accident he rushed to the hospital. The last time I had seen him we had a big argument. I asked him if he was still mad and he replied, 'That stuff don't matter anymore.'"

For many families past arguments represent "stuff [that] don't matter anymore." What happened in the past is past. Now the family's energy must be riveted on that which threatens their future.

One motivation that is powerfully rooted in our consciousness is the desire to belong to a compassionate family. No matter how we might define our "family," this image suggests that we feel most secure when we know that there are a few special people on whom we can depend.

In these interviews, those who were able to move through their misfortunes with the least amount of trauma were often individuals who had one or two special loved ones from whom they drew a quiet strength. Here are the characteristics of families who were able to survive their losses.

The first, and perhaps most striking, characteristic of families who survive a tragedy is that they simply refuse to be bitter.

Jerry Lubenow was locked in a jail cell for three and a half years for a crime he did not commit. The murder for which Jerry was sentenced was gruesome. A woman was found lying in a ditch in a country road seven miles from a small community. She had been critically injured when a long, sharp object was shoved into her vagina. For several hours she lay in the freezing cold until a passerby saw her and called the police. Five days later she was dead.[2]

It was a sensational murder case. Throughout the trial Jerry maintained his innocence. Nevertheless the court found him guilty and locked him in jail. While in prison there was little to do but paint. A sensitive chaplain worked with him and tried to show him that it was possible to think positive. "I also learned something about patience," he added.

Three years later the state supreme court reviewed his case and found that the evidence was too weak to substantiate the charges. Not only was the evidence weak, but the judge had made errors preventing Jerry from receiving a fair hearing. To Jerry Lubenow's relief he was released and returned to his family as a free man.

Why didn't he become bitter about the fact that a large chunk of his life was unfairly taken?

> There were times in Stillwater [prison] that I was angry or frustrated or feeling down or whatever you want to call it. But that doesn't do any good. It took me a while to figure that out, but with a lot of help from friends I've learned to deal with it. "I've learned to sort of *mellow out the hate*." [Italics mine.][3]

How do you "mellow out the hate"? For many it takes

considerable time. Consider Joe Heartman, a farmer who had a whole bucketful of resentment.

>   Our oldest son, Steven, almost drove us crazy. He constantly rebelled against everything in which we believed.
>   When Steven was young, he was a lovable kid. He pitched in on the farm and did whatever we asked. But that all changed.
>   He started to talk back to his mother and soon he deliberately disobeyed us. At times our home was a battlefield.
>   All of this was so hard. Heck, why would I want to fight with a child I brought into the world?
>   One night Steven was in an ugly mood. While we were gone he attempted suicide. His brother found him and called the doctor.
>   We rushed to the hospital and I couldn't believe what happened. Steven told us that this whole thing was our fault. Right in front of the doctors he accused us of causing his problems. I couldn't believe what I was hearing.
>   He recovered mainly because he didn't hurt himself too much. But during the next year Steven became silent as a stone. Finally he moved out of the house. He never bothered to tell us where he was going.
>   Can you imagine what it would be like if your child never talked to you? Can you imagine what it would be like to have a child who really hates you? It is so hard . . . I've poured so much love into that kid.

Joe Heartman's eyes glisten as he recalls the disappointments with his son. Fortunately, however, he is married to a woman who knows how to mellow out the hate. She too felt the pain. But she never permitted herself to become resentful even though she had every reason to feel betrayed.

Why the lack of resentment? Mary Ann Heartman had learned a powerful lesson at the time of her father's death:

"My dad went to his grave bitter over his misfortunes. I vowed at his graveside that I would never go to *my* grave in the same frame of mind that he went to his."

The next several years were not easy for the Heartman family. Occasionally they would see their son at a distance. But he seldom acknowledged their presence.

It took Joe Heartman several years to let go of his anger. But he was helped by a special wife, who urged restraint when he was angry and who offered hope when he felt hopeless. As time passed, he put renewed energy into his farm. He rebuilt a barn and opened a new section of land. And he spent less time thinking about his wayward son and more time on the family he still had at home. Then came the turning point:

> I went downtown and was loading some feed into the pickup. I saw Steven on his motorbike. I waved to him. To my surprise he waved back.
>
> He turned the bike around. As he came close, I noticed that he looked pale, like he hadn't been eating.
>
> I asked him how he was doing. He said, "O.K."
>
> I looked at him again and for some reason he looked more like my little boy than a grown man. I said, "Do you want something to eat?"
>
> We went to a restaurant and I told him to get a big steak in order to put some meat back on his bones. We didn't talk much but he sure did eat.
>
> When we were done he reached out and picked up the tab and paid for the dinner. I just about dropped over out of surprise.
>
> We said good-bye and I went home and told my wife what had happened. I mean, he would pay for *my* meal? I still can't believe it.
>
> But my wife just kind of smiled. I guess she knew that some day he would get this whole thing resolved.
>
> My son and I are still not on the best of terms. But I see him almost every week and we often eat together

in that same restaurant. Sometimes we even have a pretty good conversation.

Can you really mellow out the hate? Can a wife who has been faithful for twenty-five years to her husband and then finds out that she has been abandoned really let go of her hurt and hate? What about a child who through no fault of his own learns that the gymnastic accident will put him in a wheelchair for the rest of his life? Can that person let go of the hate?

All of them can if they live in the present. This is the second characteristic of families that are able to cope successfully with a crisis event.

A tragedy can force families into two unhealthy postures. The first is to be resentful of that which has occurred in the past. This was Joe Heartman's Achilles' heel. Like a record needle stuck in a groove he repeatedly thought about what he might have done in order to avoid the pain he was now experiencing. Repeatedly he raised the questions that yielded no answers: "What if I had more severely disciplined Steven—would he have turned out differently? What if I had given him more freedom—then would he have developed such a dislike for me? Perhaps I should have spent more time with him as he was growing up." The litany of different ways that life could have been lived is endless.

Unfortunately, even if it were possible to prove that there was a better way of handling a past event, it does little good to replay it. The only healthy thing to do is to accept what has happened. And perhaps learn from it.

For some individuals the future can be even more threatening than the past. At least the past represents a known entity. But the future is filled with uncertainties. Will I have a job next year? Will our savings be ravaged by renewed inflation? Will we be able to afford to send our children to college?

Few would deny the importance of such issues. But it is easy to become obsessed with future events. And once you become preoccupied with the future it is largely impossible to experience the simple joys inherent within today.

Today is all that any of us have. Far better to wrench every single drop of meaning out of today than to project scenarios that may not come to pass. As Bertrand Russell perceptively noted:

> The wise man thinks about his trouble only when there is some purpose in doing so. At other times he thinks about other things.... When misfortune threatens, consider seriously and deliberately what is the very worse that could possibly happen. Having looked this possible misfortune in the face, give yourself sound reasons for thinking that after all it would be no such very terrible disaster.[4]

Joe Heartman will tell you that the turning point in his life was that thirty-minute dinner that he had with his son. Gradually they were able to reestablish their relationship and, after a number of years, their friendship.

But if truth be known, the turning point for Joe was not on that fateful day. His turning point came as he started to live one day at a time. It came in those moments when he refused to blame himself for his past mistakes. It came about after he quit worrying about whether his son would ever speak to him. But most of all his joy returned as he redis-covered a sense of satisfaction in working in his fields, rebuilding a barn, and fixing an old tractor. Because when he was out in the fields or creating a shelter for his cattle or tuning up an old motor, he was living in the present.

In summary, healthy families refuse to be bitter over their misfortunes. They accomplish that feat by living in the present rather than by replaying old defeats and anticipating future threats.

Yet most who have recovered from their heartbreaks will tell you that it was not an easy pilgrimage. And the reason it is so difficult is that heartbreaks often accentuate family tensions. Indeed, many families will tell you that the worst part of going through a crisis is having to deal with the family tensions that emerge in the weeks, months, and even years following the heartbreak.

This brings us to the third characteristic of healthy families: *They creatively manage their conflicts*.

Conflict is an inherent part of family living. Whenever individuals live in close proximity to one another, there are bound to be periodic tensions, disputes, and sometimes outright disagreements. As Saint Jerome aptly put it, "He who lives without quarreling is a bachelor."[5]

Families who appear to have the greatest difficulty resolving their heartbreaks are those who have never learned to manage their family conflicts. Once a crisis occurs they simply do not have the necessary skills to resolve opposing points of view. Indeed, there is a crucial difference among families: Those who except conflict and address their problems in a rational manner are able to find solutions enabling them to move into a new era; those who can't, find that their families splinter apart.

There are a number of debilitating ways that families manage their disputes. Some family members deliberately avoid discussing certain topics. A husband might say: "I don't want to hear about Junior's problems at school. I've had enough problems today at work to last a year."

When individuals are asked why they seek to avoid conflict, they often become defensive and shift the blame for their lack of communication to somebody else. "My wife sulks around the house for days if I bring up a sensitive topic. I have learned that it is far easier for everyone if we don't discuss certain issues." What he does not say, but what is painfully evident to his wife, is that he becomes belligerent whenever sensitive issues are brought to center stage. She therefore also avoids discussing important family matters.

Sometimes families will avoid certain topics because they fear the discussion will drift into an examination of unresolved problems. Most families have a few ghosts rattling around in hidden closets. Some of the ghosts are personality conflicts that have their genesis in childhood jealousies and sibling rivalries. Sometimes the ghosts are fears of learning how family members perceive one another. Sometimes the ghosts are represented in resentments that have been secretly tallied in the family ledger.

Whatever the real and/or imagined ghosts might be, some families will avoid discussing current difficulties simply because they fear that the closet might be opened. If the closet were to see daylight, the carefully stored resentments might come tumbling forth. Far better to keep the closet door shut and the lips sealed.

Some family members manage their conflicts by becoming *martyrs*. Martyrs beg for sympathy. When Grace Youngstren's social security check was lost in the mail, she said to whoever happened to be listening, "I don't know why all these terrible things always happen to me." Later in the day she sighed, "Well, this is just one more cross that I have to bear."

Martyrs enjoy making other family members feel guilty. Of course they would never admit to their manipulation, but their martyrdom is an effort to engender sympathy. When Maggie Atwell lost her job, she said to her sister: "Well, you have a wonderful family and a husband to take care of you. Now I have nothing." Her sister, who was equally adept at martyrdom, replied: "Well, at least you have an unemployment check. We hardly have anything to live on."

Then there are family members who are *confronters*. Confronters love conflict! They relish it. There is nothing like a good family fight to bring out their hostile juices. Why do some people enjoy conflict? Because they almost always win.

Confronters frequently justify their aggressiveness by saying something like: "I don't believe in charades. I just put it right out in the open and tell it like it is." Under the guise of honesty, they threaten and cajole and often use their reasoning to intimidate others.

Les Atwell had long been fed up with the way his sisters played the martyr role. He had little patience with their whiny voices and long faces. So when Maggie lost her job, he gave unsolicited advice: "Losing your job is the best thing that ever happened to you. Now you will be forced to stand up on your own two feet."

As you might expect, Maggie Atwell said nothing. Quietly she withdrew. The verbal assault was simply overwhelming.

In most families there is one member who is rather forceful. If the forcefulness borders on arrogance, there will be a love-hate relationship with this relative. The family might admire the confronter's ability to reason, as well as his or her verbal skills. But they fear the judgmental attacks. The family therefore keeps the confronter at arm's length. They will do their serious talking later—once the confronter has left the room.

Forthright communication can be a virtue. But it is only a virtue if it is housed in compassion. If confrontation is not coupled with sensitivity, the family will withhold their trust as well as their confidence.

In healthy families you do not see individuals avoiding conflict simply because it engenders anxious feelings. Nor do you see family members playing the role of the martyr.

Nor do you see loved ones confronting one another in self-righteous, accusatory tones. Healthy families have one important thing in common: *they problem-solve*.

Families who problem-solve define the issues that need resolution. Anything that is bothering any family member is worthy of discussion. But they also focus their energies on the critical problems—the ones that *must* be solved if the family is to recover from its heartbreak.

Not only do healthy families define the issues, but they *persistently* and with a *steadfastness of purpose* seek solutions to their difficulties. They tend to look for creative answers. They do not dismiss solutions that appear impractical, for they recognize that every solution has strengths as well as limitations. They therefore systematically set out to find the very best solution to whatever problem may be disrupting their tranquillity.

When family members roll up their sleeves and diligently search for solutions, the clouds begin to recede. They recede because the family is beginning to believe that something can, in fact, be done to resolve their dilemmas. And when creative answers surface, the family senses a ray of hope breaking into the home. Indeed, the problem begins to be manageable.

One of the most helpful things that a family can do at a time of crisis is to draw up a list of issues that should be discussed. Here is one way to foster a spirit of creative problem-solving within the family:

Take out a pen and paper and write on the top of the page: *Identification of Issues*. Working together as a family, list all the possible issues that relate to whatever problem you are experiencing. List everything that comes to mind. Be sure to do this with your teenagers. In fact, you may find it helpful to do this with grade-school children.

After you have listed the many issues about which the

family is concerned, identify four or five of the most critical issues. Then select a member of the family who will take the initiative in gathering information about the defined topics. The goal is simple: to gather resources, ideas, and information that will help the family solve its difficulties.

Finally, list those topics that, while important, can safely be discussed at a later point in time.

After each family member has had ample time to gather information, or perhaps simply to reflect on the problem, the family should have a "conference" at which they pool their information. The most pressing problem should be discussed first. Every solution that the family can think of should be put in writing. Then the family should come to an agreement about what actions to take.

There are of course some issues that might not be appropriate to discuss with children. Figure 1 represents an example of how Sharon and Herb Worthington, working without their youngsters, were able to define issues related to his unemployment.

Figure 1.

PROBLEM-SOLVING WHEN EMPLOYMENT HAS BEEN TERMINATED

Identification of Issues

Determine how much money is in our savings account.
Determine whether it is possible to borrow on our pension.
Determine the cash values in our life insurance policies.
Determine our total indebtedness.
Call the bank; find out if we can pay only the interest on our loans.
Call the savings and loan company; determine whether it is possible/desirable to refinance our home.

List all the ways to save money.

Call Jerry to see if it is possible to borrow money.

Find out if there are other employment possibilities within the company; request boss to stay on the payroll until June 30.

Ask if a lump sum payout of our pension could be given after January 1.

Update résumé.

Determine whether Sharon could find a better-paying job.

Consider selling the old car.

Determine how best to tell children about our unemployment.

Determine how to tell parents about our unemployment; determine what to do if they offer us money to get through this period.

Determine whether or not to use an employment placement service.

Find books in the library on how to search for new employment.

Determine whether I should find a mentor to help me through this.

Determine whether to buy groceries in bulk to cut down on food costs.

Find out if the boss will give me a letter of recommendation.

IDENTIFYING THE MOST CRITICAL ISSUES THAT NEED RESOLUTION

1. Determine whether there are any employment opportunities in my present company.

2. Discuss with my boss pension payouts.

3. Obtain an accurate assessment of our financial borrowing power including life insurance loans, equity in the house, and (possibly) new borrowing.

4. List all the ways that we can begin to save money.

FAMILY MEMBER RESPONSIBLE FOR FINDING INFORMATION CONCERNING ABOVE PRIORITIES

Herb will assume responsibility for gathering information on issues one and two.

Sharon will assume responsibility for issues three and four.

ISSUES TO BE DISCUSSED LATER

Update résumé. . . . Determine Sharon's employment possibilities. . . . Use library resources. . . . Determine how best to use our savings.

To repeat: Families who manage their conflicts problem-solve. But they also decide *which problems are worthy of discussions, which can be deferred, and which can be completely ignored*. Most families have sensitivities stashed in their histories that have never been adequately addressed. Families that skillfully manage their present dilemmas seem to have an intuitive understanding as to when it is helpful to reexamine past squabbles and when it is best to simply let them die.

Sometimes it is prudent to *not* discuss certain painful conflicts, or agree to discuss them at some other time. As psychologist and philosopher William James said, "The art of being wise is the art of knowing what to overlook."

Sometimes the most helpful thing to do is simply agree to put on the shelf past problems. This is particularly true when emotional energy needs to be spent on the current crisis. Here is how a brother and sister managed a very difficult situation:

My sister and I have never gotten along with one another. Not even when we were growing up.

After college I moved to Florida. She lived in Ohio, about a mile from my parents' home. I got caught up in my work and I guess she got caught up in hers. We wrote once in a while, but that was about it. We just kind of lost touch with one another.

But then I received a rather desperate call. My father had Alzheimer's disease and he was slowly becoming nonfunctional. Decisions had to be made quickly about how to find a nursing home, how to finance it, and how to best care for Mom.

So I flew home to Ohio. My sister was at the airport and we shook hands. I guess it was impossible for either of us to give a hug. Then we started to talk. But we could hardly converse with one another. The old resentments were still present. She knew it and so did I. The issues between us were so great that we could not discuss our parents' difficulties.

Finally I felt so frustrated that I kind of blurted out without really knowing what I was saying: "I'm sorry for whatever I have done to hurt you."

To my surprise she started to cry. She is a very strong person but I saw the tears. She left the room and came back a few minutes later. "Sometime we have to get things straightened out between us," she said. "But I can't deal with all that right now plus figure out how to help the parents."

We made an agreement. I suggested that within a year we would get together and try to work out our disagreements and differences. But for now all our attention had to be focused on how we were going to get Dad into a nursing home and how we were going to help Mom adjust to a new life.

Suddenly we were able to talk to one another.

There is a fourth characteristic of families who are able to resolve their tragedies, which is truly critical if healing is to occur: *Healthy families give one another room to breathe*. Or to put it another way, healthy family members respect one another's ability to resolve their crisis *in their own way, on their own time schedule, and on their own terms.*

Healthy families share a belief—often unspoken—that family members must deal with misfortune by themselves. This is not to deny the strength that comes from genuine caring. Nor does it deny the power of collaborative problem-solving. Rather, the giving of space to one another is based on a realization that it is largely impossible to control other people's response to any situation. Furthermore, to structure how others should respond denies them the opportunity to use their own resources in confronting their private challenges.

In unhealthy families love is given with conditions, for there is an incessant struggle to control one another. The martyr controls through guilt. The confronter controls through boisterous righteousness. The avoider controls through silence.

But in healthy families there is a strong affirmation that each person has a capacity not only to confront threats *but to resolve them*. To give a loved one psychological space is to say: "I'm here to support you. To listen to you. To encourage you and, if asked, to give suggestions. But most of all I will respect you. I will respect your aloneness. And I will respect your desire to resolve this difficulty in a way that you determine."

Most family relationships prosper in such an environment. No longer are family members worried about the heavy hand of a strong member. Nor are they suffocated by unwanted intrusions and unsolicited advice.

Rather, they feel protected by tender encouragements. And they are sustained by affirmations. In effect what they have received is a gift from the heart—a gift of unconditional love.

It is admittedly difficult to give love without conditions.

And it is particularly difficult when the actions of loved ones appear to be self-destructive. We therefore give unsolicited advice. We tell our loved one what to do and how to do it. In effect we write out a prescription. Unfortunately the medicine may have little effect on that which ails the spirit.

Giving unconditional love taxes the resources of most people. It's difficult to give love without conditions because the more we care about someone, the more we have our hooks into them. We therefore give advice when it is not wanted. Even when we are silent, the furrow in our brow suggests that we disapprove.

Why is it so difficult to give unconditional love? Primarily because we have been taught to think critically and in sharply judgmental terms. For example, when we hear a statement, our first reaction is to say, "That's correct," or "That's stupid." Unfortunately we do not take the time to understand precisely what the other person is trying to say.

But we also find it difficult to give unconditional love simply because we care so much. There is an ache when we see a spouse come home from work depressed night after night because of a difficult job. There is a pain that strikes to the core of our being when we see our children not living up to their potential. And when elderly parents have lost the spark of excitement in their lives, we too feel diminished.

When we want to change a family member, our criticism usually begins with rather innocuous suggestions. For example, suppose a spouse is frustrated in his or her career. First there is a gentle admonition, "At least you have a job; you ought to be thankful for that." But then the tone becomes critical: "You've got to change. When you come home from work everybody gets depressed." Finally there is the ultimate threat, "Either you change, or I'm leaving."

Such statements may be warranted and perhaps in some instances motivate constructive action. But usually the judgments come thundering down like a ton of bricks. Instead of helping they push the loved one a bit closer to the edge of despair.

In healthy families there is a concerted effort not to make demands on one another, but rather to give all freedom to live their lives in a way that best meets their needs, hopes, and aspirations.

It is admittedly difficult to get our hooks out of the skin of loved ones. But it can be done. Listen to the struggles and the victories of Warren Eustis, a Minneapolis attorney.[6]

Warren learned about unconditional love while fighting alcoholism. His battle with the bottle was a constant struggle. In fact, he was treated twenty-six times without success. But he vowed to get well. With the help of skilled professionals he achieved his goal.

I am free from anxiety and depression—people who haven't had it can't understand. The other thing is being given back a sense of joy, the excitement of discovering the people you love, love you. . . . *Once I granted them independence in my mind*, then things happened beautifully to me, things I wanted so badly, love and concern without strings. People no longer feared my heavy hand. [Italics mine.]

With his new understanding he was able to give his family more freedom. His wife, however, was writing a book. Suddenly the old resentments, the need to control, came back.

I hated the damn thing [the book], the time it took, the worry. I was in a dither. I was so angry. The counselor told me I ought to cool off for a while and put me in a nice room. I suddenly realized this was the intensive care room I'd been in when I went through my hardest drug withdrawal, and then I realized I was acting the same way I had been then.

I shot out of there . . . and told Nancy: "Your life is yours. I'm not going to interfere or put barriers in your way. I'm going to be as cooperative as I can. I am sorry." I had come to the recognition she had to carve her own life, and that gave me . . . a lot of independence.

But then came a shocker. Six weeks later his wife was permanently paralyzed in an automobile accident.

Nancy finished her book, dictating the final chapters upside down on a circular bed in a large metropolitan hospital. Warren changed their house for the time when Nancy would return home. He installed an elevator and a ramp, widened doorways, lowered counters, rotated shelves, and put in a slate floor that the wheelchair could glide on. But his biggest challenge was to fight that old impulse to take over, to step in and do everything for her.

Then came one more blow: Warren was diagnosed as having bone cancer. Again he needed to relearn old lessons, particularly the importance of not seeking to control the reactions of his family.

Your tendency is to try to manipulate, to see that there will be a trustee, that the kids will go to the right school, your wife will have just the right attitude toward her own profession. Bullshit. It's controlling even worse from the grave than alive. They aren't under my shroud. The issue is how they can feel free and live with you. I tell my kid. We talk about cancer. It's very matter-of-fact. You let him know that you're mortal, that you're going to go, that he's off to a great start. The best you can give him is your own trust and understanding, and he's going to grow into being another person.

Today Warren Eustis states that the most important lesson he has learned has been the realization that *when you let go, you find yourself*.

Once alcoholics have started the process of a cure they get rid of false expectations. They aren't clinging, dependent, angry. They're liberated. And to use a word, it's intoxicating. You're able to accept other people's love and friendship and feel good about it, instead of wanting more, asking why don't they do this for me?

Nevertheless, the battle for control of one's priorities continues. And the big part of the battle is to do everything possible to let your loved ones live in freedom.

I ask myself: Am I really independent? Do I really mean I don't want any hooks into my family? Nancy really owes me nothing, really isn't a slave to my feelings, and that's the way you want her . . . isn't it? Yes. Why? Because so much exuberance comes out of it.

A final characteristic of healthy families is that they protect one another. Protection is defined as the ability to shelter the family from further harm. The protector is also the family member who consistently affirms that the family will in fact recover.

In healthy families someone usually evolves as the "leader." When we use the term *leader*, however, we are not referring to someone who gives unsolicited advice and who makes unilateral decisions. Nor is the leader the "head of the house" and the one to whom everyone defers.

Leadership as it is used in this context has little to do with age or even family position. Rather, the person who evolves into the leadership role is the individual who (a) helps the family gain a perspective on the problem and (b) helps redirect the family's energy into productive thinking.

To see how individuals evolve into leadership positions, consider the crew of the *Southern Star*.[7] In October 1973 the ship capsized and all ten crew members were forced to board a life raft. The crew became a "family," deeply dependent upon one another for their survival. For nine days they drifted and battled the elements with limited rations. On the fifth day one of their members died, and on the ninth two more perished in delirium.

But on that ninth day, the life raft landed on a rocky shore. Three members went looking for help through dense brush. Finally, on the thirteenth day of their ordeal, they were discovered by a local logging contractor.

How did they survive? The crew pointed to one member who had become their leader and who gave them a perspective on their situation. Within hours after their mother ship had capsized he began to display leadership ability. He demonstrated his technical abilities with a knowledge of winds, currents, and the use of survival apparatus. He set up the schedules for rowing and for rations. When crew members were reluctant to pull their weight or threatened the group's mood with displays of anger and hopelessness, he gave encouragement. And he showed gentleness and compassion, particularly to the youngest crew members. Above all, stated those who investigated the accident, "He provided a model of competence, rationality, and hope."

What is needed in a crisis situation is someone who will provide a "model of competence, rationality, and hope." When Robert Kendrick lost his job, the person who brought hope was his wife. "We have been through tough times before," she said. "All of us in this family are capable of working. All of us have our health. We have food in the freezer. We have friends we can count on. There is no reason we can't make it." The family started to row in unison.

The person who becomes the leader is given that position out of trust. The family trusts their loved one's intuition and plain good sense. They also know that their loved one will not run over their sensitivities.

Often the family member who evolves into a leadership role will do something of a symbolic nature that breaks the gloom. When Robert Kendrick told his wife that he had been fired from his job, she listened attentively. Then, while he went for a walk, she put a tablecloth on the dining-room table, brought out the wine glasses and the best silverware. "We're not in the poorhouse yet," she said. By nightfall the Kendrick family had a plan by which to attack their problem.

Sometimes a family member will present a symbolic gift and in so doing protect the family from a sense of hopelessness. If you were to walk through the corridors of a children's hospital on Christmas Eve, you would find rooms filled with symbolic gifts. You might see a bicycle given to a child who will walk again only if he is willing to undergo hours of painful therapy. Or you might find a sled given to a child who has barely enough strength to make it to the bathroom. Or you might see a severely diabetic youngster learning to master Monopoly even though her eyesight is beginning to fail.

The cynic might ask what the utility of such gifts is, particularly if the boy can no longer walk or the girl can no longer see.

But each gift is given in hope. Its symbolic value far outweighs its utility. For when the child receives the bike, he can envision himself hustling over to a friend's house. When the sled is propped up in the hospital room, it is a symbol that life will not always be spent with needles and diagnostic tests. When a Monopoly game is mastered by sight, there is a recognition that it can be played when the eyes fail.

When a family member presents a symbolic gift or quietly expresses optimism, it has a powerful effect on the entire family. Sometimes all it takes is the image of that loved one to engender a sense of confidence in the future.

When the crew of the *Southern Star* were drifting aimlessly in a swirling ocean, the men reported that they focused their thoughts on a family member who they knew cared deeply about them:

> I just kept thinking about my wife and family—that was all that I had to live for.
>
> Every night I could see my wife's face. Every time I closed my eyes I could see my wife there.
>
> Even when I paddled, I used to recite [his children's] names. . . . I'd go right through them. I think it helped. It gave me determination.[8]

But, one may ask, what do you do if there is no one in the family who is capable of giving encouragement? What if everyone is so wrapped up in the crisis that no one is capable of giving leadership? And what if you are alone?

Sometimes we need to *extend our family beyond bloodlines*. We need to trust non-family members to give us a perspective on what is taking place. If you do not have anyone in your family who can give you needed encouragement, be reassured that there are individuals who if they know about your plight will offer their special resources, insights, and ideas. Consider George Herring, who went from being quarterback for the Denver Broncos football team to being an alcoholic on skid row.[9]

While at Southern Mississippi University, he was an All-American football player. Then he had a career in pro sports. After his playing days were completed, he worked for sixteen years in the automobile business. But then alcoholism began disassembling his life.

After a divorce he went steadily downhill until he landed on Larimer Street, panhandling loose change, sleeping in an abandoned truck near the railroad tracks west of downtown Denver, and living from drink to drink.

One morning he walked more than three miles in order to check into a detoxification center. "I was so sick. I knew I had to do something."

The word about George Herring's condition became known in the Denver community. Within a short period of time past friends as well as virtual strangers came to help. They let him know that he was not abandoned.

He was offered a job by Randy Gradishar, Denver's perennial All-Pro football player, and by car dealership owner Mike Bundy. He was offered free room and board in an alcoholic treatment center by Craig Morton, the current Denver quarterback, as well as by Republican congressional candidate Arch Decker. The Denver General Hospital reported more than thirty calls volunteering help. Longtime friends, strangers, former players, religious leaders—all of them called to lend a hand. Some even offered money. Said Gradishar, "We just want to let George know that we care about him and that we're following up on him." Another friend said, "I just want George to know there's still a lot to live for."[10]

Some might suggest that George Herring received all his help because he was once a famous quarterback. I think not. Nan Robertson, a reporter for *The New York Times*, had the ends of her fingers amputated, owing to gangrene infection caused by toxic shock syndrome.[11] But she found help in the most unexpected places:

> I had decided to try a self-confidence approach to all strangers in New York. I would hail a cab, hold up my hands, and say, smiling, "I have a bum hand—could you open the door for me?" The drivers would leap

around to the back door and open it with a flourish. As we approached our destination, I would hand him my wallet, tote bag or purse, and they would hold up each bill and coin like a rosary or miraculous medal or baby to be blessed. "This is a dollar bill," they would say. "This is a quarter," and then return the rest of the money to its place.

Of course, not everyone is helpful. But even the most hard-nosed person can be turned around:

> The stinker cabbie was an elderly man who refused to roll down his window or open the back door for me. I finally asked a woman on the street corner to help; she complied without asking why. "You roll down the window, you get a gun to your head," he [the taxi driver] snarled. "You got only one bum hand; why didn't you open the door with the other?" I shrieked back: "Because all the fingers on both my hands have been amputated!" He almost dissolved into a heap of ashes. "I'm sorry, lady," he said.[12]

As Nan Robertson discovered, you can find acts of kindness anywhere. Even on the streets of New York City.

SEVEN

Getting By with a Little Help from Your Friends

A real friend is one who walks in when the rest of the world walks out.
—WALTER WINCHELL

George Burns once said of his friend Jack Benny: "Jack and I had a wonderful friendship for nearly fifty-five years. Jack never walked out on me when I sang a song, and I never walked out on him when he played the violin. We laughed together, we played together, we worked together, we ate together. I suppose that for many of those years we talked every single day."[1]

Friendships have an immense power to heal a broken spirit. Why? Because we know that our best friends would never walk out on us, no matter how difficult the crisis might be.

When a heartbreak occurs, most people are surprised by

156

how many friends they actually have. Cheryl Gilcrest put it this way:

> I have received encouragement from many people. My boss sent a dozen roses. My friends at work hugged me. I even heard from people that I haven't seen in years. I didn't know I had so many friends.
>
> It's going to be difficult living with this disease. But I know that if I feel depressed, there are a whole lot of people who will cheer me up.

A seventy-three-year-old man slipped on the ice and cracked a vertebra in his back. It was a nasty accident, leaving him partially paralyzed. But I didn't hear anger. I didn't hear regret. What he wanted to talk about were his friends. "Can you believe all those get-well cards?" he said. "Just think. All those people care about me."

It's strange, but sometimes you have to have an accident or a career reversal or an illness before you realize that there are a lot of people who care. A comment I heard over and over again was, "If there is one thing this experience taught me it is that I have a lot of friends."

There is something deep within us that reaches out to people who are hurting. Even the toughest, most hard-nosed person becomes tender when a heartbreak occurs.

In college I had a professor who was anything but soft. He had a reputation for being a tough taskmaster. Everyone admired him. But most of us feared him.

On the day that Martin Luther King died we saw a side of our professor that had been carefully blocked from view. He came to class and began lecturing in his normal way. But then he stopped as if to catch his breath. And then he said: "Martin Luther King was a man I admired. His words touched me deeply." He paused, but I could see his chin quiver. Fighting his emotions, he continued: "We have lost a great person. Our society has been diminished. . . . And each one of us in this room has been diminished."

He broke down and left the classroom.

Heartbreaks soften the human spirit. They have a way of breaking through the aloofness and carefully controlled exteriors. The rigid rules of how we are to behave are suspended.

And that which remains is what unites us: an understanding that all of us feel pain. All of us know suffering. And all of us can relate to the heartbreaks of others. Our respect for our professor went up a hundredfold on that day. We had admired him for his scholarship. But now we saw him as someone who understood the tender side of life.

It's almost a universal truth: When you let others see your vulnerability, you receive love. When you show your hurt others befriend you.

Several weeks before writing these paragraphs, I went to my office and found a foreign student waiting to see me. She had taken a class from me at the university and wanted her grade changed. She noted that she had done "A" work, but that she had inadvertently chosen a different grading system which would only give her a grade of "satisfactory."

I informed her that it couldn't be done. I explained that the university has rather strict rules and one of them is that instructors can't change grades after a course has been completed.

She thanked me for my time. But then as she left my office, I noticed a few tears trickling down her cheeks. She quickly turned to the door, embarrassed at her crying.

I was taken aback by the tears. I caught up with her in the hallway and asked her what was wrong. She explained that she was from Nigeria. Her government wanted her to go to America for schooling. But they only gave her a week's notice before she had to leave home. She left behind her family, including an eighteen-month-old daughter whom she very much missed.

When she enrolled in my class, she knew little about American education. She was unaware of all the rules and regulations that were well known to the other members of the class. But, most important, she was not aware that her choice of grading systems might jeopardize her graduate program.

I suddenly saw a person who was vulnerable: a student who was thrown into the middle of a new system and who had difficulty making sense out of a foreign language and a foreign culture.

I telephoned a university official to see if the rule could be waived. The immediate response: "A rule is a rule. She should have known what she was doing." But then I explained her situation. There was a long pause on the other end of the telephone. The voice was now soft. "Maybe we need to bend the rule for this student."

She beamed with joy when she heard the news.

There is a marvelous gift of healing that comes when you share your vulnerability. There is understanding. Acceptance. Encouragement. And sometimes even rigid rules can be changed.

Characteristics of Friends Who Know How to Help

If you are going to be helped by a friend, you need to share your pain. But it is a little more complicated than that. In fact, you must be careful in whom you put your trust.

There are people who will not help you. Some will not understand what you are going through. Others will not care to know. And still others will be more interested in telling you what to do than in listening to your problems.

After Roberta Collinswood was informed that she needed to have exploratory surgery, she drove to a friend's house. But when Roberta shared the seriousness of the situation, her friend became emotional.

> Seeing her become so upset made me feel worse. So I went home, regained my composure, and invited a friend from work out to supper.
>
> We must have talked a couple hours. It was a good conversation and I felt somewhat better as I went home.
>
> But I was unprepared for what happened next.
>
> About a week later I discovered that everyone in the office knew about my problem. Not only did they know about my problem, but they knew all the intimate details.
>
> I felt betrayed. I had shared some pretty personal things and just assumed that she would keep it to herself.
>
> At that point I decided that maybe all this stuff about friendship was a lot of hot air. So I didn't talk to anybody for the longest time.

You need to select carefully the person in whom you confide. What kind of person will help you the most? Here are the characteristics of a good friend:

First, good friends are curious. They are inquisitive. They don't just sit there hoping you will say something. They ask questions. And they seem interested in everything that you have to say.

Beth Olson was having difficulty coping with the demands of her job. After a trying day she called her best friend, who asked some questions: "Why was today so difficult? What made this day different than others? Did you get enough sleep last night? Is something else bothering you?"

None of the questions was asked in an accusatory tone. But they were pointed, enabling Beth to take a second look at her difficulties. Later she said: "My friend has a way of helping you see all sides of an issue. She doesn't let you get away with a lot of "poor me" thinking. Rather, she asks questions, helping you gain insights into what's going on."

Curious people are a true joy. They ask questions that help you refocus your thoughts. Equally important, the questions themselves let you know that they care.

Helpful friends are not only curious, but they listen intently. Good listeners shout a message: "I'm interested! I really want to know what's going on! I want to understand what you are thinking and what you are feeling! I care!" If I were to point to the most important characteristic of a good friend, it would be the ability to listen.

Richard Lindaman was only twenty-three years old when he had a heartbreak that almost resulted in a nervous breakdown. He desperately wanted to get into medical school. For four grueling years he had taken biology and chemistry courses. He studied when other students were playing. He did everything he could, including getting a near-perfect grade point average, in order to become a doctor.

But apparently he didn't do enough. A rejection notice came from the medical school on the very day that he was graduating from college.

> My first reaction was a good cry. Then I went through a bunch of rationalizations: "It's all for the best. It's God's will."
>
> That made me feel better for about a day. But the next morning I woke up angry. I said, "It's not for the best; and what about *my* will?"
>
> I knew that I needed to talk to someone. I needed to explode and get a lot of things off my chest. But most of all I needed to be with someone who cared.
>
> I called up my roommate. We met in the student union.
>
> I just let out all my feelings. And my anger.

He sat there for three hours listening. That's all he did—listen. He didn't offer advice. He didn't give me false reassurances. He didn't try to convince me that everything was going to be O.K. All he did was listen.

And that's *exactly* what I needed.

If you are going to get a little help from your friends, you need to find a good listener. But you need more than that. You also need someone who is upbeat. Optimistic. Positive.

What you need in this period of life is someone who doesn't get all emotional and caught up in your difficulty. What is needed is someone who remains objective, even a bit detached from the feelings being expressed.

When a heartbreak occurs, we are often flooded with negative thoughts. We convince ourselves that nothing good could come out of the situation.

A good friend is one who opens the door a crack and lets light into the room. A good friend is one who points out your strengths, not your weakness. A good friend is one who helps you rediscover that tough core that has enabled you to solve other problems. A good friend is one who assures you that you can meet not only this challenge, but any challenge that life might put in your path.

Finding an optimistic friend does not mean looking for someone who falsely reassures. You don't need someone who is glib and who offers advice without knowing the magnitude of the problem. But what you do need is a friend who will affirm your strengths and offer encouragement.

Christine Jensen had very ambivalent feelings about giving birth to another child. She decided to talk with a neighbor.

I told her that I really had mixed feelings about being pregnant. After all, I was thirty-seven years old and already had three children.

She listened. But then she shared something that really made a difference.

She said that she had watched how I was raising our three children and that I was a role model for her. She said that if there was one person in this world who could manage four kids, it was me.

Hearing those things really made me feel good. I thought about how much I enjoyed being a mother. In fact, I started to think more positively about adding a new member to our family.

There is one characteristic of strong friendships that is particularly important: Good friends are honest with one another.

When you've had a heartbreak, you need to talk in an open, uninhibited way. You should be able to talk about your fears and your hopes, your failures as well as your successes. You should sense your friend's respect. And you should be assured that whatever you say will be kept in confidence.

But honesty must be reciprocal. Your friends need to be forthright as well. They should be able to inform you when your thoughts are self-defeating or when your perceptions may be in error. And they should be able to share their own experiences and offer new insights and fresh ideas.

Sometimes you need to encourage honesty in a relationship. You may find that your friends respect you so much that they don't want to do anything that might hurt you or make the situation worse. If so, give permission for them to share their ideas. Tell them that you need their knowledge and want to benefit from their experiences. Ask them how they would manage a problem similar to your own.

Good friends will respond to the invitation. And you will have a depth of sharing and understanding that will be cherished long after the crisis has passed.

The last characteristic of good friends is that they give unconditional love. What is unconditional love? It means that no matter how difficult your problem and no matter how many times you may fail in trying to solve it, your friends will stick with you.

They will not put demands on the friendship. They will not tell you that you must respond in a certain way or do certain things. And they will never imply that their way of coping with life is better than your own.

Rather, they will listen. They will ask questions. They will share their knowledge and experience. But most of all, they will love you.

One of the few positive outcomes of the Vietnam War was that young men learned the power of friendships. As Philip Caputo said in *A Rumor of War*:

> Communion between men (in infantry battalions) is as profound as any between lovers. Actually, it is more so. It does not demand for its sustenance the reciprocity, the pledge of affection, the endless reassurances required by the love of men and women. It is, unlike marriage, a bond that cannot be broken by a word, by boredom or divorce, or by anything other than death. Sometimes even that is not strong enough. Two friends of mine died trying to save the corpses of their men from the battlefield. Such devotion, simple and selfless, the sentiment of belonging to each other, was the one decent thing we found in a conflict otherwise notable for its monstrosities.[2]

Soldiers throughout history have learned one important lesson: Friendships matter. If you must enter any field of battle, have one good friend who will stick with you.

Why Friendships Fail

You will be surprised at the number of people who offer encouragement in the weeks following a heartbreak. But a strange thing happens. Approximately six months later, they may no longer be available.

> When my wife died everyone wanted to help. Friends stopped by to visit. Neighbors brought in food. People I hadn't heard from in years telephoned.
> All this support helped me through the first couple of months. I never knew that so many people cared.
> But a few months later everything seemed to stop. My friends no longer asked how I was doing. It was like they were saying: "O.K., Chuck: We gave you six months of support. Now you are on your own."

The most difficult period in recovering from a heartbreak is not the first few months. The hardest time often begins six months later when the sympathy cards stop coming. And when the telephone ceases to ring.

Earlier it was noted that we expect people to get over their heartbreak quickly. How long should it take? Progress is expected to six months. And in a year you should be back on your feet.

But healing can't be timed by a stopwatch. For no one turns the corner at exactly the same moment.

You would think that friends—particularly good friends—would give support no matter how long the healing may take. But sometimes even good friends aren't aware of the setbacks and the prolonged struggles.

> I had a friend who gave me a great deal of support. But it tapered off.

I used to see her every week. But then it was once every two weeks. Then a whole month went by without even a telephone call.

I stopped by her house. She apologized for being so busy.

As we talked it became apparent that our lives were taking different paths. She was involved in PTA and their boy's hockey team. Her husband was climbing the hierarchy at work and they were doing a lot of socializing.

And I was barely surviving.

We gave each other a hug as we left. But it wasn't that warm hug we use to give each other.

Why do friendships wither? Why can't friendships continue to be strong in the years after a heartbreak, as they were when the heartbreak occurred?

The main reason why friendships erode is that interests shift. There are different priorities. Different agendas. Sometimes different lifestyles and values. Consequently even good friends become involved in new tasks and new problems. And the more involved they become the greater the likelihood that old friendships will lose some of their meaning.

When you sense that your friendship is not as solid as it once was, you will feel sad. Perhaps a bit angry. But don't take your friend's absence personally. It's not your fault. And it's probably not the fault of your friend either. It's the nature of friendship.

Friendships change. There are periods of closeness followed by periods of separateness. There are times when you talk often and there are times when the telephone seldom rings.

Sometimes when you need your friend the most, your friend is preoccupied. Sometimes with new interests, sometimes with new problems. If your friendship has grown cold, be patient. Do not try to force a friendship, for coercion and friendship are strangers.

Rather, be kind. Stay in contact. Believe the best about one another. For there may come a time when your paths will again join together.

Why do friendships fail? Sometimes it's because interests diverge. But for others it's because the heartbreak creates too much tension. Too much pain. Too much dissonance.

Some friendships are based only on what might be termed "happy talk." These people frequently socialize together. They have fun on weekends. They celebrate birthdays and promotions and the good times in life. But the friendship may not be able to stand the strain of adversity.

Some individuals simply do not know how to respond when a friend is having a problem. They don't know what to say. They may not know how to act. One man, perplexed by his friend's illness, said:

> We used to hunt and fish together. But then he got real sick with cancer.
> I would go to the hospital and try to cheer him up. You know, joke around. Make him feel good.
> But it wasn't the same. After a while I didn't want to go to the hospital. It would make me feel so sad.
> So I just stopped going. I know it doesn't seem right. But I just couldn't handle it anymore.

There are people who want to stay as far away as possible from adversity. They don't want to be near depression and they don't want to be reminded of how the fortunes of life suddenly change. So they don't go to the hospital. They don't visit a sick friend. And they rarely get involved.

It is easy to be upset with such people, especially if we have enjoyed their company during the good times in life. But if they don't want to be with you in bad times, let them go. It's not that they don't care. It's just that they don't know how to respond.

There is one final reason why friendships fail. Sometimes

a friend will not have the strength to help.

Doug Malowski spent many evenings trying to help his buddy survive a divorce. They would meet at his friend's apartment, drink coffee, and sometimes talk until late at night.

> But it was too much. After being with him three and sometimes four evenings a week, I knew it was getting to me.
>
> And it was getting to my family as well. My wife told me that the family needed me as much as my friend.
>
> So the next time Jack asked me to come over to talk, I said "no."
>
> I told him that I really cared and wanted to help, but I really had to start backing off. I told him that my family needed me too.
>
> He was very nice and said he understood.
>
> But now he hardly ever calls. And when I call him, he is noticeably cool.
>
> Can you blame me? Isn't there a limit as to how much of myself I can give?

There *is* a limit as to how much anyone can give. And there are times in everyone's life when it is nearly impossible to give the love and support that a friend may need. If you have a friend who isn't offering help, try to be understanding. Your friend probably cares but at this point in time may not have any resources to share.

What do you do if your friends let you down? Where do you go to find people who understand and truly care?

The answer is to find a support group. Because in a support group you will find people who care. And you will find people who will give you all the practical help you need.

What Is a Support Group?

My first experience with a support group came on a hot, muggy August evening. I was observing a group composed of parents of congenitally deformed children. This was the first meeting, sponsored by a community hospital. None of the parents knew one another.

I could see apprehension in their eyes as they entered the room. Many of the men appeared to have a chip on their shoulder—an attitude of, "I don't need any help."

The meeting was convened by a pediatric nurse. She began by asking, "How many of you really wanted to come tonight?" Most everyone was shocked by the honesty implied in the question. No one raised a hand. "Then why did you come?" she asked.

The answers were generally the same: They had been referred to the group by a minister or a physician and, in one case, by a friend.

The nurse then began to bore into the most tender feelings within the group. "You, sir—why didn't you want to come tonight?" she asked a gruff-looking man in his late thirties. You could see anger in his eyes.

Without hesitation he shot back, "Because there isn't one thing you can do about my son's birthmarks."

A person sitting in the rear of the room joined in. "Everyone has a lot of problems. Why would anyone want to listen to mine?"

Another man simply said, "The only reason I am here is because my wife insisted I come."

There was silence in the group. Finally, a woman said: "I came here to ask some questions. I need to find out where you can get a wheelchair and where I might find some financial help. I just can't manage this on my own."

Quietly the leader asked, "Should we get on with our business?" Half the group nodded affirmatively; the other half remained silent. Then she asked, "What is the worst thing about having a handicapped child?"

The floodgates burst open. One member talked about not being able to look at her child who was born with a severe disfigurement. Another cried as she told about how her father looked at his grandchild and then advised her to put "it into a home." Still another said she didn't have the mental strength to think about braces and crutches that her child would eventually need.

But as people talked, healing was taking place. There was even some gentle humor as individuals mentioned the bizarre reactions of relatives and friends to this misfortune.

During the next three months everyone talked about what had happened in their family. In small but tangible ways a sense of hope was being instilled. Several members of the group were assigned the task of obtaining the names of physicians who had specialties that could help their children. Two members were asked to compile a list of social service agencies. Another member contacted parents of handicapped children who were managing their lives very nicely and invited them to one of the meetings. Everyone's spirit soared after that meeting. They concluded that maybe they too could transcend their situation.

But the best thing that happened in the group was not the transference of information, although that was needed and valued. Rather, friendships were formed that last to this day. As the gruff-looking man said a year later:

> We had to go through a lot of surgeries with our child. There was one guy in that group who was always at the hospital whenever we had to go through these things.

He never said a lot, but we would sit together when the surgery was being performed. He's turned out to be the best friend I ever had.

What are support groups? And why are they so popular?

Most self-help groups are composed of ordinary people confronting difficult problems. Sometimes they are sponsored by a parent organization such as Alcoholics Anonymous, American Diabetes Association, Cystic Fibrosis Foundation, Gray Panthers, or the National Society for Autistic Children. Others are sponsored by hospitals, churches, and educational institutions.

Hospitals frequently sponsor weight control programs, groups of prospective parents, and "I can cope" groups for people with cancer. Churches sponsor family life groups, marriage enrichment groups, and groups designed to help people deepen their faith. Educational institutions offer support services for low achievers and high achievers and individuals who have learning disabilities as well as groups for intellectually bright students.

But many self-help groups are formed spontaneously. I know one men's group that has been meeting every Friday morning for breakfast for nineteen years. There is no agenda. No leader. They just get together to share what is on their minds and in their hearts.

According to the U.S. Public Health Service, 15 million Americans are members of over 500,000 support groups. The concept has become so popular that on any day there will be literally hundreds of groups convened in any urban area. And in rural America self-help groups are rapidly being formed to help farmers and their families cope with declining land values and economic uncertainty.

How did the self-help movement get started? Anthropologists state that primitive man's survival was predicated on helping one another. Small clans gathered fruits and vegetables. Hunting parties trapped animals. There were informal agreements that "families" would assist one another if threatened.

As time passed, farmers learned that they could obtain bigger harvests by working with other farmers rather than by working alone. Teams were formed to clear the fields, till the soil, plant the grain, and harvest the crops.

In industrialized America workers jointly protested working conditions and low salaries. Those protests were the embryonic beginnings of labor unions and insurance organizations.

With the coming of the Depression in the 1930s the first formal self-help groups were formed. Some were designed to barter food, others to trade essential skills. An organization called Unemployed Cooperatives, which rationed food, was started. Groups were formed to help farmers deal with drought and poor crops and land foreclosures.

There was a phenomenal growth in the self-help movement in the 1940s and 1950s. Survivors of the concentration camps helped one another find work. Alliances were formed among parents of handicapped children. Workers began assertively to address health and safety hazards in mines and in factories.[3]

The most important development, however, was the establishment of Alcoholics Anonymous in 1935. The founder of the movement, William Griffith Wilson, was profoundly touched by the power inherent in a simple concept: Alcoholics are the best resource in helping other alcoholics.[4]

The growth of AA has been remarkable. Today the worldwide membership stands at more than 750,000 members. In addition, AA has been responsible for the evolution of hundreds of other self-help groups, many of whom had adopted the AA philosophy.[5]

According to the World Health Organization, self-help groups now exist for almost every disease entity. Here is a brief list of the types of problems addressed in contemporary support groups:

Amputation	National Amputation Foundation
Arthritis	Arthritis Foundation
Asthma	Asthmatic Children Foundation of New York
Blindness	National Federation of the Blind
Cancer	Candlelighters
Deafness	National Association for the Deaf
Diabetes	American Diabetes Foundation
Disfigurement	Society for the Rehabilitation of the Facially Disfigured
Down's syndrome	National Association for Down's Syndrome
Gambling	Gamblers Anonymous
Grief	National Association for Widowed People
Heart attack	Mended Hearts
Learning disabilities	Association for Children with Learning Disabilities
Mastectomy	Reach to Recovery
Paralysis	Paralyzed Veterans of America
Physical handicaps	National Association of the Physically Handicapped
Single parents	Parents Without Partners
Stroke	Stroke Clubs International
Stuttering	National Council of Stuttering
Sudden infant death	National Foundation for Sudden Infant Death

Weight problems   Overeaters Anonymous

Today support groups represent one of the fast-growing social trends in America. If you feel friendless or if you do not feel you are getting all the help you need, you might want to consider joining a self-help group. Here are some of the benefits:

Why Join a Support Group?

Every Saturday night seven men meet in the basement of a church in a St. Louis suburb. Two are executives employed by major corporations. Three are salesmen. One owns a construction company. And one is a minister. All share a similar problem: They are alcoholics.

The meeting begins with a short prayer. And then the question that has been opening their meetings for four years is asked. "How did it go this week?"

One man nervously begins:

> My boss took me out for a drink. He ordered a round and I couldn't push it away. I didn't want to offend him. I didn't want him to know that I had a drinking problem. "It was just one little drink," I said. But I bought a bottle on the way home. I lost four years of sobriety.

There was silence. There were no reprimands. No judgmental statements. Everyone acknowledged how easy it would be to have "just one little drink."

They talked about their embarrassment in turning down drinks from friends and the fear that others might discover their alcoholism. Said the minister, "If my congregation knew I was an alcoholic, it would cost me my job." Another admitted that he too almost went into a liquor store during the week.

Everyone understood. And that is probably the single biggest benefit of joining a support group: Everyone in the group understands the seriousness of the problem.

Thus there is no need to feel ashamed or embarrassed when things don't go quite right. And there is no reason to explain why you are having difficulty coping. After all, good friends don't demand explanations.

But there is more than empathy in support groups. There is practical help. New ideas. Fresh perspectives.

After the meeting was over, one of the members went to the home of the man who had been drinking. They poured the liquor down the sink. Then they went into the living room and talked.

They talked about how easy it would be for both of them to get drunk. How easy it would be to go to a liquor store that was but a scant block from where they were sitting. But, more important, they talked about how easy it would be to let alcohol destroy that which they had so carefully built during the past four years. They didn't want that. And they vowed that it wouldn't happen.

Around 2:00 A.M. they both knew that neither one would drink that night. Nor the next day. Nor any day in the future. But they made a pact with one another to talk in the morning. Just to be sure.

In "The Ambitious Guest" Nathaniel Hawthorne writes, "Is not the kindred of a common fate a closer tie than that of birth?" The answer is, yes. Because if you have a common fate such as the same illness or the same type of emotional problem or a similar career problem, there is understanding. And a reaching out to one another for help.

The friendship among those seven men is one of the strongest bonds of friendship that I have ever seen. They telephone each other several times a week. Even when the executives are traveling on business, they make certain that they fly home for the Saturday night meeting. It's just too precious to miss. One member put it this way:

> In this group it doesn't matter whether you are wealthy or poor; whether you are educated or uneducated. The only thing that matters is that we have the same problem. And we need each other if we are to stay sober.
>
> We have become like brothers. Oh, we have our disagreements. But when the chips are down, these are the people I count on. They've never let me down.

One of the principal benefits of belonging to a self-help group is friendship. And out of that friendship flows concern and an eagerness to help one another regain confidence and self-respect.

A high school counselor told me that when teenagers are in academic difficulty the hardest thing to do is help them regain self-respect: "What tends to happen is that they stop believing in themselves. They have grown accustomed to thinking of themselves as 'average' and in some cases 'failures.' To get themselves to think positively about themselves is the biggest part of the battle."

If you haven't been able to cope with a problem, you may sense that you have failed. And you will feel that most strongly when you meet someone who appears to have mastered an identical problem. A parent of a handicapped child said: "My neighbor has a chronically ill child. But I never see her discouraged. She doesn't seem depressed. In fact, she enjoys life. Seeing her happy makes my problem worse. Because I can't be happy."

Sometimes it is nearly impossible to think positively. If you are an unemployed executive, it may be difficult to think of yourself ever again putting on your suit and heading for work. And if you have been divorced by someone whom you love, it may be impossible to think of yourself as being lovable. But support groups send reassuring messages: You can change attitudes. And you can regain confidence and self-respect.

During the past decade many women have joined support groups. In fact today there are more than twelve hundred support groups for women in the United States. There are also support groups in Canada, Europe, Australia, New Zealand, and South America. Most are designed to help women sort out the economic, work, and health issues associated with life in the mid-1980s.[6]

There are groups for the newly divorced. There are groups for single parents. Some women's groups focus on health issues. Others on grief.

Among the fastest-growing support groups for women are those that help them find careers. Once the career has been found, group members help one another cope with the demands of full-time employment and sometimes full-time parenting.

Claire Freeman joined such a group. But only after a dream had burst. She had spent eighteen years raising three daughters. Now she was going to find a paid job. Unfortunately she didn't know how tough it would be to resume a career after an eighteen-year interruption.

I'll never forget the day I started my job hunt. I was so full of enthusiasm and very idealistic. But I quickly became disillusioned.

The first interviewer hardly gave me any time. The second interviewer said I had no skills. Within a month I had been turned down fourteen times. The response was always the same: We don't have any jobs.

I went to my old employer, whom I worked with before the birth of our first child. But the personnel officer hardly looked at me. He mumbled something to the effect that he would keep my name on file.

I was angry. I had given that company six good years of my life and even though that was eighteen years ago, I thought they would show some respect.

Out of frustration I said, "Don't you have job openings right now?"

He leaned over the desk and said: "I'll put it to you straight, lady. You worked here eighteen years ago. The whole world has changed. What happened eighteen years ago has little resemblance to what we are doing today. Frankly, we just don't have too many jobs for forty-three-year-old people. I can get a hundred fresh M.B.A.s who don't need to be retrained."

Claire went home numbed by the rejection. It was the last straw. She told her husband that she would never again look for a job. She hardly went out of the house during the next couple of months. She didn't talk to anybody. She stopped seeing friends. She avoided social gatherings. "I was so depressed. I didn't want to see anybody," she said.

But then a friend told her about an organization called "Women Together," an organization designed to help women through mid-life transitions.

I was very hesitant about going to a group. I have never needed a group in my life and I didn't know why I needed one now. But I was told that this group had helped a lot of women.

With some apprehension I went to the first meeting. Everyone in the room talked about the difficulties they were having in finding employment. Some have been looking for jobs for two years.

One of the women stated that she had been rejected by four different employers during the past month. Without thinking, I blurted, "That's my story—only I have been rejected fourteen times!"

There was a lot of laughter. They all knew what I was talking about.

That evening we talked about self-confidence and most admitted that we hardly had any left. Just knowing that there were other women who felt like I did made me feel better.

The next few meetings were helpful. We discussed how to write a résumé. No one had ever taught me that there was a proper way to write a professional-looking document about yourself. We discussed the job interview and how to dress and how to make a good presentation. One week was particularly helpful because it dealt with how to keep our family together during this difficult time in our lives. I needed that session because we were having some problems at home that were related to my job difficulties.

Each week I received new ideas and new encouragements. Soon I began to feel that maybe I could get rejected a fifteenth time and not be completely demoralized.

I kept interviewing in different companies. And the group kept supporting me. And when I got turned down the group encouraged me to keep trying.

Finally, I found a company that would hire me. It didn't seem like much of a job. But as the group pointed out it was a start. They encouraged me to take it. And I did and have I ever been grateful.

If you were to see Claire Freeman today, you would never guess that this was the same person who only a couple of years ago said that she had "no skills, no experience, no future." What you would see is a professional woman handling a company's payroll. More important, you would see a woman who is deeply valued by her boss and by her company.

After all of those rejections I quit believing in myself. I had convinced myself that my work life was over. I was sure that no one would hire me.

But my support group changed all that around. Everyone knew what it is like to be a middle-aged woman seeking employment. Everyone knew the frustrations, the rejections, the feelings of incompetence.

But they also knew how to help one another. To encourage you to do things that you don't feel you can do. To take some risks. And most of all, to believe in yourself.

Probably the most difficult part of the journey in recovering from a heartbreak is to take risks. To actually believe that you can find a new job, a new way of life. And it is particularly difficult to take risks if you have convinced yourself that your situation will never change.

Fortunately support groups help you re-examine rigid perceptions and self-defeating thoughts. And they encourage members to test out assumptions that might not be true.

Janice Hastings was a member of a mastectomy club (composed of women who have lost one or both breasts to cancer). One evening she shared her greatest fear with the group: "I fell in love with a wonderful man. But I keep wondering: Will he love me when he finds out that I have cancer? Will he love me when he sees my disfigurement?"

Now we are at the marrow of human existence. "Will I be promoted if my boss learns that I am an alcoholic?" "Will my girlfriend marry me when she finds out that I have diabetes?" "What will our friends say when they learn that our son is gay, or when they find out that our daughter is a lesbian?"

Unfortunately there are few places in society where we can talk about such issues. Usually they rumble around in the privacy of our minds. Sometimes they are shared with a spouse. Perhaps a close friend. But beyond that they are usually hidden from view.

That's why support groups are so valuable. You don't need to keep problems hidden. They can be discussed with concerned friends who will listen.

Janice Hastings tells what happened the night that she shared her greatest worry:

I told the group my worst fear which was that my friend would abandon me if he found out that I had cancer.

Everyone in the room became quiet. But in the quietness everyone understood what was being said. Everyone had been there. Every one of the women has had the same feelings and the same fears.

We talked quite a while that night. One woman said that after the surgery she felt like half a person. Another said that she never looks at herself in the mirror. Another confessed that she didn't know how her husband could love her, given the way she looked.

But then one of the members turned to me and said: "Do you think your friend will actually abandon you if he finds you have cancer? Do you think his love for you will change because you do not have breasts?" I said that I didn't know. The group suggested that I find out. And I needed to find out right away.

As I was driving home, I thought about going to see my friend. But I didn't know if I had the courage. I drove by his house once. Then a second time. Finally I parked the car and walked up the steps. My heart was pounding.

"There's something I need to tell you," I said. My voice cracked with emotion. Then I told him my secret.

He put his arms around me. Then he looked at me and said softly: "It doesn't matter. I have never loved you more."

That night two lovers loved. And the important things in life were reaffirmed.

Why are support groups helpful? They provide us a place where we can be honest. A place to share our fears. A place to try out new ideas. But they also encourage us to act.

If you are having difficulty in getting over a problem, a support group may be for you. The names and addresses of some of the major organizations that help people in crisis are listed in Appendix B.

But if you cannot find an organization for your particular

problem, do not become discouraged. Because one probably exists. Consult with a physician, a social worker, a nurse— anyone who knows the resources within your community. Or contact your community hospital, a YMCA or YWCA, your church or synagogue. Make inquiries. Eventually you will find a support group that will help. And there will be an added benefit: You will discover some very good friends.

E I G H T

Finding Competent Professional Help

Do I recommend counseling? I think it was the difference between being sad the rest of my life and being happy.
——FORTY-ONE-YEAR-OLD
UNEMPLOYED EXECUTIVE

One of the most important tasks in overcoming a heartbreak is to obtain competent professional help. Fortunately such assistance is close at hand. In most communities there are skilled individuals, including physicians, ministers, psychologists, and social workers who want to help.

But how do you find good help? And how can you best use their services? Perhaps the starting point is to assess whether a counselor could be of help at this point in your life.

How Do I Know If I Need Help?

There are a number of signs that suggest that professional counseling is needed. One of the most important is depression. It is possible to live in a depressed state for months, even years, after experiencing a loss. At times the seriousness of the depression is not recognized. But then something happens that sensitizes us to our sadness. We find ourselves crying for no apparent reason. We think pessimistic thoughts. The usual things that bring joy no longer break the gloom.

As time passes, we pick up other clues to our depression. There is a lack of energy and drive. There are tiredness and sleep disturbances. We feel irritable. We may even find it difficult to get out of bed and go to work.

Depression is not an isolated phenomenon. In fact 15 percent of the adult American population suffers from significant symptoms of depression.[1] And it seems to be increasing among young people in the fifteen to thirty-five age group.

How do you know if you are depressed? Answer the following questions as honestly as possible:

1. Do you experience abrupt changes in mood?
2. Do you feel lonely—that no one understands your problems?
3. Do you have difficulty finding fun in hobbies and avocations?
4. Do you feel tired most of the time?
5. Do you wake up most mornings dreading the day?
6. If you had your life to live over, would you do most everything different?

If you answer "yes" to any of the above, it is a sign that you could benefit from counseling. And if your answers are affirmative to all six questions, you should obtain help as soon as possible. This does not imply that something is gravely wrong. But it does suggest that you could benefit from the helpful advice of a sympathetic counselor.

A second reason for seeking professional help is to diminish feelings of loneliness. Most of us want periods of solitude—time to collect our thoughts, reflect on our heartbreak, and figure out how we can best manage our future.

But loneliness means that there is no one in whom we confide. There is no one to share our pain, our sense of loss, our frustrations.

Sometimes depressed people choose to be lonely. I have known individuals who were surrounded by caring people but who avoided sharing their concerns. More than one person told me that they didn't talk about their problems because they might break down and cry.

There is nothing wrong with wanting to be alone. But if you avoid other people it may be a sign that you feel guilty over what has happened—perhaps a bit embarrassed that you are not handling the situation as well as you would like. If that is the case, you could benefit from professional help.

Loneliness is a complex phenomenon. You don't cure loneliness by simply being around people. If that were the case our loneliness would evaporate when we go to work. But as many know, one of the most lonely places in the world to be is at work or at a cocktail party where people talk. But never share.

Loneliness means estrangement. Estrangement from the people we love; estrangement from the people with whom we work. It's something all of us periodically experience. But when the estrangement doesn't go away, professional help may be needed.

There is one type of estrangement that is important to recognize. As we saw in Chapter 6, on families, it is not uncommon for spouses to withdraw from one another after a heartbreak. Communication ceases. Problems are not shared. Kissing, touching, and small acts of kindness are no longer evident. Sex becomes a duty. In fact, sexual relations might cease altogether. One wife said, "We always had a good sex life. But when he lost his job he lost his tenderness. He became quiet and withdrawn. Sex no longer interested him."

If you find it difficult to express love to family members, it may be a sign that your problems are getting worse rather than better. Sexual relationships in and of themselves are not a barometer of mental health. But avoiding meaningful relationships is a sign that one is having difficulty coping with the new demands that life has imposed. If this is your case, you could benefit from sympathetic help.

A third reason for considering professional help is if the crisis is hurting your career.

It is a myth that we can keep our personal and work lives separate. A college professor dealing with a mid-life crisis said: "My lectures rambled. My temper was short. I graded my students harshly. Finally I recognized that all this was due to my personal problems. It was then that I realized that I needed help. I just couldn't solve the problems by myself."

Are your personal problems influencing your employment? Do you find yourself irritable with coworkers? Do you find yourself upset by petty office politics that you used to take in stride?

If your personal problems are negatively influencing your work, consider making an appointment with a counselor. The last thing you need is to have personal problems affect the status of your career.

A fourth reason for seeing a counselor is if the crisis is eroding your physical health.

Emotional problems are often the basis for physiological complaints. Headaches, chest pains, stomach cramps, fainting spells may all be caused by unresolved psychological dilemmas. If you suspect that your health is deteriorating, you should have a complete physical examination. But if the physician suggests that your symptoms are not physiological, then you should share your problems with someone whose focus is mental health.

Now you may say: "I am not anxious. I feel close to people. My work is going O.K. And my health is good." You may still benefit from counseling.

Many individuals see counselors not because they are depressed but because they want an informed opinion about their situation. They want to see new possibilities and new ways of looking at old problems. And they want the wisdom of someone who has helped other people in similar circumstances.

Whatever the reason for obtaining professional help, remember this: It is no disgrace to say, "I can't deal with this problem by myself. I need help."

There are times in all of our lives where it is difficult—perhaps impossible—to unravel the forces that suddenly swirl around us. To see a counselor does not imply that we are at our wit's end or that we are falling apart.

And it certainly does not imply that we are incompetent in other areas of life. A successful executive, for example, might feel like a failure when he learns that his child is on drugs. A farmer may have skills in planting crops but not know how to handle the foreclosure on his land. A self-assured physician may go to pieces when he discovers his own cancer.

All of us at painful points in life can benefit from professional help. When you admit that you need help, there is relief. And when you actually obtain it, a conviction begins to emerge that life can be put back together again.

Dick Remland never thought he would need a counselor. But neither did he believe his marriage would fall apart.

> The lowest moment that I can remember occurred at O'Hare Airport. I went out to meet my wife, who was returning from a business trip.
>
> Before we had picked up the luggage she informed me that she wanted out of the marriage. She had made a decision on the trip to leave me.
>
> I was dumbfounded by the suddenness of it all. I could barely cope. Soon I was having headaches and feeling disoriented. One night I almost fainted. I knew I needed help.
>
> It was a big step to ask for help. But from the moment I arrived at the counselor's office until the moment I left, I felt trust. I felt that I could say whatever I wanted to and it would be O.K.
>
> It took a couple of months before I felt like my old self. But gradually I felt the load lift. Seeing the counselor was the best decision I ever made.

What to Expect from Professional Counseling

The first thing you will receive from a competent counselor is acceptance. A competent counselor will accept you as a unique person with unique goals, a unique history, and a unique future.

A good counselor will not treat you as a number. Rather, you will feel that your counselor is interested in your well-being and will spend the necessary time to sort out the troubling aspects of life.

But a good counselor is also honest. In fact, good counselors will tell you whether they can help. One psychologist tells his clients that by the end of the third session they both should see progress. If they don't, the client is advised to see another psychologist.

Of course honesty has a painful edge. Most counselors will provide ample emotional support. But you should expect to hear things that might make you uncomfortable. If your beliefs and attitudes are harmful to your recovery, you should be prepared for an honest assessment.

Sometimes it is this aspect of counseling that we fear. Most of us live with a certain illusion that we see the world correctly. We don't want to be told that our perceptions are inaccurate.

Nevertheless the primary goal of counseling is to help us see our world a bit differently. It does not necessarily imply that our perceptions are wrong. But it does imply that there are other ways that we can view life—ways that can help us regain hope and inner peace.

An acquaintance of mine was deeply troubled by what was happening in his company. He was caught in the middle, between his boss and his subordinates. He knew that he wasn't handling the situation well and began to wonder whether his promotion was jeopardized. I could see him lose enthusiasm for work. More troubling, he was losing confidence in himself.

Finally he visited a psychologist. Two months later he viewed his work problems from a different perspective:

> I learned that I didn't have to get involved in all the disputes. I take everything in life so seriously. If something goes wrong in the department I just assume that it is my fault.
>
> The psychologist helped me differentiate those problems that I have control over from those that I don't. He encouraged me to step back and gain a perspective on each problem. He told me to pick my wars carefully.
>
> Now when a problem comes up at work I step back

and say to myself: "Do I need to get involved in this dispute? Is this a fight that I must wage? And if so, how can I wage it so that everybody wins?"

It's amazing what I learned in six weeks. It's also amazing how good you feel when you pick your battles carefully.

A primary goal of counseling is to help us gain new understandings and new tools to deal with our problems. But a secondary goal—and a very important one—is to help us become aware of community resources.

As noted earlier, in every community there are many organizations whose primary mission is to help others. An effective counselor will inform you of these resources and help you identify those that might be of help after the counseling has been completed.

Randy Henderson's wife was about to be discharged from St. Luke's Hospital. With some hesitation he went to get the bill. It was worse than he had imagined—$6,650 for the twelve-day stay.

Randy was a truck driver with meager savings. He had no idea how the bill would be paid and indicated that to a hospital employee. He was referred to a social worker, who listened attentively to his financial difficulties.

Randy learned that there was financial aid available within the hospital and through the state welfare office. He was told about a public health nursing program that could assist him in caring for his wife once she returned home. He also learned about a support group that could help him cope with his wife's illness. Suddenly new options appeared. Everything no longer seemed quite so hopeless.

None of us wants to be faced with unhappy dilemmas and unpleasant choices. But I can tell you one thing: If you have a problem, you could not be living in a better era. In most communities there are scores of organizations and hundreds of professional people who want to help. Use them. Their wisdom and experience are there for the asking.

How to Find a Competent Counselor

A number of resources can be used in locating counseling services. You might begin with your personal physician. Inform the physician about the nature of your problem. Be honest. Don't hide the fact that you are having difficulty coping with the situation. Indicate what steps, if any, you have already taken to solve your problems.

Your physician will ask questions and probably will give you a physical examination to be certain that you are in good physical health. If you are healthy and there is no physiological cause of your problem, you will be referred to a therapist.

The type of therapist your physician recommends will be based in part on the nature of the problem to be treated. There are counselors skilled at dealing with depression. Others are effective in diminishing anger, hostility, and abusive behavior. Still others are effective in dealing with problems associated with divorce, unemployment, rape, grief, marital discord.

Sometimes physicians will recommend a colleague who is a partner in their practice. It is not uncommon for medical clinics to employ psychologists and family therapists. I know one medical clinic that employs a pastoral counselor who helps patients sort out the spiritual issues related to their problems.

Once you have been given the name of a mental health professional, make an appointment. Don't make the mistake of putting the name on a slip of paper and stashing it in a drawer. If you need help, now is the time to get it.

An excellent resource for finding psychological help is the clergy. In fact, millions of people will go to their pastor, priest, or rabbi before visiting anyone else. Most members of the clergy are well equipped to give psychological as well as spiritual counseling. The reason for this is that most pastors, priests, and rabbis are trained in mental health as well as theology.

Seminary education is far different than what it was a decade or two ago. In fact, previous generations of ministers would receive but one watered-down course in psychology.

But today the curriculum in most seminaries is heavily endowed with psychological as well as biblical studies. The reason is simple: If members of the clergy are to be helpful, they need to understand human problems and human dilemmas. And they need to be able to give practical advice to those in need.

Many members of the clergy, by virtue of either their seminary education and/or continuing education, will have counseling skills. Some will have a certificate indicating that they have had Clinical Pastoral Education (CPE), which is an extensive program in counseling and pastoral care. If your minister has had such training, you can be assured that your problems will be treated with sensitivity and the utmost care.

One of the advantages of obtaining help from a member of the clergy is that a heartbreak can shake the theological foundations of life. Many question their religious beliefs and wonder why God let them down. Some unfortunately believe that they are being punished.

Because human dilemmas have spiritual implications, your pastor, priest, or rabbi may be particularly useful. And even if you do not belong to a church or synagogue you may still want to request their services. By virtue of the vows that are taken, as well as their personal commitment, most members of the clergy will help anyone who knocks on their door.

Professional help can also be found by consulting the Yellow Pages. But you need to be careful, because it's difficult to know which organizations are credible and which aren't. Nevertheless a quick review will indicate hundreds of social service organizations in a typical community. There are child guidance centers, family counseling programs, mental health organizations, marriage enrichment centers, as well as the names of specific counselors. If you are confused by the long list of agencies, consult your mental health association. Or you may want to call your city health department.

There is one other resource that should not be overlooked. Sometimes the very best recommendations come from friends, acquaintances, and business associates.

Neighbors, for example, might be able to refer you to skilled physicians and counselors whom they have found effective in dealing with the bumps and bruises of life. School nurses can refer you to pediatricians and child psychologists. Social workers can refer you to psychiatrists and family counselors. Bankers can usually give you names of attorneys, financial planners, and certified public accountants.

Unfortunately, in spite of the many resources that are available, there are those who put off getting help. The fear is that it will cost too much money.

Counseling can be costly, particularly long-term psychoanalysis. But it need not be. Many organizations ask you to pay only what you can afford. Others request a modest donation. And some services sponsored by philanthropic organizations are free.

Don't make the mistake of thinking that because services are free or low-cost they are ineffective. Some of the most

highly skilled counselors that I know are employed by charitable organizations. Their salaries are modest. But they are
living out a commitment to help people in need, regardless
of ability to pay.

But suppose you want to see a psychiatrist who charges
hourly fees. Does a tight budget automatically exclude you
from such help? Not necessarily. Call the psychiatrist's office
and ask for a statement of costs. Explain your financial
circumstances and ask whether the fees can be negotiated.
In some instances clinics will lower fees and/or provide
additional time to make reasonable monthly payments.

One form of financial reimbursement that should not be
overlooked is medical insurance. We usually think of insurance as paying for a broken arm or leg. Increasingly, however, medical insurance will reimburse counselors who help
us cope with a broken spirit. This is particularly true if you
work for a company that has a comprehensive protection
policy for its employees.

Before entering any counseling relationship, consult with
your insurance company. Ask whether your policy reim-
burses for mental health services. If it does, determine if
there are specific organizations, clinics, and/or agencies that
you must visit in order to be eligible for financial reimbursement.

In summary, if you want to locate good help you need
to be curious. Ask questions. Consult with friends. Visit
agencies, clinics, and private practices. Request literature
from the mental health association and visit your city health
department. The more information you discover, the greater
the likelihood that you will find competent and compassionate help.

How to Spot a Quack

While there are hundreds of legitimate organizations and professional therapists, there are a few who will try to con you out of your money. They may even make recommendations that will endanger your health.

Health quackery takes many forms. There are "Dr. William's Pink Pills for Pale People" and the "Famous Arisian Depilatory" to get rid of unsightly hair. There are worthless drugs, bust developers, and penis enlargers. There are restorative juices that come from calf's liver and zinc disks worn in shoes to allegedly cure aches and pains. There are mechanical devices such as the "Detoxacolon," which treats twenty-eight different diseases.[2]

These products are usually benign. But the hopes that are raised are not. And when the ulcer is not cured or the cancer does not go away, there is disappointment. Often a sense of deep betrayal.

Why do many people seek out false gurus, palm-readers, pseudo-doctors? Some people want simple solutions to complex problems. They don't want to go through medical tests. They don't want prolonged treatment programs or lengthy hospital stays. What they want are quick and painless cures.

Others see quacks because they have lost confidence in the medical system. They sense that it is a high-tech system, one devoid of human touch. Not finding hope, they turn elsewhere for care.

False healers exploit two diseases in particular: arthritis and cancer.

The Arthritis Foundation reports that almost a billion dollars is spent each year on unproven remedies such as copper bracelets, "immunized" milk, and now, "green-lipped mussel extract."[3]

There are Mexican physicians whose business is almost entirely devoted to arthritic patients. One such doctor will see as many as 120 individuals per day during a ten-hour workday, although most of his appointments last between seven and ten minutes. Some of these patients will have made appointments many months in advance of their trip. Nevertheless they may have to wait in long lines once they arrive.[4]

The claims for cancer cures are numerous and sound scientific. There are "Escharotics," which are salves to "draw out" the cancer from the body. "Krebiozen" is a remedy allegedly obtained from the blood of horses, although scientific analysis has proved that it is mainly mineral oil. Then there is the "Spectro-chrome," which will treat disease through "attuned color waves."[5]

There is no scientific justification for these products and there is no empirical evidence that they work. But the most important reason for avoiding them, particularly for cancer patients, is that you lose valuable time—time that could be spent in obtaining competent help.

How can you spot an imposter? Here is a handy checklist:

- Do the sellers claim that they are battling the medical profession or the federal government, which is trying to suppress the latest advances in science?

- Are you told that the typical medical program involving surgery, chemotherapy, and X rays will do more harm than good?

- Does the seller have a secret remedy or an instant cure?

- Does the seller use testimonials "guaranteeing" his product?

- Does the seller try to scare you into purchasing the product?

- Is the remedy sold door-to-door by a "health adviser" or a "health technician"?[6]

Would you spot a charlatan if you saw one? Don't be so sure. Charlatans are often sophisticated businessmen who know how to advertise their products and exploit your fears. They also know how to present their credentials so that they sound impressive.

But the credentials are neither impressive nor legitimate. Most come out of mail-order diploma mills. One organization boasts that it has issued 1½ million doctoral degrees at twenty-five dollars each through its mail-order program.[7]

In seeking medical, psychological, legal, or financial help, work with reputable professionals. If you question their credentials, ask where they went to school and where they received their training. Inquire as to how long they have worked in their profession and the length of time they have practiced in your community.

Answers to your inquiries will not guarantee competent help. But the information will give you an indication of their professional preparation and work experience. If your questions cause defensiveness, find another helper.

Practical Strategies for Working with Professional Helpers

Here are several important suggestions that will help you work effectively with physicians, counselors, and members of the clergy.

Be assertive. Some individuals walk into a physician's clinic or a psychologist's office and say: "Heal me. Do what you want—just get me well."

There is no curiosity about the healer's education or experience. No questions are raised about costs or referral services. No inquiry is made as to how long the treatment program will last or whether it has proven effective in similar situations.

A better approach is to interview a number of professionals before determining one who might offer the most help. This is particularly true in locating a skilled counselor, given the fact that there are many different therapies and approaches to human problems. Here are some questions you might ask:

What has been your experience in treating my problem?

What type of treatment program is followed?

How long will the treatment program last and how long will it take until I feel better?

Can I call you in an emergency?

Do you encourage second opinions? Can I feel free to consult with other professionals if need be?

How much do your services cost?

What do you expect from me as your patient/client?

What can I do to help myself?

The concept of interviewing a professional person might seem somewhat strange, for we are taught to be respectful of authority. We therefore don't ask questions or verbalize misgivings.

Nevertheless, it is important to be curious. For how can you assess skills without understanding the nature of the professional's training and experience? And how can you find out about costs unless you come right out and ask the charge?

One of the primary benefits of asking questions is that it involves you in the healing process. You are in effect saying: "This is my life. Ultimately I have to be responsible for what I do and for what happens to me."

When you receive thoughtful answers to your inquiries you will feel reassured. You will know what to expect and what your treatment might entail. You will also know that you are respected and that your wishes will be carried out.

Now you may say: "This all sounds a bit overwhelming. I have never related to a doctor in that way. I don't even know if I could do it."

Michelle Linstrom has those same feelings. She had never been very assertive. But as she was sitting in the waiting room of a psychologist's office, she decided that maybe she'd better get a few answers to her questions.

I had never gone to a psychologist before. So I was quite apprehensive. And what made me particularly fearful was the thought that in a few minutes I would be sharing with a stranger the intimacies of my life. I would be telling him things I probably have never told anyone. That frightened me. How do I know whether I can trust him? How do I know if he can help?

I told him that before we discussed my problem I would like to ask him about his practice and how he would help me. I asked him whether he had worked with many people who had lost their husband like I had.

He told me that he had been helping grieving patients for over twenty years. He mentioned that he had recently lost a close friend and knew firsthand what it was like to lose someone you love.

Then I asked him how long it might take for me to feel better. He said that was a difficult question to answer but that usually his clients began to notice a difference in a couple of months.

Then I asked what his costs would be and whether any of this might be covered by my insurance.

He answered all my questions to my satisfaction. He was very kind. He didn't seem rushed. The only thing that mattered was that I felt comfortable.

I started to look forward to the next session.

Be honest. If you are going to get well in body, mind, and spirit, your caregiver needs a complete picture of your frustrations, worries, and hopes.

Some patients hedge with their physician about why they

are seeking help. They might discuss vague physical symptoms but never get to the heart of the problem. They might talk about their headaches or their fatigue but not mention the struggles that they are having with a job or with a child or with finances.

Your caregiver cannot give you an accurate diagnosis or prescribe a plan of action unless the problem that is bothering you is honestly explained. Should you really tell your family physician about how things are going for you at home, at school, or at work?

The answer is yes, particularly if it has a bearing on your physical problems.

Physicians are increasingly aware of the close relationship between mental and physical health and of how emotions influence physiological processes. It is known, for example, that both streptococcal infections and respiratory infections occur more frequently after major life changes, and that one's ability to get over illnesses, such as influenza and mononucleosis, often correlates with the amount of stress that is being experienced.[8]

Your physician needs to be aware not only of the ache in the stomach but of the ache in the heart. For it is only then that he or she will be able to treat you as a whole person.

One important reason for being honest is that it may significantly reduce the amount of time it takes to get well. Patients who reveal their symptoms obtain the most accurate diagnoses. They receive the most appropriate medications. And they obtain specific help for specific dilemmas.

When you enter a physician's clinic or a counselor's office, share what's on your mind. And in your heart. You do not need to portray yourself as the competent executive, the self-assured business person, the super mom or dad.

Rather, share your hurt and confide your pain. Be vulnerable. It's the quickest way to recovery.

Understand your medications. Drugs are increasingly prescribed for both medical and psychological problems. The drug business has grown by a factor of 100 during this century. One of the fastest-growing sectors of the pharmaceutical market is medications that influence the central nervous system. Dependence on tranquilizers and other sedatives has increased by 290 percent since 1962.[9]

You need to be cautious in taking any medication. You need to understand what you are taking, why you are taking it, and whether the medication could harm you.

Contrary to public opinion, adverse side effects strike more than half of all consumers who take medications. Fortunately most side effects are minor. But some are severe, as evidenced by the fact that 300,000 people are hospitalized each year for adverse drug reactions.

You need to be curious about what is being prescribed for you. Some drugs, for example, need to be taken on an empty stomach, while others should be taken with a full meal. Some lose their effectiveness when used with other medications. And still others should never be taken with alcohol. More than 2,500 people will die from mixing medications and alcohol this year.[10]

To minimize the negative effects of medications, remember this: Never leave a physician's office without information about the medication: when to take it, how to take it, and whether there may be adverse side effects. Request the information in writing. If your physician does not have the information, ask your pharmacist.

One way to obtain additional information about medications is to consult *The Physicians' Desk Reference for Nonprescription Drugs* or *The United States Pharmacopoeia—Dispensing Information*. Those references will give you concise drug information. They can be found in most pharmacies and community libraries.

Obtain second opinions. An important strategy in getting

well is to use more than one caregiver. This is particularly true when you question the accuracy of a diagnosis or the merits of a treatment program.

For example, suppose you are a jogger and are experiencing discomfort in your knee. You go to a physician who suggests that you may have strained a ligament. Rest is prescribed. But the pain doesn't go away. In fact, it gets worse. You decide to obtain a second opinion.

This time you see a specialist in sports medicine. Several sophisticated diagnostic tests are used in assessing your problem. The diagnosis: torn cartilage. You may not need to check with anyone else, given the thoroughness of the examination. Surgery will be suggested and a rehabilitation program outlined.

But if you hesitate about accepting the second diagnosis, there is nothing wrong with obtaining a third opinion. Even a fourth. Your goal is clear: You want an accurate diagnosis and the best possible plan of action to solve the problem.

It is important to remember that in spite of the sophistication of medical practice, it is an art as well as a science. Consequently you are relying on human judgments. Therefore you need second opinions on anything that significantly affects your health. Unfortunately many people don't obtain them. Why? Because they feel that they would be disloyal to their primary doctor.

You should dismiss such feelings, or at the very least talk them over with your personal physician. It is standard medical practice to obtain second opinions. In fact, most health insurance companies pay for them. And if the second opinion conflicts with the first, they may even pay for a third assessment.

I learned the importance of second opinions several years ago when we had to make some important decisions concerning our seven-year-old son. Our boy had a chronic ear infection. A pediatrician informed us, rather dogmatically, that the only way to solve the problem permanently was to have surgery. The surgical procedure was called a myringotomy. An incision would be made in the eardrum, permitting the inner ear to be ventilated.

I wasn't expecting that type of recommendation. Furthermore, when someone tells me that there is only one way to solve a problem, I become a bit suspicious. So I began to ask questions: Were there other ways that our son could be treated? Were there new medications that he could be taking? Could there be negative effects from the surgery?

The physician became quite uncomfortable and visibly upset. My wife asked one more question: "What if we did nothing—could our son's problem clear up on its own?"

Well, I wish that you could have seen the reaction. In a deep, authoritative tone of voice, he said: "He needs the surgery. And if you don't like what I recommend, find another doctor."

Well, we did just that. We found a physician who specialized in ear, nose, and throat problems. He was perhaps thirty-five years old. But he had the maturity of a senior statesman.

The first thing I noted about this doctor was that he talked to our boy. He asked him questions about school and basketball and about what he did on the weekends. A sense of peace came over me as I watched this quiet interchange. He was gaining our son's trust. And he was rapidly gaining our respect as well.

After the physical evaluation was completed, the physician informed us that there were several options. First, he could do surgery. Second, there could be what he termed a "holding action"—a period of time in which we would wait to see if our son's problem could straighten out on its own. And finally, he could treat the child conservatively, with some medications. The advantages and limitations of each option were carefully explained.

We thought about it overnight and called him the next day. I told him that for the time being we would like to try the medications that he had recommended. "That's fine," he replied. "If need be, we can do the surgery later."

I hung up the telephone with a warm, good feeling about the care our son was receiving. And the care we as parents were receiving as well. To make matters even better, the medications worked and the surgery was never scheduled.

It really is important to obtain second opinions. At Cornell Medical Center the cases of 700,000 patients were reviewed. Of those who received a second opinion, 25 percent were informed that they did not need the surgery that was recommended by the first physician. Most refused the surgery and *did not have any ill effects*. It is interesting to note that the bulk of the initial recommendations were for knee surgery, hysterectomies, and prostate removal.[11]

Second opinions can save you not only emotional and financial costs—they might even save your life. A congressional investigation found that there are approximately two million unnecessary operations a year, responsible for 12,000 deaths.[12]

If you take the time to obtain a second opinion, one of two things will happen. Either the second opinion will corroborate the first, thus giving you peace of mind, or you will receive conflicting advice. If that is the case, obtain a third opinion. Even a fourth, until you are positive that the procedure that is being recommended is in your best interest. That's what it means to be a full partner in the healing process.

Insist on quality care. If there is one thing that my son's experience taught me, it is this: If you do not like the help you are receiving, go elsewhere. For within your community are numerous competent and compassionate caregivers—

individuals who will respect your autonomy and value your intellect.

Sometimes you don't have to look very far to find quality help.

Millie Jameson told me an interesting story of how she switched ministers. I listened attentively because most people stay with the same church or synagogue out of a sense of loyalty even if the minister or rabbi isn't effective.

One morning while she was reading her Bible, the telephone rang. It was the principal of her daughter's school. Millie's daughter had been caught smoking pot and admitted to having taken LSD.

The news was a shock. A wave of panic came over her and the only thing she could think of was to drive over to her church and see her minister. Tormented with anxiety, she rushed into the minister's study. "What have I done wrong? Why would my daughter take drugs?"

Her minister wasn't sympathetic. In fact, he implied that she should have been alert to her daughter's drug use. He indicated that he didn't have a whole lot of time because he had to prepare his sermon for next Sunday. He told her that the only way to deal with kids on drugs is to be very tough. He also stated that Millie's daughter would need to be reinstated into "the good graces of the church" and suggested that she apologize to the congregation at the next midweek prayer service.

Millie was humiliated. On the way home she pulled the car to the side of the road and put her head on the steering wheel and sobbed. She finally brushed away her tears and noticed a rather large church on a distant corner. She walked up to the church and looked it over. According to a sign on the front lawn, the minister's name was the Reverend Nelson. Maybe someone else could help. She asked to see the minister.

To Millie's surprise the woman she was talking with was

the minister. "I saw kindness in her eyes," reported Millie, "and I started to cry. I felt her arms around me. And I knew that I was in a safe place."

Millie shared her pain and her anxiety. Finally, when there were no more tears to be shed, she showed the minister a picture of her daughter.

"You're so fortunate," said the Reverend Nelson. "You have a beautiful child."

Then the minister gave some quiet advice. She told Millie to go to school and give her daughter a big hug and stand by her no matter what the consequences might be. She said that her daughter needed her now more than ever and that Millie should have the courage to be strong and kind.

But then her voice became firm: "The most important thing, Millie, is to be loving. Whatever else you might do, make certain your child knows that you love her."

A year later Millie reflected on the meeting with the Reverend Nelson:

> I left her office and practically flew down the church steps. Sure, my daughter was in trouble—but she was my daughter. And she needed me.
>
> I drove to the school. I could see the fear in her eyes. I told her not to worry, that everything would turn out O.K. As I was leaving my child took my hand and squeezed it and quietly said, "You're the best mother any daughter could have."
>
> The last year hasn't always been easy. But my daughter is off drugs and we have had some frank talks that have been tender and beautiful.
>
> I really don't know what I would have done if I hadn't met Reverend Nelson. I hate to think about it because I left my own minister's office feeling so guilty. But the other pastor was kind.

There is nothing quite so powerful as finding someone who helps you change your perception of the world. But what is important is not the new idea or the new perception or the new plan of action—as important as these may be. What is important is that you have a sense of confidence within yourself. Insist on that type of care.

Trust your intuitions. Now we come to an important point: You need to trust yourself. You need to trust your experiences and intuitions, your intellect as well as your faith.

When the physician told us that our son needed surgery, it simply didn't feel right. Now mind you, I am not a surgeon. I don't have knowledge about the inner ear, hearing disabilities, or medications.

But I am a father. And I know my son. And at that point in time I knew deep within my bones that surgery wasn't the answer.

Now some will suggest that as patients we are too emotionally involved to make important decisions like this. Perhaps there is truth in what they say. Sometimes when lightning strikes, we become so confused that we can't think straight about matters that affect the essence of life.

But that's why you obtain second opinions. And third opinions as well. And then, in the quietness of your own being, you make the decisions that will affect your life. And at times the life of your family.

Obviously it is difficult to make such decisions. I think, for example, of cancer patients who must decide whether treatment should be initiated or whether it should be discontinued.

My advice is this: Listen carefully to your physician. Learn all you can. Ask questions. But then request second and third opinions from qualified medical personnel. If possible talk to other patients who have had to face similar choices.

But then in the quietness of your soul ask yourself, "Given my situation and all that I have learned, what path is best?"

Now you need to trust yourself. You need to trust your

knowledge, your experience. Most of all you need to trust your faith. Don't push for an answer if one does not come. Be patient. In time the answer will come and you will know what to do. Remember these words:

> Any path is only a path, and there is no affront to oneself or to others in dropping it if that is what your heart tells you. . . . Look at every path closely and deliberately. Try it as many times as you think necessary. Then ask yourself and yourself alone, one question. . . . Does this path have a heart? If it does, the path is good. If it doesn't, it is of no use.[13]

There is one last point to be made: *Be charitable to those who offer assistance.*

It is important to remember that professional helpers are human beings. They have their good days and not-so-good days. And, perhaps most important, they too have to deal with their own frustrations and heartaches.

Sometimes the reason that a physician is late for an appointment is because there was an emergency. Sometimes the reason for the curtness of counselors is that they are helping a large number of people—all of whom are demanding immediate assistance.

This does not imply that you overlook rudeness and insensitivity. But it does suggest that there are times in which we need to look past personal mannerisms and idiosyncrasies that make us feel uncomfortable.

If you are receiving sound technical help, perhaps you should overlook the office delays. And if a counselor is helping you to sort out your problem in an efficient way, maybe you need to ignore brusque mannerisms or the insensitive comment.

Robin Ruzinski went to his rabbi's office two months after his daughter committed suicide. He was ambivalent about seeing the rabbi, for he was a harsh man. Here's what happened:

I told my rabbi that I was feeling depressed and that I didn't think I'd ever feel happy again.

Well, the rabbi sat straight up in his chair. He told me that I was feeling sorry for myself and that I acted like I was the only one in the world who had problems. He said that last year over five thousand kids in this country committed suicide and that many of them came from good homes. He said that it was just as tough for those parents, but that most of them probably were doing all right. He asked me what I was doing to make myself feel good, and of course I'm not doing anything.

I almost walked out when he was giving all that pompous advice.

But I didn't. I sat there and listened.

He told me that he wanted me to go home and count my blessings. He told me to get up before sunrise every day and say a prayer of thanks. Then I was to write down three things for which I was thankful.

I decided to try it, although I thought it would have been nice to have received a little sympathy.

I got up at 5:15 the next morning and went outside to my patio. The sun was starting to rise. I couldn't remember the last time I had seen a sunrise.

Then I took out some paper like the rabbi told me to do and wrote down what I was thankful for.

The first thing I put down was that I had seventeen good years with my daughter. We were close, and although I didn't understand everything she was feeling, she left me a beautiful letter before she took her life. So I put down for my second thing that I was glad I had that letter. But I couldn't think of anything else that I was thankful for. So I went into the house.

Then it hit me: If my daughter saw me now she would really be hurt. She wouldn't understand why I had given up. In fact, she would be angry with me and would tell me to get on with life. What she would want more than anything else would be to see me happy.

The more I thought about it, the more I thought I owed it to her to get over my unhappiness and to remember all the good times we had together.

Then I thought about the rabbi. I smiled. He knew exactly what he was doing. I called him up and thanked him.

The rabbi had been insensitive. But the rabbi had a marvelous gift that more than offset his gruffness. He was able to motivate a heartbroken father to take some action. And he was able to instill confidence and purpose and direction.

Don't be unduly put off by the personality of a caregiver. Don't get angry at the slight injustices or the insensitive mannerisms.

Rather, ask yourself if the technical advice is sound. If it is, you are probably receiving competent care.

N I N E

Affirming a Faith

*It is not necessary to go off on a tour
of great cathedrals in order to find the
Deity. Look within. You have to sit to
do it.*
　　　　　　　　—NORMAN COUSINS

*Every time I have a heart attack, I get a
lump in my throat and I get scared, and all
of a sudden I hear this voice inside of me
saying, "You'll be all right man, calm down.
I'll live with you. I'll die with you, and
I'll take care of you no matter what." The
lump in my throat, it just goes away.*
　　　　　　　　—TIM DODSON

Now we come to the Gordian knot in the healing process:
the matter of faith. Is it possible to believe in the goodness
of life when you have learned that your child has been given
a bleak diagnosis? Can you believe that there is a loving
God when a call from the sheriff's office informs you that
your spouse has been in a life-threatening accident? Can

you affirm vitality when depression stalks you night and day?

Theologians are quick to reassure. They tell us that if we have but the faith of a mustard seed we will resolve our hurt. But when your world collapses and everything of meaning is taken from you, concepts such as "affirmation," "hope," and "faith" tend to sound hollow. They even seem cruel when they are glibly tossed to us as ready-made answers to life's most perplexing dilemmas.

The purpose of this chapter is to examine the meaning of faith. Our examination will not come out of theological treatises. Nor will our frame of reference be philosophers who speculate on the meaning of the universe. Rather, our focus will be those special individuals who discovered the power of a simple faith while in the winter of their lives.

Spirituality: The Essence of Life

We begin with an important premise: All of us are spiritual beings. To be spiritual implies a belief in a power greater than ourselves. It means that life is sacred and has been given to us as a gift.

It is easy to lose sight of the spiritual dimension of life. We struggle with jobs that burn us out, forgetting that work, as envisioned by the sixteenth-century theologian John Calvin, is innately good, even holy. We build our pensions and our IRA's and our Keogh plans but forget that ultimately the only security that any of us have rests deep within the quietness of our being. And when we become ill, we hope that the wonders of space-age medicine will restore our vitality. Yet we forget that the root definition of the Old English word *hǣlth* is "wholeness," which includes the mending of the spirit.

The spiritual dimension of life is often trampled into the ground in a culture that rewards action rather than meditation. Yet there is a growing belief among many that when we have lost the spiritual foundations of life we have lost something that is precious. And what has been lost is the very thing that could provide a sturdy anchor to our turbulent lives.

Fortunately there is a growing desire to understand better the spiritual dimension of life. New studies aptly demonstrate that the religious pulse of the American people is quickening. Eighty percent of adults believe religion is increasing its influence, compared with only fourteen percent in 1970.[1] A Gallup poll found that three out of four individuals would like to see our religious beliefs having a greater role in our lives.[2] A *U.S. News and World Report* survey discovered that Americans are becoming more aggressive in proclaiming that spirituality "is the root of their very existence."[3]

The reassessment of the spiritual dimension of life is being pursued in diverse settings throughout America. In big cities and small towns citizens are meeting in homes in order to understand what faith means in terms of daily activities. At Michigan State University there is a tremendous demand for courses on the Bible, such that the Religious Studies Department cannot handle it.[4] And in a growing number of corporations, executives as well as staff members meet regularly for meditation and prayer and self-examination. As Colin W. Williams, professor of religion at Yale Divinity School, states: "The confident secularism of the 50's and 60's has passed and people are asking questions about what is transcendent, what is life's meaning."[5]

If there is one redeeming legacy of a heartbreak, it is that we are given an opportunity to discover "what is transcendent, what is life's meaning." When the issue of faith was raised with those that I interviewed, the conversation turned serious—as if we were beginning a pilgrimage into the most tender and most sacred parts of their personal journey.

As you might expect, responses concerning the meaning of faith varied widely. Some people without reflection stated: "God pulled me through." "If it weren't for God I wouldn't have made it." Some were almost embarrassed by the simplicity of their views. "I know it sounds trite, but I just turned my problem over to God." Still others commented, "When you know you are going to die, the only thing that comforts is a belief in the goodness of God."

I do not wish to imply that everyone or even the majority of individuals that I interviewed found traditional Judeo-Christian beliefs helpful. The belief systems varied tremendously. Some respondents were religious fundamentalists who fervently believed "in the power of prayer." Some were agnostics who had a deep reverence for life. And others were simply confused about the unanswered riddles of life. At times they relied on their faith, but in other instances they felt that religious expressions were but empty words.

But regardless of the religious orientation, I discovered one important fact: *Faith has a powerful effect in helping people recover a sense of balance, tranquillity, and hope.* Indeed, I am persuaded that there is nothing in the arsenal of medical or psychological technology that equals the power inherent in a simple faith.

The Healing of the Human Spirit: The Gifts of Faith

Those who are fortunate to have survived a heartbreak have engaged in what Dag Hammarskjöld once referred to as "the longest journey, the journey inward."⁶ The difficulties of this pilgrimage are aptly stated by Carl Jung:

> Whenever there is a reaching down into innermost experience, into the nucleus of personality, most people are overcome by fright, and many run away.... The risk of inner experience, the adventure of the spirit, is alien to most human beings.⁷

A tragedy that forever alters life makes it difficult to "run away." There is simply no place to run, for no matter where you go the existential questions follow: Why did this happen to me? Is life worth living? What do I now believe about God, life, and happiness?

The answers to these perplexing questions are elusive. What makes matters worse is that we often find little comfort in other people's explanations. A faith handed down to us by relatives often seems anemic. Admonitions from poets and priests might contain a measure of comfort, yet their explanations are often one step removed from our experience. And prayers spoken by well-meaning individuals often leave in their wake more questions than answers.

Nevertheless, you *must* ask the questions. In fact, what seems to demarcate those who survive a heartbreak from those who don't is a willingness to ask the poignant questions that relate to life and death, purpose and chaos. The answers may never be totally found, but *by becoming a friend to the questions* a small step toward inner healing is taken.

What seems to be warranted at this juncture in your recovery is a willingness to not force the answers. For when you force the answers you become like a man drowning in the sea, beating the water frantically without giving a sane thought as to how he might survive. Far better, as Rainer Maria Rilke noted, to value the questions:

I want to beg you as much as I can . . . to be patient toward all that is unsolved in your heart and to try to love the questions themselves. . . . Do not now seek answers which cannot be given you because you would not be able to live them. And the point is to live everything. _Live_ the questions now. Perhaps you will then gradually, without noticing it, live along some distant day into the answer . . . take whatever comes with great trust, and if only it comes out of your own will, out of some need of your innermost being, take it upon yourself and heed nothing.[8]

The willingness to live with questions appears to be a prerequisite for inner healing. But to ask the questions is to make yourself vulnerable. For when you cannot find a tidy answer to Job's haunting question—Why must good people suffer?—life's meaning seems to be sucked dry.

There is consternation when silence greets important questions. And there often is anger.

A young man was visiting with a chaplain after the death of his mother. On the wall was a crucifix with a ceramic corpus. The boy's eyes focused on the crucifix. The chaplain, sensitive to the young man's hostility, said, "Do whatever you need to do."

The boy reached for the crucifix, removed it from the wall, raised it over his head, and smashed it against the floor over and over again until the ceramic figure was broken into bits.

When you grapple with the irrational, no symbol is safe from destruction. Even symbols that may once have given life meaning.

After his destructive deed the young man collapsed on the couch next to the minister. The chaplain held the boy tightly as the young man poured out his grief in deep, powerful, and unrestrained sobs. His grief was bottomless, as wave after wave of emotion came over him. At the end he was exhausted, peaceful.[9]

Listen to the statements of others who have suffered great losses:

- My philosophy of life was once complex. Now it is simple. I believe there is a reason for everything. More precisely, a purpose to life. *One must act in this way even when life seems to contradict this*. We are not determined. We largely make what we want of our situation. (Twenty-two-year-old woman jilted by her lover.)

- I think that without God I probably would have had a mental breakdown. For a long time I held my emotions in so tight that I wouldn't let myself feel anything so that I wouldn't get hurt again by loving someone that I might lose. And so I held back my love. But one day I was finally able to cry for my loss. I told God how angry I was. I questioned how He could have taken my son when I thought I had been a "good" Christian. And you know, as I was venting my hostility toward God a strange thing happened. Somehow I just believed that God wouldn't get angry with me. *I believed that God knew who I was and why I was so angry and accepted me for who I am*. That belief—that I could be myself—was healing. And someday I just know that I will again see my child. (Mother of a twelve-year-old son who died of cancer.)

- Do you know what it is like to be abused? I'll tell you, because my whole life has been filled with terror. My parents abused me. My dad told me that I had a personality of zero minus and my mother said I was defective [born with an eye defect]. My husband told me that the only thing I could do was produce babies. (They were defective too, my mother-in-law said.) So what do you do when you are told all these awful things all of your life? I'll tell you what you do: You survive. I lived through it because I had to. Survival was it.

Through it all I developed a strong belief that I and only I could make me happy and I was the only person who could make me angry. Those beliefs gave me hope to start the long climb up. (Forty-three-year-old woman abused by her family.)

- Someone asked my youngest son: "How can your family laugh so much?" He responded instantly, *"If we hadn't laughed, we would have died."* (Thirteen-year-old son of an alcoholic father.)

- My wife's illness has been very difficult. But in spite of everything this experience has helped me develop a deeper faith in the richness and beauty of life. I was able to see clearly those events which caused me so very much pain were irrelevant in the larger picture. *They were painful to me because I had lost something I wanted—not because the world was unkind or unlovely.* (Fifty-seven-year-old husband.)

- I wanted God to change me because I didn't like the way I was at the height of my crisis. It was hard. Many times I thought I didn't care if I made it or not. *But I make an effort to sing every day and play my guitar.* It has lifted me out of my depression. (Thirty-three-year-old woman who lost both parents.)

- I left work early after hearing that I would lose my job. I got in my car and went to my church. Unfortunately the minister was not there. But the chapel was open. I went in and stared at the cross. I started to cry. I told God that I didn't have the strength to get through this mess. And I asked for help. I must have sat there for a couple of hours. I brushed away the tears. Suddenly a whole load went off my shoulders. *I can't explain it but I went into that chapel crushed. And I came out feeling strong.* I actually felt that I could make it. (Forty-one-year-old man.)

For those people and others in my survey, faith offered three important gifts. *The first is the letting go of fear.*

Fear can immobilize even the strongest person. Often fears seem to strike at the strangest times. Sometimes just when we think we are in the final stages of recovery a haunting memory or a disquieting thought nudges our insecurities. And we find that the fears come roaring back with a vengeance, crippling any small flicker of stability.

Whatever else faith might yield, it does have a power to diminish fear. Consider Margaret Robertson, a thirty-three-year-old nurse who went through a painful divorce:

> Our marriage was not made in heaven, but we did have some pretty good moments together. Andy was no villain. He was hurting as much as I was over our impending divorce. Nevertheless, we both knew that we would be better off not living with one another.
>
> I'll never forget the night that Andy packed his bags and left the house. He kissed me at the door and, fighting back tears, thanked me for the good times we had.
>
> That night I could not sleep. I felt totally abandoned. I feared that I would be alone for the rest of my life. I cried and, without even thinking, prayed, "God, please—don't You abandon me too!"
>
> Day after day I struggled with my loneliness. One night I knelt by my bed just like I did as a kid. I just said, "God, if You can hear this, please help me."
>
> That night I fell asleep right away and for the first time in months slept soundly. But in the morning all the terrible fears came back. But I prayed again and asked God to help me through this mess.
>
> I have been saying little prayers now for over five months. I have some terribly difficult days. But I am starting to have some good ones too. I feel stronger. I feel that maybe I can put together the fractured parts of life.

Why does faith have such a powerful effect in diminishing fear? I believe it's because faith takes us into a radically new dimension. A dimension of hope. Of possibility. Of peace.

In the weeks following a heartbreak attention is usually focused on concerns other than faith. We study the problem. We seek to comprehend it. And sometimes we analyze it to death.

But all the analysis in the world doesn't make the pain go away. As the father of a mentally retarded child said:

> I tried to examine what had happened. I read books. I talked to genetic counselors.
> But none of that helped me accept the problem.
> Finally my wife and I simply asked God to give us strength. It was the only solution to our restlessness.

Sometimes the only solution to our restlessness is to believe the best about whatever has happened. And that is sometimes the most difficult task of them all.

A heartbreak places us in the middle of bipolar forces operating within life.

The one force is epitomized by seeing the worst in everything. Fear is its major ally. There is fear of the future. Fear about medical treatments. There are fears about what other people will say and what they might think.

But the opposite force in life is love. And one can choose to see the world through this pair of lenses as well.

When a deliberate effort is made to see through love, we are simply saying that we will look for the best in people, no matter what type of personality they might happen to have, and in events, no matter how hurtful they may happen to be. This orientation not only diminishes our worst fears, but opens up a whole new way of thinking about relationships and events and the future. Inevitably, when one chooses to see love, the world becomes a friendly rather than a hostile place in which to reside.

To illustrate the power of unconditional love, consider a young man identified only as Tommy, who is talking to the Reverend John Powell, a professor at Loyola University in Chicago:

"Oh yes, [I am] very sick. I have cancer in both lungs. It's a matter of weeks."

"Can you talk about it, Tom?"

"Sure, what would you like to know?"

"What's it like to be only twenty-four and dying?"

"Well, it could be worse."

"Like what?"

"Well, like being fifty and having no values or ideals, like being fifty and thinking that booze, seducing women, and making money are the real biggies in life."

Tommy then began to share some of the values that were sustaining him during this difficult period of life.

"The doctors removed a lump from my groin and told me that it was malignant, then I got serious about locating God. And when the malignancy spread into my vital organs, I really began banging bloody fists against the bronze doors of heaven. But God did not come out. In fact, nothing happened. Did you ever try for a long time with great effort and with no success? You get psychologically glutted, fed up with trying. And then you quit. Well, one day I woke up, and instead of throwing a few more futile appeals over that high brick wall to a God who may be or may not be there, I just quit. I decided that I didn't really care . . . about God, about an afterlife, anything like that.

"I decided to spend what time I had left doing something more profitable. I thought about you . . . and I remembered something else you had said: 'The essential sadness is to go through life without loving. But it would be almost equally sad to go through life and leave this world without ever telling those you loved that you loved them.'

"So I began with the hardest one: my Dad. He was reading the newspaper when I approached him.

"'Dad . . .'

"'Yes, what?' he asked without lowering the newspaper.

"'Dad, I would like to talk with you.'

"'Well, talk.'

"'I mean . . . it's really important.'

"The newspaper fluttered to the floor. Then my father did two things I could never remember him ever doing before. He cried and he hugged me. And we talked all night, even though he had to go to work the next morning. It felt so good to be close to my father, to see his tears, to feel his hug, to hear him say that he loved me.

"It was easier with my mother and little brother. They cried with me, too, and we hugged each other. We shared the things we had been keeping secret for so many years. I was only sorry about one thing: that I had waited so long. Here I was, in the shadow of death, and I was just beginning to open up to all the people I had actually been close to.

"Then once I turned around and God was there. He didn't come to me when I pleaded with him. I guess I was like an animal trainer holding out a hoop. 'C'mon, jump through. C'mon, I'll give you three days . . . three weeks.' Apparently God does things in His own way and at His own hour.

"But the important thing is that He was there. He found me. He found me even after I stopped looking for Him."[10]

Pierre Teilhard de Chardin knew the truth inherent in this young man's experience: "Some day, after we have mastered the winds, the waves, the tides and gravity, we will harness for God the energies of *love* and then for the second time in the history of the world man will have discovered fire."

The first gift of faith is that it moves us into a new dimension. It shifts the staggering loads of life off our shoulders and onto what theologian Paul Tillich aptly called the

"Ground of All Being." Through faith we come to understand, as author Corrie ten Boom noted, that "worry does not empty tomorrow's sorrow; it empties today of its strength."

When you begin to turn your attention from fear to the giving of unconditional love, there is an inner transformation. Out of that transformation comes a clearer understanding of that which is important in life, that which is transient, and that which is irrelevant.

This brings us to the second gift of faith. And that gift is *the rediscovery of enduring values—values we would not give up for anything in the world.*

All of us live by a set of values. When everything is going well, there is little need to question their merits. But a crisis experience forces us to sharpen our perception of that which is important. Kareem Abdul-Jabbar, the famous basketball player for the Los Angeles Lakers, said after a fire had destroyed his Bel Air, California, mansion:

> My whole perspective changed after the fire. I think it's more important now for me to spend time with my son Amir and appreciate other things beside basketball. There are a lot of things that are more important. Like friends.[11]

In the months following a heartbreak, there is a strong need to re-examine our values. Often the struggle is intense and confusing. As one fifteen-year-old said upon learning of his parents' impending separation: "I don't understand it. How can they love one another one year and not the next?"

Nevertheless, out of the confusion new values take root. And almost without exception those who recover from their setbacks state that the most important thing about the tragedy was that it *forced them to reconsider that which is important*.

On January 14, 1983, Howard Hoy was skiing down a Utah mountain. Suddenly he hit a patch of ice and went whirling out of control on a forty-five-degree slope. "I went from almost a complete stop to what they estimate was about fifty m.p.h. when I hit the tree." There were massive internal injuries. The space in his pelvis was widened by eight inches and his right thigh was fractured. He required more than 124 units of blood products and, ultimately, fourteen trips to surgery.[12]

Today Howard Hoy does not look much different. But he states that his life has been changed. His suits don't fit quite right. His hips are wider and his sedentary life has kept him away from things he loves to do such as skiing and tennis.

But out of this experience have come new learnings. He has rediscovered the value of relationships. While he was spending 100 days in the hospital, he received heaps of cards and visitors. He was included in prayer chains at home and in Salt Lake City.

Today he has a lot of empathy for people who are physically disabled. He expressed gratitude to his wife, who was "always there pushing and prodding.... She is about the strongest person I know in a crisis." But he has also come to understand how important it is to have a period in life in which you are forced to reevaluate what is important: "It sounds a little schmaltzy, but I think everybody should have some kind of traumatic experience like this; it makes them appreciate the little things in life more."[13]

No one wants to hit a tree at fifty miles per hour. No one wants to lose health or face financial ruin. Yet individuals in this survey commented: "This was the best thing that ever happened to me." "It took the accident for me to get my priorities straightened around." "I wouldn't wish my illness on anybody, but I can tell you that I am living at a level of contentment that I had never known."

At first I did not know what to make of such statements. Do these people really mean what they are saying? Or are such claims cognitive dissonance—efforts to rationalize a misfortune?

I have concluded that the majority of statements are pure as gold. These are not attempts to put an optimistic interpretation on a ghastly affair. Rather, in the darkest periods of life new values have appeared that give comfort in ways that the old ones never did.

The rhythms of life seem to influence even the most humble members of the animal kingdom. Deep on the ocean floor, at a certain point in the life cycle of the lobster the back of its shell breaks open. The creature has been growing but the shell cannot expand. This is a time of distress and pressure and change.

In the darkness the lobster begins to form a new shell. Gradually it hardens. Soon the creature emerges from the ocean floor reborn. It then goes about its business of living.[14]

For many people a heartbreak shatters the old shell, leaving them vulnerable and defenseless. The old values by which they structured their lives now seem curiously out of whack with new realities. The faith that had nurtured no longer sustains. The future that was once clearly in focus is now blurred.

At this point some discard the canopies that had shadowed their lives. Some realize that they were consumed by careers that left them lifeless. Now they vow that work will no longer be the singular orbit of meaning in their lives.

Others jettison old notions about God and faith, for they are not equal to the challenge. A victim of multiple sclerosis stated: "I always believed that God would take care of me. But when I was lifted into a wheelchair for the first time,

I knew I had to find a faith that would sustain me in ways that my old one never could have done."

Most of us, however, do not feel a need to discard totally our former beliefs. The old shell might need a little reconditioning, but there is little to be gained by rejecting values that have comforted. "My faith has always been important to me," said Jerry Richter. "But now I want to live it out a bit differently. I don't want to be so critical of my children or my employees. And I don't want to hurry through life."

Of course, there are those who never take the opportunity to re-examine the old shell. At a time in their lives when they should be probing and learning about themselves and about their faith, they tenaciously cling to old systems of belief.

Some deeply religious people in this study were confused by what had happened in their lives. They had trusted the Lord yet the Lord had not protected them. In mechanistic ways they repeated their biblical chants. But in the process they refused to ask the searing questions, about the meaning of faith and the meaning of life and how they might transcend their situations. And the more they sought to hunker down in the old shell, the more enslaved they were by it.

But for most people in this survey a crisis provided them with a rare opportunity to reflect on life and to sharpen the values that sustain, comfort, and give meaning.

How are new values formed? New values usually do not come out of a sudden burst of energy or in a blitzkrieg of new ideas. Rather, new ideas are formed gradually. Quietly. And they usually emerge after regrets have been abandoned. Indeed, there is a powerful correlation: Before joy is rediscovered, self-reproach must be surrendered.

Most people make an uneasy truce with past mistakes, misplaced priorities, and small joys taken for granted. But when a crisis arrives, regrets rush to the surface.

John Hinkley, Sr., testified on behalf of his son after the boy shot President Reagan. Prior to the shooting the family received a telephone call from their son, who was in New York. The boy was incoherent, broke and hungry, begging for a ticket home. The boy flew to Denver and was met at the airport by his father who said: "He was dazed, wiped out. He could hardly walk from the plane."[15]

They went to a waiting room and talked. "I told him how disappointed I was in him, how he had let us down, how he had not followed the plan we had all agreed on, how he left us with no choice but not to take him back again." Mr. Hinkley gave his son a couple of hundred dollars and suggested he stay at a YMCA.

At this point in the trial, John Hinkley had trouble speaking. But he reported that his final words to his son were: "O.K. You're on your own. Do whatever you want."

"In looking back on that, I'm sure that was the greatest mistake of my life. I am the cause of John's tragedy. We forced him out at a time in his life when he just couldn't cope. I wish to God that I could trade places with him right now." Mr. Hinkley began weeping quietly into his handkerchief.[16]

At times the desire to rewrite our personal histories is so powerful that we are overwhelmed by the fact that it can't be done. "I would do anything to recall my anger," said Lewis Cranford, who unleashed his hostility at an aged parent, "but I can't. I have to live with a bad mistake."

How do you let go of regrets? There are probably many ways, but perhaps the starting point is to ask one important question: *What is life trying to teach me?* When you ask the question, you are approaching the future with an empty cup. No longer are you blaming yourself for past mistakes. No longer are you in the quagmire of self-doubt. Rather, you are emptying yourself of judgmental attitudes.

Nan-in, a Japanese Zen master, was visited by a university professor who wanted to learn about his religion. Nan-in graciously brought tea to his guest. He poured until his visitor's cup was full. But then he kept pouring.

The professor watched the overflow until he could no longer restrain himself. "It is full," he shouted. "No more will go in!"

"Like this cup," said Nan-in, "you are full of your opinions and speculations. How can I show you Zen unless you first empty your cup?"

Most of the major religions of the world point to a similar conclusion: Before you can form new values, life must be approached with an empty cup. When Jesus spoke about being "born again," he was not referring to ecclesiastical rules or rigid performance requirements. He was referring to a new state of being. A state that was predicated on a new openness to life. And when Moses commanded the Jewish people to move to higher ground, he was not simply referring to a geographical place, but was stating an important fact: There is a new plane on which life can be lived.

When you ask, What is life trying to teach me? you begin to sharpen your priorities. Your values become refocused as well.

On a frigid January morning when the wind chill registered 37 degrees below zero, I parked my car and began walking to the office. As I trudged through the winter landscape, I found myself preoccupied with disquieting thoughts. The icy winds cut through my parka. Winter never seemed more brutal. To make matters worse, six hours of nonstop teaching were on the agenda, coupled with four hours of committee meetings. My mind darted from one negative perception to another as I thought about the day. By the time I was a block from my office I felt quite tense.

For some reason I took my eyes off the icy sidewalk and

looked up. In front of me was the Masonic Cancer Center at the University of Minnesota. To my utter amazement I read a sign appearing in a patient's window: "I need a large sausage pizza!"

A smile came to my face. In fact, I stopped in my tracks and reread that sign. Here was a patient, possibly living out the last days of life, who had retained a sense of humor.

Suddenly my problems did not seem so great. I straightened my posture and with a new step walked toward the office.

Throughout the day my mind kept going back to the sign in the window. Finally my curiosity could stand it no longer. I asked a nurse whether she had seen the pizza sign. A soft smile came across her face. "Oh yes. You ought to meet that patient. He has one of the most virulent forms of cancer, but his spirit is amazing. He just won't give up."

I couldn't resist asking: "Did anyone bring him a pizza?" The reply: "By noon his room was lined from door to window with large sausage pizzas. We had enough pizza to feed everyone in the unit."

There was a lesson in this that I needed to relearn. A lesson about not letting my small problems escalate into World War III encounters. A lesson about inner peace. A lesson about human generosity. On a frigid Minnesota morning I relearned one of the important lessons that life can teach.

Sometimes life's lessons are right on our doorstep. Unfortunately, the psychological fog is so thick we do not see the searchlight.

In his brilliant play *No Exit*, Jean-Paul Sartre describes the meaning of hell. There are three people in a room, a man and two women. The room has no windows and no doors. The man loves woman A, but woman A is a lesbian in love with woman B. Woman B is straight and in love with the man. Each person in the room is in love with someone who does not return his or her love. There seems to be no exit from that despair.

But there was an exit. Unfortunately, they were each so wrapped up in their agony that they did not see it. Any of these individuals at any point in time could have turned around and loved the person who loved him or her. At any moment any one of the group had the possibility of finding a relationship of love, tenderness, and hope. Unfortunately, they did not see it.[17]

It is possible to redefine life's problems so that they don't seem so "awful" or "intolerable." And when you see a way of redefining your situation, you begin to be healed spiritually. Even physically.

In an important study conducted by physicians at the Australian National University, heart attack victims were given personality tests, as were individuals who had never experienced cardiovascular problems. The tests were designed to measure the various stresses the subjects had been experiencing related to family pressures, work experiences, and deaths of relatives.

The researchers discovered an important fact: The amount of stress that the heart attack victims had experienced was no greater than that which was experienced by the individuals who did not have heart problems. But there was a difference when they asked the heart attack victims to rate the *seriousness* of their problems. The heart attack victims rated the stresses as far more upsetting than those without heart difficulties did. Those without heart problems would say that a negative event was an "inconvenience." Those who had heart attacks rated it as a "catastrophe."[18]

Is it really possible to approach life with an empty cup? Is it possible to let go of regrets and to redefine life events so that they don't seem so terrible? Steve Skallerud was pinned between his parents' car and another automobile as he was filling up the gas tank. His right leg had to be amputated. When the anesthetic subsided, he had to stare at the cold truth of life in which he would no longer be able to run, ski, bicycle, or kick a football like most teenagers.

Nevertheless, a mere ten months after the accident Steve Skallerud was again skiing a mile-long mountain run at sixty-eight miles per hour. In so doing, he won the second National Handicap Ski Championship at Winter Park, Colorado.

Jim Klobuchar, a reporter for the *Minneapolis Star and Tribune*, chronicled the young man's journey and concluded, "It is comforting to be bitter about bad luck, but it is more practical to create." What can a twelve-year-old boy create with one leg and a stump?

> He can squat on a water ski one-legged, and remember enough and struggle enough to stand up the first try when the boat begins churning. And not long after, he can be skiing barefooted on the slalom course. . . . And a little later, he can swing a driver on one good leg, and the artificial one, and shoot within five strokes of his old score the first time down the course.

Steve Skallerud once again does things that other kids enjoy. Why? He has changed his perceptions about something that could have shattered his life:

> I think I'm better for what happened. Three years ago, schooling didn't mean much. It was skiing and ball and things, and the rest didn't matter too much. I study more now. It's still great to have fun, but you know you aren't going to do that for a living, and now is a pretty good time to realize that.
> When you have to do things with one leg, you find yourself thinking more about people who don't have the

advantages others do, and that isn't only the physical advantages.

I guess you just think more about people who are trying to make it, and you feel for them and you know how much they have to work and try.

I even get along better with my sister now.[19]

What does faith impart? First, faith diminishes fear. Second, it helps redefine values. Finally, a meaningful faith permits us to *accept the outcomes of life's predicaments*.[20]

A young woman going blind was a puzzlement to her friends. She seemed to be in good spirits in spite of her problems. Finally, their curiosity peaked. "How can you seem so peaceful when you are going blind?"

"It's simple," she replied. "I have learned to accept the outcome—*whatever it may be*."

You know that you are healed spiritually when you can accept the outcomes of life's uncertainties. But how do you do it? How do you get to the point where you can accept what has happened? And accept what might happen?

The teachings of psychoanalyst Erik Erikson are instructive.[21] Erikson suggests that one of the determinants of happiness is whether or not *we will trust life*. This is a situation thata is confronted at birth and is confronted again and again until the day we die.

At the moment of birth an infant is thrust into a strange environment. Within minutes the child receives a stream of messages as to whether the world is a friendly or a hostile place.

Most infants are reassured. They are stroked and warmly cuddled. Tender hugs affirm thata this is an inviting world. It is a place that can be trusted. But as infants grow into childhood there are new occasions to reassess their fundamental posture toward life. Children test and tease one another. Teachers make evaluations. There are rejections from peers and from lovers. Finally, there is the struggle to find a job and to discover one's role in life.

If these challenges are satisfactorily resolved, a young person will reaffirm that life is good and can be trusted.

But then comes a major setback. Parents might obtain a divorce. A lover finds someone else. A job cannot be found. Perhaps health fails for the first time.

Suddenly we are forced backward in time. The initial crisis at birth is again confronted. But this time a choice must be made. Will we respond to life with acceptance? With apprehension? With love? With hope? With trust?

Those who survive come down on the side of trusting life, *even when the evidence suggests that they should turn against it*. Emil Fackenhein is a case in point.

From his own experience with Nazism he understands the evil and the horror of the Holocaust. Yet he continues to affirm that life can be trusted. Why? Because for him there would be no greater mistake, no deeper tragedy, than to give up on God and thus do for Hitler what he could not do for himself—destroy Judaism. "Jews are forbidden to hand Hitler posthumous victories.... They are forbidden to despair of the God of Israel, lest Judaism perish."[22]

It is true that the Holocaust severely tested the faith of the Jewish people. But for the majority of Jews the Holocaust did not destroy their faith. As Howard Burkle, author of *God, Suffering and Belief*, says, "They continued to believe in God whether or not they could find good reasons for doing so."[23]

There are many gifts that come our way when we reaffirm that life can be trusted—even if there are not always good reasons for doing so. For many people the most important gift is a deep assurance that a loving Creator will see them through their misfortunes.

Saint Paul, who had a serious and some believe a life-threatening ailment, summarized many people's belief: "Who shall separate us from the love of Christ? Shall tribulation or distress or persecution or famine or nakedness or peril or sword? . . . For I am sure that neither death, nor life, nor angels, nor principalities, nor powers, nor things present, nor things to come, nor height, nor depth, nor any other creature shall be able to separate us from the love of God."[24]

Others do not frame their affirmations in theological terms, yet their beliefs are equally powerful in dissipating the effect of life's misfortunes. A father who had lost his teenage son to cancer said: "The turning point for me was the realization that it was better that Jeff lived seventeen good years than not to have lived at all. I started to reaffirm all the great times we had together. I stopped feeling that I had been cheated."

When you affirm that you can again trust life your healing begins in earnest. A remarkable study was made of five hundred patients with detached retinas. The researcher wanted to know the following: "How well does the patient accept himself, his retinal detachment, the surgery, his surgeon, the hospital situation, the fact that this is a world in which things like retinal detachments happen? How well does he come to terms with these things? Does he say 'Yes' or 'No' to life? Can he take this experience into his world of meaning and go on?"[25]

Patients who scored high in acceptance were those individuals appropriately frightened by the damage to the eye yet who were confronting the danger and were willing to do whatever was necessary to remedy the situation. They trusted their surgeon and they were optimistic about the outcome of the operation.

Nevertheless—and this is very important—those who ranked high in acceptance had confidence in their ability to cope, *even if the surgery was not successful*. They felt little need to project an image. They took the bad with the good in life. They asked no favors. And when they prayed it was simply for strength to meet the troublesome news and for grace to accept whatever a day might bring.

At the opposite extreme were individuals who ranked low in acceptance. They were panicky and anxious about the damage to their sight. They tended to be distrustful of the surgeon and pessimistic about the outcome of the operation. They despaired at the thought that their sight might be forever gone. They resented hospital personnel and they disliked the chaplain. If they wanted anything from the minister, it was to demand that the Reverend put the screws to God. In brief, these patients were utterly miserable, sulking, and angry.

What were the results of the study? Those patients with high acceptance experienced rapid healing. Those with low acceptance healed slowly if at all.[26]

It *does* matter whether you say "yes" or "no" to life. For when you say "yes" your perceptions begin to change. That which seems so senseless no longer seems quite so terrible. Soon an inner power is felt. A belief begins to emerge that, no matter what the odds, it is possible to move life forward.

What does it mean to say "yes" to life? We are not referring to cute little homilies about looking on the bright side of things. Nor are we suggesting shallow optimism presented in catchy slogans. Rather, what is being suggested is a radical reorientation toward life in which we actively believe that *life can be trusted*.

What does it mean to "trust life"?

- Living in the present. Taking one day at a time.
- Pushing aside doubts that you can ever again be happy.
- Relying on friends. Asking them for comfort.
- Telling others how you feel: Lonely. Fearful. Hopeful.
- Affirming that you are good. Your intentions are good. Your past has been good. Your future will be good.

• Meditating. Asking for strength.

In several places in this book I have referred to the experiences of parents who have lost a child. I have done so because they have much to teach about trusting in life. I think of Mickie Sherman, whose four-year-old daughter became ill with what appeared to be a virus. The child did not respond to medications. Her legs became swollen. She complained of pain in her ankles.

Mickie took her daughter to the hospital, where a diagnosis of rheumatic fever was made. But after more tests the initial diagnosis was discarded. The words "lymphocytic leukemia" were uttered. Her daughter would live for only two and a half to three years.

Elizabeth died in her mother's arms. The months that followed were difficult, yet in their own way healing:

> Initially, I was overwhelmed by the urge to speak often of Elizabeth to my other children and to friends who had known her well. She had died—but I could not bear that she be forgotten. She had to continue to live in their memories, to form a substantive part of their experience, I felt—it was the only immortality I could offer her. We still speak of Elizabeth occasionally, the children and I, as sometimes do friends or other family members. Usually, it is with happiness because we are sharing her.
>
> Perhaps in time a balance will be achieved. The pain is diminishing. Just a few months ago I could hardly bear to see a young blonde-headed child walk before me down the street. I revisited Elizabeth's school, but only with great difficulty. I was unable to remain in the new playroom of the Oberlin Hospital, where Elizabeth's many toys, games, and books, and stuffed animals have now found a home. But it becomes easier.[27]

It does become easier. And sometimes the sacred speaks through other people.

One day Mickie Sherman had lunch with a professional acquaintance. He asked whether she was reacting excessively to the death of her daughter. Said Mickie: "I acknowledged with, 'Perhaps.' He asked, 'Did she die with her spirit intact?' 'Yes,' I affirmed, 'Yes.' And then he put to me another question, his last: 'What more can we really ask of life?' "[28]

What If the Pain Doesn't Go Away?

T E N

Death Wishes

It's a good thing God doesn't let you look a year or two into the future, or you might be sorely tempted to shoot yourself.
— LEE IACOCCA, CHAIRMAN, CHRYSLER CORPORATION

Sometimes we do all the necessary things to recover from a heartbreak. We select competent help. We protect our family. We talk to friends. We ask for divine strength. But the pain does not go away. And suicidal thoughts begin to surface.

The purpose of this chapter is to help us understand self-destruction. We will learn what to do when we feel suicidal and what can be done when a mother or father, son or daughter, is tempted to pull out a gun or swallow a fistful of pills. Finally, we will learn what can be done to comfort ourselves when suicide touches our family.

Who Commits Suicide?

When this project started, I did not intend to write about suicide. It seemed like such a depressing subject and at that point in time not that important.

But then something happened. An executive volunteered to be interviewed about the pressures and disappointments he was having at work. He was in his mid-fifties, the president of a small manufacturing firm. He had a good income and a wonderful wife. But he felt like a failure. His heartbreak was that his company was going bankrupt.

After completing a written questionnaire he wrote these words on top of the first page: "In my anxiety I hope this helps others." I read his questionnaire and put it away. I felt sorry for him, but at the time I didn't think his problems were that unusual. Or even that serious.

Two weeks later he killed himself.

I was stunned. I simply could not believe that this talented man would have ended his life.

I reread his questionnaire, trying to find a motive. A comment jumped off the page: "You want to get out of the problems so badly you don't care how.... You consider everything from suicide to hospitalization to running to a foreign country."

I wanted to shout: "Don't give up. Life is a gift! Life is precious! Tomorrow will be a better day, a new day." But of course it was too late.

I decided to talk with counselors who work with suicidal adults. And I spoke with researchers who seek to understand the emotional health of adolescents. Here is what I discovered.

Suicide is a major public health problem. According to

the U.S. Public Health Service, between 28,000 and 30,000 Americans "officially" commit suicide every year. The actual total is closer to 90,000, for it is often difficult to judge whether a death is an accident or a suicide.

In addition to those who commit suicide, an estimated one million people attempt to end their lives every year. Assuming a realistic average of four family members for each suicidal attempt, over four million Americans are directly touched by suicide.[1]

One of the saddest parts of the whole suicide story is that the young are killing themselves in ever greater numbers. Seven thousand teenagers kill themselves annually, triple the figure of three decades ago. And the kids who kill themselves are often the high achievers—teenagers loaded with talent and ability.

Suicidal adolescents are usually not social misfits. Many come from good homes and are surrounded by loving families. Unfortunately they feel helpless. And in one awful moment, they terminate life.

Melissa Putney was fourteen years old and nine months pregnant. She finished her picnic lunch and swallowed the last of the wine. A tiny fleck of light appeared far down the railroad tracks. Seconds later the crescendo of engines going 100 miles per hour could be heard. Amtrak 141 was right on time.

Melissa ran to the tracks, knelt between the rails, and clasped her hands in prayer. She made the sign of the cross. The engineer applied the brakes. But it was too late. Her suicide note read:

> You always ask me if there's anything wrong. I said, "No, I'm O.K."
> Mom, I wasn't telling the truth. I was never O.K. I was very depressed. I ran away from all of my problems. I am taking the easy way out. I am admitting to myself

that I am a weak person not able to handle the weight of life.

I'm very sorry to put you all through the troubles. I think everything I have to do is done.

I drank some wine and took some pills. But before I did all that I prayed to my Father God in heaven. I asked Him to forgive me but He won't. I don't blame Him for that.

Please pray that I won't be sent to hell, because then I won't be able to come back and watch over you and help you. I want to do that.

Mom, please don't have a nervous breakdown and be crying all the time. I don't want you to. I want you to live forever and ever, the way you want to and I will always love you very much. Please try and forgive me.

I love you always and always,

Love,
Melissa[2]

Suicide notes often contain statements of love. These are not superficial comments. Suicidal kids generally love their parents and suicidal parents love their children. Yet they part company.

Suicide happens in the best communities. It happens in the best schools. And it can happen in the most loving family.

What to Do If You Are Tempted to Harm Yourself

If you have experienced a heartbreak, do not be surprised if you feel self-destructive. Eighty percent of us have toyed with suicidal ideas, often in the darkest moments of life.[3] There are, however, constructive things that can be done to help us over those difficult moments. Where do we begin?

If you are suicidal, you need to obtain professional assistance. There are a number of people who can help. Most communities have crisis intervention centers or a suicide "hotline" that you can telephone twenty-four hours a day. These organizations are staffed with mental health professionals or volunteers specifically trained in crisis management.

They will listen to your problems. They will make suggestions. But perhaps most important, they will let you know the seriousness of your problem. If it is critical they will refer you to someone who can give immediate care.

If your community does not have a crisis center, contact a physician. Be very specific with the receptionist about the nature of the problem. State that you feel suicidal and that you are calling for help. If the physician is not in, request the telephone number of a professional who could be of assistance.

At the same time you are seeking professional help, rely on friends. Tell them you are depressed and need to be with them. If your friends are unavailable, go to the nearest church. Confide in the minister or priest or rabbi. Simply say, "I need to be with someone today." They will understand.

It is important to be with loving people in this time of life. I cannot emphasize this too strongly. More than one death has been averted simply because a friend was there to help.

When you ask friends to help, be sure to tell them your problems. Because if you aren't honest they will not know that your situation is serious. Nor will they be of much help.

The importance of being honest was brought forcefully home to me several years ago. I worked with a man whom I greatly admired. But one day his wife called from the hospital. He had attempted suicide.

As I was driving to the hospital, a thousand thoughts went through my mind. Why hadn't I been more observant? Why hadn't he confided his problems?

I then thought about how much I liked my colleague. He was loyal and trustworthy. And he had a good sense of humor.

But I obviously did not know my associate.

Cautiously I went into his room. A soft smile came across his face and his eyes filled with tears.

He held my hand for the longest time. No words passed between us. Finally I told him of my friendship and my affection.

He pulled his hand away and turned his face toward the wall. "I couldn't tell you," he said. "I wanted to, but I couldn't. I couldn't tell my problems to anyone."

I understood his reluctance. For who wants to share the dark side of life? Better, we reason, to put on the air of the executive. Self-assured. Self-confident.

But inwardly we cry. We may be able to lead committee meetings, make public presentations, and discuss the future of our companies. But inside we are dying.

It's far better to be vulnerable and share the pain with someone you trust. Admittedly it takes courage to telephone a suicide hotline number or to share intimacies with a physician or minister. And sometimes it takes a double amount of courage to share problems with a friend.

But an amazing gift comes to us when we do. Guilt has a way of dissolving. The problems tend not to look so awesome. And we realize that there is a special person who can gently guide us through a difficult period of life.

In addition to sharing your problems with others there are a number of important things to do.

First, follow a routine. Get up at the same time every morning and eat a good breakfast. Don't call in sick. Rather, go to school or to work and follow normal routines. Try to be with people as much as possible.

Second, make a short list of things you want to accomplish. But be careful—you don't want to list all the things that have been left undone for weeks and about which you may already feel guilty! Rather, put down one, two, or perhaps three things that you want to do during the day. Try to complete them before nightfall.

Third, do something special for yourself. Something that is fun. Go for a walk or see a movie. If you enjoy sports, go to a ball game. If you like music, attend an uplifting concert.

Fourth, think about the advice that you would give to a friend who was having a problem similar to your own.

I asked a counselor at a midwestern college how she helps depressed students. Here is her reply:

> I first give them a lot of support and try to help them realize that not everything is as bad as they feel.
> Then later in the conversation I say: "Suppose your best friend had the very same problem that you have. What advice might you give?"
> That question really makes them think.
> One student thought about that question for the longest time. Then she replied: "Well, I would tell her that the situation is not hopeless. I probably would tell her to do something that is just plain fun. And I probably would tell her not to take life quite so seriously."
> The student then paused and reflected on what she said. A big smile came across her face: "That's not too bad advice, is it?"

It certainly isn't bad advice. In fact, it is excellent.

Sometimes we need to think of ourselves as a counselor giving helpful suggestions to someone who has the very same problem we are confronting. Listen to your suggestions. And if they seem wise, use them.

Fifth, at the end of the day recall one thing that brought some joy. Maybe you received encouragement from a friend. Maybe you had one good idea that gave your confidence a boost. Perhaps you saw a child smile. Or maybe you enjoyed the quiet of your apartment or home. Focus on that enjoyable moment. Hang onto it. Because when you focus on one good thing in life you soon learn that there are many more good things waiting to be discovered.

There is one last thing that should be mentioned: You do not need to be perfect nor do you have to meet another's idea of what you are supposed to be.

Many suicidal individuals feel that they need to be the perfect parent, the perfect teacher, the perfect boss, the perfect student. But we are imperfect. We make mistakes. We fumble the ball. And occasionally we come in last in the race. It's the nature of being human. But life can be rebuilt. Maybe not all at once. But it can be done. Slowly. Gradually. And with increasing joy.

What should you do if you are suicidal? Remember the following:

- It is not a sin to feel suicidal. Most people experience such feelings.

- Telephone a suicide hotline or a crisis intervention center. Or call a physician. Explain that you are suicidal and need help.

- Do not be alone. Stay with friends.

- Live for today. Do not permit yourself to get worked up over future problems. They may never come to pass.

- Do one thing *today* that makes you feel happy: take an invigorating walk, see an upbeat movie, listen to some inspiring music. Maybe have dinner with a special friend.

- Be nice to yourself.

- And above all else remember the following: there are a host of people, including members of the clergy, neighbors, friends, loved ones, acquaintances, who want to help. Let them.

How to Help the People You Love

Family members usually panic at the first hint of suicide: Should they talk about their suspicions, or would that make the situation worse? Should they be sympathetic, or would that be misread as a sign of permission? Should they obtain professional help, or will their loved one "get over it" in due time? There are no easy answers. But here are some practical suggestions that might help.[4]

FIRST, TAKE ALL COMMENTS ABOUT SUICIDE SERIOUSLY

Researchers agree on the following: Any comment about ending life, even if it is made in jest, should be carefully pursued. More than one family has lamented, "I didn't think he was serious."

Do you receive a warning that a suicide is about to happen? Usually. In one study of 134 suicide victims, 69 percent had communicated their self-destructive thoughts. Forty-one percent had made their intentions crystal clear as they discussed their plans with many different people in the preceding weeks.[5]

SECOND, BE HONEST ABOUT YOUR SUSPICIONS

You might ask: "Do you ever think about harming yourself?" "Do you think about ending life?" But be tactful and compassionate. And remain calm and reassuring no matter what the answer may be.

Many families are hesitant about discussing suicide, for they fear a conversation might push their loved one over the edge.

But talking about it does not increase suicidal risk.[6] Nor does it give permission to do the inconceivable, particularly if you give assurance that help can be found.

Talking about suicide usually reduces tension and lowers stress. When the question is finally asked, "Do you ever think about ending life?" there is a healing catharsis. Someone finally understands the magnitude of the problem. With that reassurance suicidal intentions are at least temporarily put on hold.[7]

THIRD, BE AWARE OF CLUES THAT POINT TO SELF-DESTRUCTIVE BEHAVIOR

Here is what they are:

Depression. Adults tend to be immobilized by depression. But teenagers frequently become reckless. Adolescents may exhibit boundless energy and sport black eyes, fractured bones, bruises, and cuts. Not infrequently they enjoy the fast life, both on the highway and in their relationships. It is not uncommon for a teenager to wreck a car soon after the wreckage of a relationship.

Depressed adolescents often have trouble at school. There may be personality conflicts with teachers. They may skip class, using elaborate cover-ups to keep parents from knowing what is going on.

But depression in both adults and adolescents can take on other forms. Some explode at the slightest reprimand. Others become despondent when perfection cannot be achieved or when a goal cannot be obtained.

Others appear to be in a daze: When asked what they are watching on television, they may not know. When asked what they are thinking, they can't recall.

School counselors will tell you that hardly a week goes by that they do not see depressed young people. Estimates by the National Institute of Mental Health indicate that one in five children may suffer from depression. In a recent study of 5,600 high school students, depression was second only to colds, sore throats, and coughs in frequency of illness.

Even children become depressed, and they may plot the end of life as carefully as an adult. They may even leave a "will," as did one eight-year-old:

> I want to not
> live no more.
> Michey gest my
> bank and Mommey my stamp book.[8]

If you are having difficulty knowing whether a loved one is depressed, keep a daily journal, writing down what you observe. If your concern is a child, share your journal with a school psychologist. Upon a review of your observations as well as through comments from teachers, the psychologist will be able to give you an interpretation of your child's behavior. If your concern is a spouse, talk with a family physician.

Inability to concentrate.   Most depressed people find it difficult to focus their thoughts. Assignments cannot be completed. Homework is pushed aside. Deadlines are not met. In short, it is difficult to concentrate.[9]

Sometimes depressed people find it difficult to complete simple tasks. For Conrad Jarrett in Judith Guest's novel *Ordinary People*: "Morning is not a good time for him. Too many details crowd his mind. Brush his teeth first? Wash his face? What pants should he wear? What shirt?"[10] Sometimes the smallest task is an insurmountable obstacle.

Mood swings.   An important clue to suicidal behavior is frequent and volatile mood swings. Listen to what one young man wrote in his journal:

> *Golly gee I'm glad I'm me.*
> *There's no one else I'd rather be.*
> *I smile on every bird and tree.*
> *Life is a ball. I'm in love with me!*

A couple of pages later he wrote, "I pretend I've got lots of confidence and I'm a big jock...but deep inside I'm a frightened, insecure, can't-make-it-failure."[11]

Personality changes take many forms. The extrovert withdraws from friends and social occasions. The introvert becomes the jokester, the hit of the party, the carefree romantic.

One young man explained his personality modifications as a "last-ditch effort to change." Unfortunately it wasn't convincing or successful. He attempted suicide, concluding that he was no happier in his new personality than he was in the old.[12]

It is particularly important to be aware of positive mood swings following periods of melancholy. These dramatic improvements are mistakenly taken as a sign that the crisis is over. "He's snapping out of it," a loved one may comment. Unfortunately, he may be snapping into a presuicidal state.

Tranquillity is not necessarily a sign of health. It may reflect a terrifying truth: A decision to kill oneself has been made.

Sometimes the tranquillity is reflected in kind comments and beautiful gestures. There may be spontaneous hugs and expressions of affection. Friends may be called to assure them that "everything is all right."

The crisis may be over. But then again, it may be reaching a terrifying climax. A mother commented after her twenty-year-old son committed suicide:

> Looking back, I recall the night he bought ice cream for everybody. Earlier that day he had gone to a drugstore and charged boxes of candy, Valentine's Day cards, and all kinds of gifts for his girlfriends. Then he took them one by one . . . and presented his Valentines. It was his way of saying good-bye. When he came home he bought ice cream for everyone in the house. It was the night before he died. There was a look about his eyes that last night; he had never bought ice cream for the family. Sure, that was a sign right there. He didn't spend much money because he didn't have much. For him to have brought ice cream home for the whole family was a sign that I might pick up today. It was peaceful, it was wonderful. Everybody was loving and having a marvelous time— but he looked strange. I followed him to his room and said, "Are you okay?" And he said, "Well, no worse than any other night." Again I assumed his sadness was due to the girlfriend matter, and to the pain of being rejected.[13]

Sometimes death threats are crystal clear. But they may be obscure, reflected only in a gift of ice cream or a Valentine's Day greeting.

Lack of friends.   "Nobody likes me; nobody wants to spend time with me" are frequent comments of depressed individuals. A nineteen-year-old enrolled at Northern Illinois University remarked:

> I feel like a total nonentity. At college I have a room on a co-ed floor.... I'm an outsider, a lone wolf who's noticed and tolerated by the rest of the floor, but is not really a part of things. I feel like I'm living inside a glass booth, cut off from everyone even as I sit next to them. I'm one of those awkward, self-conscious people who sits a little off to the side of the group, wearing a papier-mâché smile that's beginning to crack.... There are nights when people are laughing and talking out in the halls while I sit inside my room, door closed, biting my knuckle to keep from crying because I so desperately want to be part of the group.[14]

Being friendless is a major predictor of suicidal behavior. In a study of suicide in the New Jersey public schools, the researchers discovered that in every single case of suicide the child was friendless. There was no one to share confidences; no one to give psychological support.[15]

Alcohol and drug abuse.   Any family member who is abusing chemicals should be considered a suicidal risk. Two authorities on adolescent suicide, Mary Griffin and Carol Felsenthal, put it this way: "Red lights should start flashing, for substance abuse is a key warning sign—second only to depression as a spur to suicide."[16] Nearly 50 percent of all adolescents who commit suicide are drunk or "high" shortly before their death. That figure jumps to an astonishing 85 percent for adolescents who attempt suicide but survive.[17]

Why is alcohol a precipitating factor in suicide? Alcohol increases depression as it decreases judgment. It tempers the fear of dying.

In summary, these are the major clues to suicidal behavior: depression, inability to concentrate, mood swings, being friendless, substance abuse. If your loved one exhibits any of these symptoms, stay close at hand. Be observant. And calmly discuss any problems that may be shared.

FOURTH, OBTAIN SKILLED PROFESSIONAL CARE

If your loved one is missing work or school and is spending a great deal of time alone, encourage your loved one to call a crisis center or a family physician. But if he or she doesn't seem interested, make an appointment and go together. This is not a time for timidity. This is a time to assertively find the help that is needed.

Don't be surprised if your suggestion meets resistance. Frequent responses to the suggestion about finding professional help are, "I'm feeling better," or, "I can manage my own problems."

If you receive such a response, back off. But don't back off for too many days if you sense that the condition is getting worse rather than better. If nothing else, go to a counselor yourself in order to determine how best to manage the situation.

But suppose your crisis is acute. What if your loved one is so depressed that he or she might not make it through the night? Then what should you do?

Go to the emergency room of a hospital. There you will find physicians and nurses skilled in helping suicidal individuals. They probably will admit your loved one to the hospital to monitor his or her condition. But if the crisis is not acute, they will recommend outpatient therapy and will put you in contact with a skilled therapist.

FIFTH, REMOVE ALL POSSIBLE WEAPONS

You should make your home free of poisons, barbiturates, and other potent drugs. And of course guns, since they are used in three out of four teenage suicides and in 43 percent of all suicides.

Children are particularly attracted to guns, for they do not see them as lethal weapons. When children point guns at themselves, they expect to get up again—just like their heroes on TV. Fifty percent of all children aged six to eleven actually believe that death is a reversible event.[18]

The primary reason for removing potential weapons is to create a roadblock. It is a fact that many individuals do not have a firm resolve to end life. One authority on suicide states: "Most people who try to kill themselves are ambivalent about it. What they really want is not to die but merely to achieve a change in the conditions of their existence."[19] If a family member is ambivalent about life, you do not want to have weapons nearby. For if they are available, they might be used.

If you are asked why you are removing the pills or the guns or the knives, be honest. Your loved one will know of your concern and may begin to share frustrations with you.

SIXTH, DON'T ADD TO THEIR BURDENS

Family conflict is a major predictor of suicide. In fact, family discord is the most common event triggering childhood and adolescent emergency psychiatric referrals, many of which are associated with suicidal attempts or threats.[20]

Some parents become angry when children first confide their suicidal thoughts. "How could you think that way?"

"How in the world, after all we have done for you, could you ever have such thoughts?"

When family fights escalate, psychological reserves weaken. And when children observe conflict between parents, their own stress heightens. One child was interviewed for ABC-TV's "Hotline":

> INTERVIEWER: *So you feel like you had to choose . . . between your mother and father?*
>
> YOUNG BOY: *I sort of feel sometimes that the fights that go on between my Dad and my Mother . . . pull me apart . . . so it's like I've got to choose sides. . . . I can't . . . it's difficult for me to just stay in the middle. . . . I was asking for help . . . by attempting suicide. . . . And that's why I told my Mom, you know, sort of asking for help in a way.*[21]

If you want to help a suicidal loved one, diminish family squabbles. Put a halt to accusations. Try not to induce guilt. If you are successful in diminishing family conflict, one of the major rationalizations for ending life will have been taken away.

There is one additional suggestion that might help. Ask your loved one to write down his or her problems, whether they be at school or work or in the family. Discuss them calmly. Be judicious about giving advice. Draw the person out so that you can learn of hidden feelings and beliefs.

Next, try to find solutions to one of the problems. Try to be creative and imaginative in your approach to the difficulties. If your loved one suggests a realistic solution, be sure to reinforce its merits. In so doing you begin to build a quiet optimism.

As you go through the exercise, do not become discouraged if promising solutions are thrown out. Depression creates a mental filter that sees little good in anything and a whole lot of bad in everything. It is likely that there may be pessimistic and even caustic comments, especially when you voice confidence in the future. And if your loved one wants to stop, do so. You can always resume later.

When practical solutions are rejected, you will become aware of your loved one's depression. Nevertheless, if you can discover one small solution, you have made progress. And if one tiny irritant can be diminished, it will be a sign that other difficulties can be discussed.

As you carry out this exercise, remember one crucial point: Finding solutions to problems is actually less important than affirming your love and concern. The greatest gift that you can give to a troubled individual is your presence. For it is the kind word that diminishes the pain, rekindles the hope, and finally generates a feeling of strength.

In time the crisis will end. But do not be surprised if you never receive a thank-you or even an acknowledgment of your role in helping resolve the problem. Most suicidal individuals never fully comprehend the amount of worry and concern expended by friends and relatives.

Nevertheless take great pride in your accomplishments. For without love and tenderness, a life may never have an opportunity to flourish.

What about Those Left Behind?

A Message for Mothers and Fathers, Brothers and Sisters, Husbands and Wives

Sometimes you do everything possible to prevent a suicide. You remove the weapons. You obtain professional help. You reassure. Yet in spite of various preventive measures, self-destruction occurs.

Barbara Bell Foglia asks rhetorically, "Who suffers more

in a war—the fallen victim who survives only in the memory of the survivors, or the survivors who die daily in remembering?"[22] The answer is clear, states Arnold Toynbee. "Death's sting is two pronged and in the apportionment of the suffering, the survivor takes the brunt."[23]

A suicide is generically different from other crises. When an unfavorable diagnosis is received, there are a host of people who support. When careers are dead-ended, solace can often be found in new avocations.

But suicide has its own language. Curiously, it is spoken in private. For when suicide occurs a hush comes over friendships. Unspoken judgments are rendered. And there are awkward moments of silence.

How do you survive the self-inflicted death of someone you love? It is again important to realize that suicide takes place in the best of homes—homes where there is a generous spirit and a loving heart.

Mr. and Mrs. Bolton and their four boys were a close-knit family.[24] They owned a cabin at Lake Burton in the north Georgia woods. Throughout the summer the family would trek to the cabin for joyous weekend outings.

Iris sought to be a perfect mother. By her own account she was the team "mother" for every sport in which the four boys played.

One day, returning from the grocery store, Iris found people standing in her driveway. A neighbor said, "We have to go to the hospital."

"The feeling in the pit of my stomach tightened. I said: 'Who?' The neighbor replied, 'Mitch.' I said, 'Motorcycle?' He was twenty and had a motorcycle. The neighbor replied: 'No, worse.'"

They arrived at the hospital. Unfortunately it was too late: Mitch was dead.

Iris went straight to Mitch's hospital room although she

was instructed not to look at him. She found him lying on
a table. He had shot himself with two guns, once in the
temple and once in the mouth, while talking to his girlfriend
on the telephone.

> I had to look at him. He was naked but covered with
> a white cloth and I needed to touch him—I needed to
> take off his bracelet. He was breathing, because he was
> on a machine. I told the nurse he was alive, but she said
> no. The machine was keeping his kidneys alive so that
> they could be given to someone. It seemed impossible
> to accept the fact that he was dead because he was breath-
> ing. . . .
> I remember needing to leave the room on my own
> terms. They said that I would have to leave now and
> started to take me by the elbow. It was very important
> for me to not let people guide me by the elbow. Every-
> body was doing this with me, as if I were disabled. I
> was disabled, but I was not an invalid. It was important
> for me to decide when to leave the room. I told them I
> would leave when I was ready to leave.
> I finished touching him, and took off his bracelet.
> That bracelet was very important to me and still is.

You need to say good-bye. Unfortunately, however, fare-
wells are often frustrated by well-intentioned yet misin-
formed people. On the day Mitch died, Iris Bolton noticed
neighbors who were looking into the back of a truck. Why?
The cleaning lady determined that it would be best that Iris
not see her son's bloody mattress. She put it into a truck
and took it to the dump.

One of the hardest parts of the whole experience, states
Iris Bolton, was not being able to see everything she needed
to see. "I could face the things I saw—the things I experienced—but I had the hardest time facing the things I could
not see or was not allowed to." The cleaning lady had also
closed Mitch's room and put a sign on the door that said,
Do Not Enter.

To recover from a loved one's self-inflicted death, you need to enter all the rooms left behind. As you enter them you will sense the good and the bad. You'll see hobbies and avocations, the small and significant joys that captured life. You will probably come across letters and notes and even plans for the future.

And then you will be hit with an unanswerable question: "Why—why, when there was so much to live for—why would life be taken?" That question may brutalize your spirit for months, perhaps years.

Guilt—that is what makes the crisis of suicide different from all other crises. If you become ill, you might feel remorse for not living a healthier lifestyle. If you lose your inheritance, you might blame yourself for poor judgment. But now you are faced with an excruciating possibility: In some way you are responsible for the death of your loved one.

The weeks following a suicide are spent reviewing the psychological remains. Omissions are dredged up and are interpreted as the cause of the death. "Again and again, the survivor replays the ninth inning," states Earl Grollman, "devising plays that might have won the game and preserved the life."[25]

Guilt leads to another terrifying thought: Maybe I too am suicidal. Maybe I am not strong enough to withstand this tragedy. As one person said: "I keep thinking that I am losing my mind. I may kill myself someday. My father did, and I am just like him."[26]

Kurt Vonnegut, Jr., wrote, "Sons of suicides seldom do well." Neither do daughters or moms and dads. But you are not going insane. And there is no evidence whatsoever that suicide is inherited.[27]

How do you diminish the guilt? The starting point is to understand that the suicide was not your fault. You could not have prevented it.

But you might say: "It was my fault! I didn't see the signs. I wasn't observant."

Many loved ones blame themselves for a suicide. But in most cases, family members are blameless, for it is difficult—if not impossible—to prevent that final act. Listen to the words of one mother:

> Scott was a caring person. He was a normal teenager with normal adolescent problems. We were able to communicate, but Scott kept a lot of his feelings inside and never wanted to burden anyone with his problems.
>
> My husband and I provided a nice, comfortable home for Scott with lots of love and concern. We were the best parents we could have been to Scott. We were the best parents we knew how to be.
>
> Scott was getting ready to leave home for college. . . . Even up to the last hours before he shot himself, he called me and told me of his plans for the weekend of moving all his belongings to school.
>
> Scott couldn't tell us about this pain. We had no idea he was suffering. I thought I knew my son so well. I, his mother. I, who was so close to him, couldn't even help him because I didn't know he was hurting.[28]

Sometimes it is impossible to know the hurts of others. And even if you are aware, you may not be able to do anything about it. Suicides are rarely anyone's fault. If your spouse committed suicide, the problem that drove him or her to that desperate act was present long ago. It may have been there before you were married.

You need to absolve yourself of imagined wrongs. And you need to reaffirm the good days that your loved one enjoyed.

Unfortunately there is a tendency to judge an individual's entire life by his act. When suicide occurs, it is not uncommon to think of the victim as "weak," "confused," or "mixed-up." These assessments may reflect the last months or even years of life. But they rarely reflect the entire life span.

It is important to remember all the joyful, playful times and the moments of love and tenderness. It is also important to recall your loved one's hobbies and avocations and all the things that brought joy.

Few of us would want to be judged by considering only one period in our life. Particularly if that period was filled with confusion and turmoil. If we are to judge others, let us consider the entire life. For within that life were moments of inner peace. And possibly great joy.

There is one other way to diminish guilt and it is embedded in a simple but powerful concept: *You must agree that suicide for your loved one was the only path that he or she could have taken.* This is the most difficult concept we have discussed in this book—to pardon the one who committed the unpardonable.

There are a thousand objections that surface when it is suggested that permission be given for an act of self-destruction. "Didn't she realize the pain that this would cause us? I can never condone what happened."

You may never condone that final self-destructive act. But a liberating feeling comes over you when you begin to understand that for your loved one death was the only recourse.

The crisis of suicide is different from all other heartbreaks. As such the remedy must be potent: Your recovery will only begin when you give an unconditional pardon. And it will only end when you sense that your loved one is better off in death than in life.

There is much that is not known about suicide. But this much we do know: There is a limit to the load any person can bear. And at that moment of self-destruction your loved one could no longer bear the burden. She was not weak. He was not a coward. *The load was simply too much to bear.*

There is a special gift that we can bring to this moment

of turmoil. It is alluded to most poignantly in Thornton Wilder's *Bridge of San Luis Rey*. A bridge collapses and plunges the persons crossing it to their deaths. In seeking to discover what it was in each person's life that brought each to the ill-fated bridge of self-destruction, Wilder enunciates one certain truth: "There is a land of the living and a land of the dead and the bridge is love, the only survival, the only meaning."

E L E V E N

Ordinary Heroes

> *I don't want to die, but I'm not
> afraid to die.*
> —STACEY CUMELLA, TWELVE-YEAR-
> OLD LEUKEMIA PATIENT

It took one year to interview people for this book. After many hours of analyzing information it was time to record what I had learned.

There was, however, one last visit to a hospital that had to be made. It was to have been a routine visit, thanking a group of nurses for their assistance in this project. The visit proved far from routine.

After our meeting a head nurse said, "There is another department in the hospital that you need to visit before you complete your research."

I was taken aback by her assertiveness. From my point of view more than enough information had been gathered. Yet her demeanor was determined. It suggested that there were secrets that had not yet been told.

My curiosity quickened as I followed her down a long corridor and up four flights of stairs. We came to two large doors over which hung a sign: *Hospice Unit.*

When I saw that sign, I realized that I had walked near that unit on a number of occasions but had managed to avoid it. Perhaps it was a reflection of my own fear of death. A thousand thoughts rushed through my mind. What would I see? Why was this nurse so insistent that I come here?

Images of darkness swept over me. I thought I would see depression. Gloom. Patients with tubes emanating from all orifices.

But I was mistaken. What transpired in the visits to that hospice unit, as well as to the oncology department of another hospital, represents the philosophical foundation on which this book rests. In truth, my education about psychological coping was about to begin. Only this time it wouldn't come from books on philosophy or from the latest theory on stress. What I was about to learn would come directly out of the experiences of ordinary people confronting the ultimate crisis.

There are heroes who live in oncology wards and in hospice units. Genuine heroes—individuals who cling to life with a tenacity that contradicts all that we know about failure and finitude.

Even as life ebbs away, these ordinary heroes act kindly toward others. They express optimism. They offer encouragement to those who are closer to death than they. And they comfort friends and loved ones.

William James believed that the high point for the human spectacle was in its heroism. He said that the demand for courage is incessant. It is as much a part of our nature to be heroic as it is to breathe.[1]

Twenty years ago I categorized such thought as naive. Too many wars. Too much violence. Too much self-interest.

Now I am not so sure that William James wasn't highlighting a universal truth: Acts of heroism occur every day in villages and cities throughout our land. There is heroism in education institutions as teachers patiently work with handicapped children. There is heroism on assembly lines and in blue-collar jobs as workers struggle to bring meaning to soulless work environments. And there is heroism in oncology wards as patients die in dignity and peace.

I felt unprepared to witness the tiny acts of heroism within that hospital. I knew little about oncology and had given little thought to how people die. But wanting to learn more, I scheduled a meeting with a nurse who was a veteran of many years of work in hospice care.

I arrived early. I took my time as I walked down the corridor, for I reasoned that if I was to write about death, I wanted to smell it. I wanted to look into the eyes of the dying and capture what I thought would be a sure sense of despair.

I looked into Room 526 and a middle-aged man gave me a warm smile. In Room 528 an elderly woman waved a hand but said not a word. Three doors down a patient asked me if the weather was turning cold. Everyone was far more alert that I had projected, although there were those who were comatose. As I walked by each patient's room, there often was a reassuring "hello" or a simple "hi."

All my prejudices about death and dying were challenged. The air smelled clean and fresh. Some of the patients were wearing street clothes. Flowers were seen on little stands; pictures of relatives adorned most rooms. Bright sunshine came through the window of a conference room at the end of the hall. There was—I hesitate to use the word—a *cheerfulness* in that place.

I was about to return to the nursing station when my eyes lit on a sign: *Peace to all who enter here.*

Peace? Peace when you are dying? Death and peace seemed strangely juxtaposed. The sign seemed almost cruel.

My curiosity about the entire place quickened. "Who are these people?" I asked myself. "Why are they here? Were they forced to come by a physician, perhaps a relative? How do they cope with despair? Can there actually be peace in this place? And most of all, how can there be cheerfulness when cancer has wasted life—indeed, all possibilities?"

I commented to a nurse that everything seemed pleasant. She was quick to caution: "It's not as idyllic as it may appear, although we do try to make everyone as comfortable as possible."

"How do people die?" I asked. The words rushed forth: "Is it possible to die with a sense of coherence, integrity? How do relatives respond when they bring their father or mother, or son or daughter to this place?"

The nurse went to the heart of the matter. "Some people meet death in a violent way. And I want to make it clear that it is not the physical pain, although that can be difficult. What I am talking about is psychological pain.

"Some patients angrily fight every inch toward their death. They curse the physicians. They fight the nurses. They despise relatives who represent the life that they do not have. And when they finally take in their last breath, they are bitter that life ended in such a wretched condition.

"But there are the others..." She paused to reflect on the meaning of her words. "Maybe one of the advantages of having a terminal illness is that it is possible to plan *how* you want to die. And believe me, people plan their deaths. But instead of anger, there is peace. And instead of agitation they express love. And when they die they do so with a strong sense of dignity and inner vitality. They had lived each day to the fullest—right to their last breath."

In the quietness of a nearby office I reflected on what

had been said. I found my thoughts riveted on the distinction between people who die in bitterness and those who die in peace. I frankly wondered whether it wasn't too simplistic—a neat way of categorizing patients when in reality most meet death in varying shades of hope and despair.

I later discovered that her categorization was not simplistic. Indeed, her insights seem to be on target: When death is near, we cast our lot on one side or another of a philosophical fence.

Some, believing that life has dealt them an empty hand, become withdrawn, cynical, and angry. Suicidal thoughts dance in their heads. They plot their deaths and the methods of self-destruction. It is not uncommon for despairing patients to stuff Kleenex into tracheal openings or to hoard pills to be taken in one final gulp.

But other patients, confronting the same mysteries, find an inner strength. They are confident for they are engaged in living, not dying. For them there is a realization that while it may not be possible to be well physically, it is possible to be well mentally.

What lessons did I learn about death, dying, and living in the hospice unit? *The very first thing I observed was the tranquillity in the hospice*. Everything moves purposively, slowly. People talk to one another. They meet one another. They help one another.

There is a peacefulness in the hospice unit, but I do not want to imply that there is silence. Far from it. Laughter can be heard. Birthdays are celebrated. Gifts are given. Humor is shared. There are even celebrations when someone's child gets straight A's or when the football team wins a big game.

The peacefulness to which I refer is moments of solitude in which patients reflect on the meaning of the day. Sometimes this reflection takes place in support groups. Sometimes the solitude is seen as patients look at one another, sharing few words yet sharing everything that is important.

As you listen to conversations, you do not hear the superficial quip about having a good day. What you do hear are quiet affirmations that it is possible to get through the day with a bit of hope and considerable dignity.

After my visit to the hospice I made my way to the parking lot, trying to comprehend the emotions that had overwhelmed me. It was now 5:00 P.M. and the December sun had already set. A winter storm was rapidly moving into the city.

As I turned onto the freeway, I sensed that it would be a long trek home. Cars were lined up in an angry procession. Horns expressing agitation could be heard. A driver cursed with his eyes as I signaled a turn into his lane of traffic. The tension of life was deeply etched onto his face.

The contrast between the tranquillity of the hospice unit and the noise and exhaust of the freeway was stark. Waiting for my exit from the freeway, I sadly concluded that the highway was a more accurate symbol of life than the quiet calm of the hospice unit.

Yet in one sense the values that sustained life in the hospice unit seemed far more enduring and important than the chronic urgency experienced on the highway.

How does one move from a state of constant motion to that of inner tranquillity? I believe inner peace is arrived at when we change our understanding of time. In a hospice unit there is a totally different view of minutes, hours, and days. For when life is fragile, time takes on a new dimension. Life is lived in the present, not in the past. Nor in the future.

I once asked a nurse what oncology patients think about as time ticks away. "Time is not ticking away," she said. "That's how you look at it. For them every moment is savored. Every moment that is free from pain is *lived*."

Silence. Tranquillity. These concepts evoke ambivalence, especially as we struggle to get the kids on the bus, work an eight-hour shift, prepare dinner, pay bills, do the shopping.

Yet most of us acknowledge a tug in our souls for quiet. For when we experience those precious moments of reflection and meditation, there is a release of anxiety. A slower beat of the heart. A new focus on life.

One woman on the verge of death was asked, "Do you have any regrets?" "None," she shot back. But then she looked to her window and said, "Well, maybe one." There was silence. And then a quiet judgment: "I wish I would have slowed down. I wish I would have *consciously* decided to enjoy each day."

The first lesson I learned in the hospice was *the value of living one day at a time*. There is no need to rush into uncertain tomorrows. The joys of today must be claimed.

The second lesson was this: *It is important to complete all unfinished business*.

Unfinished business. I first heard that expression from a nurse who said her goal was to help her patients experience a "good death."

"A good death?" I asked. "What makes it possible to have a 'good death'?"

"There is one prerequisite: All important tasks must be completed."

My curiosity intensified. I pressed hard. "What is the unfinished business that needs attention?"

"It varies from one patient to another," she said. "Some need to see that their lives were a success even if there was failure. Some need to resolve anger toward a parent, a child, an unfortunate happening. And sometimes the unfinished business is letting go of the anger they feel toward their illness."

She then told me of Bill Restin, who was brought to the

hospice unit one day before his fifty-eighth birthday:

When Bill was admitted I sensed his anger. He was hostile and abrupt. And very restless. When he finally fell asleep he would moan as if something terribly wrong had happened.

I asked him if everything was O.K. He didn't answer. So I asked again. No response. It was then that I knew he had some unfinished business that needed to be completed if he was to die a good death.

His physical signs were rapidly deteriorating. But he wouldn't die. He wouldn't let go. It was as if there was something deep within him that would not permit death.

I talked to his son: "Something very deep is bothering your dad. I don't know what it is. But unless it is resolved your father will never die in peace."

The son's eyes filled with tears. The family secret was about to be told.

"I am not the only child. I have a sister who lives in Baltimore, Maryland. My dad disowned her nine years ago because she married someone of another race. From his point of view, she committed the unpardonable sin. He said he would never forgive her."

When I heard that confession I knew what his unfinished business was all about. I told the son to call his sister and tell her to get to Minneapolis as fast as possible.

Five hours later she arrived. I went with them to their father's room. For the first time in nine years he saw his daughter. He said nothing but just stared at her. Then he opened his arms to his daughter and with all the strength that was left in that frail body hugged her. She brushed away his tears and sat on the bed. They said nothing for the longest time.

Finally he looked into her eyes and said two words that freed him forever: "I'm sorry."

There were many tears. They held one another and talked about old times. The dad learned that he was a grandfather and there was much laughter.

I checked his vital signs later that evening and they seemed stronger. But then an amazing thing happened.

Around 10:30 P.M. the father said he was very tired. But he didn't want the children to leave the room. I sensed what was about to happen and told the son and daughter to stay.

Each child held his hand. And then he died. But his expression was serene. The bitterness was gone. Grievances had been resolved. All unfinished business put to rest.

"All of us have unfinished business," said the nurse. "You have it; I have it. And most of these patients have it. If there is one thing that twenty-one years of bedside nursing has convinced me of it is this: It is impossible to die in peace unless the unfinished business is put to rest."

I have thought about her concept many times as I have reflected on the passing of friends and relatives. Her assessment was correct: Those who died in peace had completed their business.

Why is it so difficult to complete our unfinished tasks? Why is it so easy to let unresolved problems drift into old age?

One woman who longed for a reconciliation with her mother could not bring herself to take the first step. "A thousand miles and a thousand years separate us," she said wistfully. An executive troubled by a mistake that had wounded a colleague could not apologize. "Too much water over the dam," he rationalized. A husband tormented by his secret infidelity said: "That happened six years ago. I still can't get it behind me."

We do not complete our unfinished business because we believe it is too painful. We fear the rejection and the blame that could be heaped upon us by admitting a mistake.

Forgiveness is a subject that evokes ambivalence. "The prevalent style in the world," says Lance Morrow, "runs more to the high-plains drifter, to the hard, cold eye of the avenger, to a numb remorselessness. Forgiveness does not look much like a tool for survival in a bad world. But that is what it is."[2]

There are many reasons that thwart the impulse to forgive. Says Colman McCarthy:

> As much as religions teach that forgiveness is the bone-deep essence of faith, learning it is lifetime's lesson mastered by few. Grudge-bearing skills are applauded, not those of personal clemency. Governments have departments of justice, not departments of mercy. For individuals and nations, a change of heart is difficult enough. Forgiveness demands a change in thinking.[3]

We tend not to forgive. We tend to forget. Yet years later words spoken in anger can be recalled. Small insults are remembered. It is then we realize that we have not forgotten. We have put our problems on hold.

Nevertheless, when the act of forgiveness is forged, there is an explosion of goodwill. Gone are the recriminations. Gone is the hate. Gone are the destructive emotions of guilt and anger. And in their place there is healing.

There have been many instances in this book in which the concept of forgiveness has been evoked. And for one very important reason: It is the prerequisite to inner peace.

Many quiet acts of forgiveness take place in a hospice. Sometimes the staff overhear confessions as loved ones exchange apologies. But usually the acts of mercy take place behind closed doors.

Even when the reconciliations are private affairs, they become public knowledge. For the signs of peace are everywhere.

There is one other type of unfinished business that must be mentioned. Unfinished business usually centers on fractured relationships and unresolved grievances. But not always.

At times the unfinished business is reflected in a need to say good-bye. Sometimes the good-byes are directed toward loved ones. Sometimes to friends. Sometimes to routines. And sometimes to material goods.

Carolyn Smith gradually came to believe that it was futile to fight the biological enemy that would eventually claim her life. She had put up a magnificent fight. Against all odds she had triumphed.

But there came a time when she realized that the fight was over. She was not giving up. Nor was she caving in to the darkness. Rather, in the marrow of her being she knew that it was time to move on.

Carolyn asked permission to leave the hospital. She said that there was one last piece of business that needed attention. No one asked what it was. Privacy is a sacred commodity in a hospice. Carolyn Smith returned home. Not to repair relationships, which were in good order. She wanted to say good-bye.

As Carolyn approached her house for the final time, she quietly gazed at the surroundings, the landscape, the swing tethered to a large tree. It was a place of serenity. A place of love. A place of quiet strength.

She rearranged flowers and with the help of a daughter prepared a family meal. She sat in a favorite chair and reread a favorite book. Then she asked to be alone.

Sitting at the kitchen table, Carolyn wrote letters to each of the children telling them of her love and how happy they had made her. She instructed them to work hard, but to have fun. She wrote to her husband and in the most tender of ways thanked him for a friendship that had spanned twenty-three beautiful years.

The letters were neatly placed in the middle drawer of a desk. A note was attached: "To be read after my death."

An hour later there was a searing pain and a call for help. An ambulance was summoned, and an oxygen mask was placed over her face as the vehicle made its way to the hospital.

With siren blaring the ambulance moved down Highway 12 and onto Interstate 94. But at some point between home and hospital, Carolyn Smith made a decision to die.

Before death came, Carolyn made several requests: The siren was to be turned off. The vehicle was to slow down. The oxygen mask removed. Then she reached out for her husband's hand and grasped it firmly.

In that silent embrace a lasting friendship was affirmed. And in that moment of grace and with an understanding that all business had been completed, she died.

There is much we do not know about death. But I am convinced of one thing: People do will their deaths, but only after their unfinished business has been completed. Then death is no longer a stranger. It comes gently, quietly, even as a friend.

There was a third lesson I learned in the hospice. It was a lesson in optimism: *No matter how difficult the situation, life can be celebrated.*

Once the unfinished business has been completed, there is a flood of joy and a renewed sense of purpose. Suddenly one feels liberated and everything of value takes on a sharper focus. Friendships are enjoyed. Acts of kindness are noticed. Relationships are valued. And the hospice becomes a place where Easter is celebrated every day.[4]

Albert Camus once observed that "there is only one liberty, to come to terms with death."[5] Until my visits with the severely ill I had never fully grasped the meaning of this concept. I had an intellectual understanding of Camus's vision. Simply put, he suggested that once the fear of death is put aside, we engage in life. Or to put it another way: When you know in the fabric of your being that you are going to die, you choose to live. And then you are free to celebrate life.

But what is intellectually tenable is often difficult to comprehend in the heart. Do patients really choose to celebrate life on a deathbed? Can one be surrounded with chaos and create meaning? Can one live joyously when death is nearby?

David Carlson would say yes. And it wouldn't be a meek yes; it would be a resounding affirmation. I spotted David sitting in the hospital coffee shop, sketching on a large posterboard. I asked him what he was designing, and with pride he revealed a drawing of a log cabin surrounded by tall pine trees.

"All my life I wanted to have a cabin," he said. "But there was never enough money and I was always too busy. But when they discovered my terminal illness I decided that maybe it was time to build."

I asked, "Do you think you will see the day that it will be built?"

"Probably not. But that isn't important. It's going to be built in my mind. And I am going to enjoy it as much as if I was there."

We started talking about the north woods and how he was going to insulate the cabin and the type of lake on which it would be constructed.

"Some people would probably think I am crazy for thinking about building a cabin, given my diagnosis . . . but if there is one thing I believe, it's you never chop down your options." He added with a smile, "Wouldn't it be something if I surprised them all and actually got this thing built?"

There was a joyful look in his eyes and amusement in his expression as he contemplated the fulfillment of a dream. I left the coffee shop with his words ringing in my ears: *You never chop down your options.*

How easy it is to chop down options. But why do we do it? Why, when we have so much potential and latent possibilities and creativity, do we cease to celebrate? Why, when there is a deep reservoir of hope within us waiting to be tapped, do we permit ourselves to fall into despair?

It is easy to blame a tragedy for everything. But I think that is too convenient an excuse. Most people do not give up on life because of a catastrophe. They give up because they *no longer see the small joys worthy of celebration*.

Some of the happiest individuals I met in this study were those *determined* to celebrate life—even in the days and hours before death.

A grandmother lived for the visits of her grandchildren. When they came to the hospice, she entered into their joyous play and affirmed her legacy. In the evening she diligently worked on her needlepoint, determined to give a final gift to her child.

One young man brought a tape deck with him into the hospital. His days and evenings were filled making recordings of his favorite jazz compositions. Then he gave them away as gifts.

A young cancer victim had an elaborate stamp collection. "Just because I am in a hospital doesn't mean that I can't have a hobby," he affirmed. His hospital room—with books stacked high—looked like a historian's office.

Gradually I was beginning to see a correlation: When patients celebrate the small joys of life, they live without fear. *When they create, chaos is put aside*. But when fear consumes all thoughts, death may not be far behind.

Is it possible to celebrate life even as the last breath is being gathered? Vince Meyers asked his son for a piece of paper. Weakly yet meticulously he scrawled one word. When he had finished he looked up. He appeared to be smiling although his lips were not easy to read.[6]

He wrote one word: "Pennant." His thoughts were on his favorite baseball team. After years of futility there was an outside possibility that the Minnesota Twins might win a championship. His eyes reflected a simple joy: Wouldn't it be wonderful if they actually won the whole thing?

Baseball in a hospice unit? Thoughts of pennants and World Series on a deathbed?

To those unfamiliar with suffering it might seem strange. They would think that thoughts should be a bit more profound. After all, baseball isn't life. War and taxes are life. But in Vince Meyers's final moments, baseball was on his mind. And a celebration was in order.

How do you summon the courage to love life when surrounded by gloom? You search and search and search. Until you find *one person, one idea, one avocation* that is so powerful that it penetrates the gloom. And you keep your sense of humor.

Dorothy Peterson would not want to be eulogized as a saint. She had no illusions about her imperfections. As a mother she had been fierce in her high expectations of her children. And she was equally fierce in their defense, which could be testified to by many teachers, school principals, commanders of air force bases, and persons close to the President of the United States whom she felt played war games with her children's lives.

Even during her last weeks she wanted to protect her family and prepare them for what was ahead. In the eighteen months after the diagnosis of lung cancer there was a renewed and magic love affair with life and with her family. And in the days preceding death there was a peace—accompanied by a marvelous sense of humor.

Dorothy Peterson saw the humor in life's raw edges. When her children became solicitous, they were told: "Stop asking how I'm doing. I'm fine." When they pressed for more reassurance, they were instructed, "I'll tell you when it's time to worry . . . until then, I'm fine."

As the time for her dying drew near, she kept a promise

made months before. The family was called together for a final meal, which was lovingly prepared and shared on November 14.

Nostalgic recollections were encouraged. She invited a neighbor to take some family pictures. Silently every member of the family hoped that they would be together again at Christmas, but it was not to be. On November 23 her condition turned grave.

"I remain in awe of her last days," said a daughter. "I am flooded with bittersweet memories of precious hours shared with her and the family which she nurtured.

"Her waking hours were spent nudging the family toward acceptance of her death, graciously acknowledging the family's love, gracefully involving us in the minuscule tasks which eased the feelings of powerlessness, openly pushing us to care for one another."

When the tensions became too great, this strong, tenacious woman had one-line quips for everyone:

Hearing the waking of fellow patients and their movements in the halls at 7:00 A.M.: "The geriatric parade begins."

Seeing an intravenous solution started, she said to the machine: "Well, machine, it's you and me against the world."

Feeling burdened by twelve people in her room: "Now this is enough. You've all been here . . . now some of you scoot."

Preparing for the arrival of a priest for anointment: "I have a message: Tell him I fought long sermons to the last day."

Of a patronizing nurse who said she wanted her to take a sedative she inquired: "Why do I have to take it?"

"Dorothy," said the nurse, "we want to find out if it's a potentiator."

With a sparkle in her eyes she said: "Don't use big words with me. Why don't you just say you want to find out if it will knock the old broad out!"

To her doctor: "Put on the chart: Give her anything she wants."

To her husband, after awakening from an uncomfortable sleep: "This has got to end; go chase blondes."

To her God, an hour and a half before she died: "I love you. I love you."[7]

I do not understand how such great peace is evoked from such great suffering. But I know celebrations happen anywhere, anyplace, and at any time.

And now we come to the final lesson: *Love heals*; *fear destroys*. In the words of Katherine Anne Porter: "Love must be learned and learned again and again; there is no end of it. Hate needs no instruction, but wants only to be provoked."[8]

It is admittedly difficult to love when darkness surrounds life. There are just too many fears.

Fear knows no boundaries. It overwhelms those who are sick, but it also overwhelms those who are well. It finds its way into an oncology ward, but it also finds its way into our homes.

A young adult might worry about selecting the right college, the right major, the right career. A salesman might worry about marketing strategies and fluctuating economies. A senior citizen might be consumed with dread over finances, health, and children.

Fear knows no gender. It strikes the old as well as the young. And it takes a deadly toll, as attested to in East Indian folklore:

> The Spirit of the Plague passed by an old man sitting under a tree. The old man inquired: "Where are you going?" The Spirit replied: "To Benares, to kill one hundred people."
>
> The Spirit walked by the old man and ravaged Benares.
>
> Later the old man heard that ten thousand had died.

Once again the Spirit passed by the old man on its return journey. With anger the old man said: "You lied. You said you would kill one hundred but travelers tell me you slew ten thousand."

To which the Spirit of the Plague replied: "I slew but one hundred. Fear slew the others."[9]

Fear casts an awfully long shadow. You cannot walk the corridor of a hospice without confronting your own anxiety about death. Nor can you listen to the agony of a rape victim or an abused child without sensing anguish.

But in those moments when bitterness threatens to destroy the essence of life, it is important to remember that fear and hope are intertwined. The French words *espoir* (hope) and *désespoir* (despair) and the Dutch words *hopen* and *wan-hopen* form a symbiotic relationship. Or as Paul Tillich observed, chaos and creation belong to one another. They are not strangers. They live and breathe in unison.

As strange as it may seem, hope has its roots in despair. It is a derivative force. It evolves out of hopelessness, and it probably would not arise otherwise. Indeed, if reality did not give us grounds for despair—it could never give us reasons for hope.[10]

Perhaps the redemptive legacy of a tragedy is that in time we can again hope. But when I use the word *hope* I am not referring to quick fixes: new spouses for banged-up marriages, new jobs for burned-out careers, miracle drugs for terminal illness. Nor am I referring to stoic acceptance of the inevitable, as if a jutting jaw or a clenched fist could substitute for a courageous heart.

When I use the word hope, I am referring to a clear understanding that life is at best a risk—an uncharted voyage in which we know little about jutting shorelines and drifting debris. But it is a voyage we want to take.

And so we purchase the ticket and set our sails into

strange new worlds. And when the ill winds blow, we may wonder why we left the safety of the harbor. But even then we cannot resist looking into the teeth of the storm. Nor can we resist summoning the courage to protect all that is of value.

Aldous Huxley knew that risk was at the heart of life. In the closing pages of his *Brave New World* the Savage, a young man brought up outside the programmed, controlled world of the new society, engages in a magnificent dialogue with the Controller of that society. The Savage says: "What you need is something *with* tears for a change. Nothing costs enough here."

The Controller admonishes him to have a chemical treatment to get rid of such notions comfortably. The Savage replies: "But I don't want comfort. I want God, I want poetry, I want real danger, I want freedom, I want goodness. I want sin."

The shocked Controller suggests that the Savage wants to be unhappy.

> "All right, then," said the Savage defiantly. "I'm claiming the right to be unhappy."
> "Not to mention the right to grow old and ugly and impotent; the right to have syphilis and cancer; the right to have too little to eat; the right to be lousy; the right to live in constant apprehension of what may happen tomorrow; the right to catch typhoid; the right to be tortured by unspeakable pains of every kind."
> There was a long silence.
> "I claim them all," said the Savage at last.[11]

This, then, is our challenge: We must affirm the perilousness of our journey. *But we must affirm that we would not want it any other way.*

Hope. It is a word that has been worn so smooth that it has lost its bite. We can recite Alexander Pope's admonition,

"Hope springs eternal in the human breast," or Cicero's observation, "Where there is life, there is hope."

But in a world that values scientific knowledge, such expressions are frequently cast into the backwaters of wishful thought. For, as the argument goes, you cannot qualify hope. You cannot build hope into bell-shaped curves. It cannot be dispensed as a medication. But for survivors hope is the greatest therapy. It is the one force that safely guides through unknown lands.

Is it possible to live in peace when surrounded by impersonal technology, beeps coming from strange machines, drugs that leave us nauseated and depleted? Is it possible to live sanely in an environment that could drive you mad? *Is it possible to love again, when that which you have loved is lost forever*?

The answer from ordinary heroes is yes. And what comes from their lips is now being confirmed by scientific investigations.

The New England Journal of Medicine recently stated that it is a myth that patients with major illnesses are likely to fall apart emotionally.[12] Said a researcher, "The stereotype of someone with a major chronic illness, particularly cancer, is that they're despairing and that they're emotionally wiped out, and that is simply not the case." In fact, these patients had significantly higher mental health scores than individuals who were physically healthy but under treatment for depression.[13]

Within the chronicles of medicine are joyous case studies of patients who beat the odds. In fact, many who were diagnosed in the bleakest terms discovered that the best years of life came after receiving the pessimistic pronouncement.

Said Abraham Maslow, after suffering a third heart attack:

> The confrontation with death . . . makes everything look

so precious, so sacred, so beautiful that I feel more strongly than ever the impulse to live it, to embrace it, and to let myself be overwhelmed by it. My river has never looked so beautiful. . . . Death, and its ever present possibility makes love, passionate love, more possible. I wonder if we could love passionately, if ecstasy would be possible at all, if we knew we'd never die.[14]

And now we come to the final part of our journey. What enables us to put fear aside? What permits hope to once again spring forth?

Ultimately, it is simple, unadulterated acts of love.

When Gus Kirzinski was brought to the hospice, he felt great fear, anger, and cynicism. "Why did I get cancer?" he repeated, as if for some strange reason he should have been exempt from the disease. "What does God have against me?"

One day he stomped down the corridor because he hadn't received the service he demanded. Then an event happened that transformed his remaining weeks of life.

"I couldn't believe it," he said. "I was just walking down the hall and I saw a five-year-old kid. Can you imagine, a five-year-old kid in a hospice? I went to a nurse and said: 'What is that kid doing here? This is a place where old people die, not little kids.'"

He was told that the child had fallen off a tractor, temporarily cutting off oxygen to her brain. The accident resulted in paralysis. She could not talk nor could she see. Nevertheless she was able to hear and respond to simple instructions.

Gus stared at her through the doorway. He couldn't fathom how something like this could happen. "She's only five years old," he said repeatedly. He later learned that her parents lived 600 miles away and could only visit on weekends.

The next morning Gus again walked by the child's room.

"Who's taking care of that kid?" he shouted at the nurses.

After one such blast a nurse replied, "Maybe you ought to do it."

Shocked at the thought, he went back to his room. "Who's taking care of that kid?" he kept asking.

After most of the patients had gone to bed, Gus put on his slippers and went into her room. He turned on a soft light and said, "Hi, kid." There was silence. Louder, he intoned: "Hi, kid. My name is Gus." Still no response as his large hand grasped a small finger.

At that very moment the little girl squeezed his hand. And in that very moment Gus was transformed—from a bitter, fearful, angry person to one who could love.

For six weeks they "talked" to one another through handshakes. He read her stories. He turned on her favorite music. He found a little red wagon, propped her safely within it, and they would go on little "trips" around the hospital. As time passed, they developed an intricate language of communication as they snapped their fingers back and forth.

"When Gus died," said a nurse, "he died smiling. He was no longer Gus the fearful patient. Now he was Gus . . . the friend of a five-year-old."

Love is the ultimate therapy. For when we love we are transformed. And then we move into a region beyond science. It can be called the spiritual world, the psychic universe, the inner spirit. But call it what you want, it is a world that knows no fear. And harbors no grudge.[15]

Victor Frankl knew of the power inherent in love. One night the Nazi guards came for him as well as for other prisoners in the death camp. The guards forced him to walk from one unknown destination to another. He describes what happened.

. . . as we stumbled on for miles, slipping on icy spots, supporting each other time and again, dragging one another up and onward, nothing was said, but we both knew; each of us was thinking of his wife. Occasionally I looked up at the sky where the stars were fading and the pink light of the morning was beginning to spread behind a dark bank of clouds. But my mind clung to my wife's image, imagining it with an uncanny acuteness. I heard her answering me, saw her smile, her frank and encouraging look.

A thought transfixed me: For the first time in my life I saw the truth as it is set into song by so many poets, proclaimed as the final wisdom by so many thinkers. The truth—that love is the ultimate and the highest goal to which men can aspire. Then I grasped the meaning of the greatest secret that human poetry and human thought and belief have to impart: the salvation of man is through love and in love.[16]

APPENDIXES
CHAPTER NOTES
FURTHER
READING

A P P E N D I X   A

Survey on Human Loss and Recovery

Your help is needed. Please take a few moments to answer the following questions on a separate piece of paper. You do not need to include your name.

The purpose of this questionnaire is to learn how people cope with difficult life events. *Your experiences could be of great help to others confronting similar situations.*

The aggregate results of this questionnaire will eventually be published. Direct quotes may be taken from the answers; however, no individual will be identified by name. The answers to all questions are voluntary. If you do not want to answer a question, feel free to skip it and go on to the next one.

1. Describe the most *difficult problem* that you have had to face in your life. Be descriptive. Include as many details as possible.

2. Describe how the problem affected your *family*, including spouse, children, and/or parents. Who was most helpful? Who was least helpful? Why?

3. How did the crisis affect your *faith*?

4. Did you seek *professional help* (physician, psychologist, member of the clergy, and/or others)? If so, how would you evaluate the effectiveness of the help?

5. How did your *friends* respond to your crisis?

6. If you were faced with a *similar problem*, would you manage it differently at this point in time? If so, in what ways?

7. Were the fundamental *values* by which you live your life changed by the crisis? If so, in what ways?

8. What *advice* do you have for someone who is confronting a similar problem?

9. Was this book helpful to you? If so, what was most useful?

Please mail your response to:

SURVEY ON HUMAN LOSS AND RECOVERY
ROBERT VENINGA, PH.D.
P.O. BOX 8117
ST. PAUL, MN 55108

Note: Only individuals eighteen years of age or older should respond to this questionnaire. Thank you!

APPENDIX B

Names and Addresses of Self-Help Organizations

Al-Anon Family Group Headquarters
One Park Avenue
New York, NY 10016

For families of alcoholics

Alateen
One Park Avenue
New York, NY 10016

For teenage children of alcoholics

Alcoholics Anonymous
AA World Services
P.O. Box 459
Grand Central Station
New York, NY 10163

For adult alcoholics

Alexander Graham Bell Association for the Deaf
3417 Volta Place N.W.
Washington, DC 20007

For deaf persons

American Blind Bowling Association
150 N. Bellaire Avenue
Louisville, KY 40206

Bowling for blind persons

American Diabetes Association
Two Park Avenue
New York, NY 10016

For diabetics, youth, adults, and their families

American Ex-Prisoners of War
2306 Wilmer Drive
Grand Prairie, TX 75051

Assists former prisoners of war

American Federation of Catholic Workers for the Blind and Visually Handicapped
200 Tabor
Pittsburgh, PA 15204

For blind persons of the Catholic faith

American Schizophrenic Association
Huxley Institute for Biosocial Research
219 East 31st Street
New York, NY 10016

For adult schizophrenics

Arthritis Foundation
1314 Spring Street N.W.
Atlanta, GA 30309

For youth and adult arthritics and their families

Associated Blind
135 West 23rd Street
New York, NY 10010

For blind persons

Association for the Advancement of Blind Children
162-10 Highland Avenue
Jamaica, NY 11432

For blind children and their parents

Association for Children with Learning Disabilities
4156 Library Road
Pittsburgh, PA 15236

For children with learning disabilities and their parents

Association for Children with Retarded Mental Development
817 Broadway
New York, NY 10030

For mentally retarded children and their families

Association for the Education and Rehabilitation of the Blind and Visually Impaired
206 West Washington Street
Alexandria, VA 22314

For visually handicapped persons

Asthmatic Children Foundation of New York
P.O. Box 568
Spring Valley Road
Ossining, NY 10562

For asthmatic children and their families

Black Lung Association
907 West Neville Street
Beckley, WV 25801

For miners with black lung disease and their families

Blinded Veterans Association
1735 DeSales Street N.W.
Washington, DC 20036

For blind veterans and their families

Buxom Belles International
27856 Palomino Drive
Warren, MI 48093

For overweight women

Calix Society
7601 Wayzata Boulevard
Minneapolis, MN 55426

*For the spiritual needs of alco-
holics of the Catholic faith*

Candlelighters
2025 Eye Street N.W.
Suite 1011
Washington, DC 20006

*For parents of children with
cancer*

**Committee for Single Adoptive
Parents**
P.O. Box 4074
Chevy Chase, MD 20815

*For single persons wishing to
adopt a child*

**Congress of Organizations of
the Physically Handi-
capped**
16630 Beverly
Tinley Park, IL 60477

*For handicapped persons and
their families*

Cooley's Anemia Foundation
105 East 22nd Street
Suite 911
New York, NY 10010

*For children with Cooley's ane-
mia and their parents*

Coronary Club
3659 Green Road
Cleveland, OH 44122

*For persons who have had heart
attacks and their families*

Cystic Fibrosis Foundation
6000 Executive Boulevard
Rockville, MD 20852

*For persons with cystic fibrosis
and their families*

Families in Action
3845 North Druid Hills Road
Suite 300
Decatur, GA 30030

*For parents concerned about
drug abuse*

Fifty Upward Network
P.O. Box 4714
Cleveland, OH 44126

*A support group for women over
fifty years of age*

The Fortune Society
39 West 19th Street
Seventh Floor
New York, NY 10011

*For ex-offenders and their fami-
lies*

**Gam-Anon International Ser-
vice Office**
P.O. Box 967
Radio City Station
New York, NY 10101

For families of gamblers

Gamblers Anonymous
2703A West 8th Street
Los Angeles, CA 90005

For gamblers

Gray Panthers
3700 Chestnut Street
Philadelphia, PA 19104

*An activist senior citizens
organization*

Hodgkins Disease and Lymphoma Organization
518 Wingate Drive
East Meadow, NY 11554

For persons with Hodgkins disease and their families

Homecoming, Inc.
1132 West Pratt
Chicago, IL 60626

For former patients of mental institutions

Huntington's Disease Foundation of America
250 West 57th Street
Suite 2016
New York, NY 10107

For persons with Huntington's disease and their families

Institute for Rational-Emotive Therapy
45 East 65th Street
New York, NY 10021

A mental health organization

International Association of Laryngectomees
c/o American Cancer Society
777 Third Avenue
New York, NY 10017

For persons who have had larynx surgery and their families

International Catholic Deaf Association
814 Thayer Avenue
Silver Spring, MD 20910

For deaf persons of the Catholic faith

International Ministers' Wives and Widows Association
128 Pennsylvania Avenue
Roosevelt, NY 11575

For widows of ministers

International Parents' Organization
c/o Alexander Graham Bell Association for the Deaf
1537 35th Street N.W.
Washington, DC 20007

For parents of deaf children

Ladies Auxiliary
Military Order of the Purple Heart
419 Franklin Street
Reading, MA 01867

For wives of soldiers who have been wounded

La Leche League International
9616 Minneapolis Avenue
Franklin Park, IL 60131

For new mothers

The Learning Exchange
2940 North Lincoln Avenue
Chicago, IL 60657

For students who want to share learning/teaching experiences

Little People of America
Box 126
Owatonna, MN 55060

For midgets and their families

Make Today Count
P.O. Box 303
Burlington, IA 52601

*For persons with cancer and
their families*

Mended Hearts
7320 Greenville Avenue
Dallas, TX 75231

*For persons who have had heart
attacks and their families*

Mensa
1701 West 3rd Street
Brooklyn, NY 11223

For persons with high IQs

Muscular Dystrophy Association
810 7th Avenue
New York, NY 10019

For persons with muscular dystrophy and their families

Myasthenia Gravis Foundation
15 East 26th Street
Suite 1603
New York, NY 10010

*For persons with myasthenia
gravis and their families*

**Myopia International
Research Foundation**
415 Lexington Avenue
Room 705
New York, NY 10017

*For persons with myopia and
their families*

National Amputation Foundation
12-45 150th Street
Whitestone, NY 11357

For amputees and their families

**National Association for
Down's Syndrome**
Box 63
Oak Park, IL 60303

*For children who have Down's
syndrome and their families*

**National Association on Drug
Abuse Problems**
355 Lexington Avenue
New York, NY 10017

For persons with drug problems

**National Association for
Gifted Children**
2070 County Road H
St. Paul, MN 55112

*For gifted children and their
parents*

**National Association for the
Deaf**
814 Thayer Avenue
Silver Spring, MD 20910

For deaf persons and their families

**National Association of the
Physically Handicapped**
76 Elm Street
London, OH 43140

For physically handicapped persons and their families

**National Association of
Patients on Hemodialysis and Transplantation**
156 William Street
New York, NY 10038

*For persons with kidney disease
and their families*

National Association of Recovered Alcoholics
P.O. Box 95
Staten Island, NY 10305

For alcoholics employed in professional organizations

National Association for Widowed People
P.O. Box 3564
Springfield, IL 62708

For widows

National Association to Aid Fat Americans
P.O. Box 43
Bellerose, NY 11426

For overweight individuals

National Congress of the Jewish Deaf
9102 Edmonston Court, No. 302
Greenbelt, MD 20770

For deaf persons of the Jewish faith

National Council of Stuttering
P.O. Box 8171
Grand Rapids, MI 49508

For stutterers

National Federation of the Blind
1800 Johnston Street
Baltimore, MD 21230

For blind persons and their families

National Foundation for Children's Hearing Education and Research
928 MacLean Avenue
Yonkers, NY 10704

For hard-of-hearing children and their families

National Foundation for Ileitis and Colitis
295 Madison Avenue
New York, NY 10017

For persons with ileitis and colitis and their families

National Foundation for Sudden Infant Death
Two Metro Plaza, Suite 205
8240 Professional Place
Landover, MD 20785

For parents of children who have died of sudden infant death syndrome

National Fraternal Society of the Deaf
1300 West Northwest Highway
Mount Prospect, IL 60056

For deaf persons and their families

National Hemophilia Foundation
19 West 34th Street, Room 1204
New York, NY 10001

For hemophiliacs and their families

National Huntington Disease Association
1182 Broadway, Suite 402
New York, NY 10001

For persons with Huntington's disease and their families

National Multiple Sclerosis Society
205 East 42nd Street
New York, NY 10017

For persons with multiple sclerosis and their families

National Organization of Mothers of Twins Clubs
5402 Amberwood Lane
Rockville, MD 20853

For mothers of twins

National Rare Blood Club
c/o Associated Health Foundation
164 Fifth Avenue
New York, NY 10010

For persons with rare blood diseases and their families

National Society for Children and Adults with Autism
1234 Massachusetts Avenue N.W.
Suite 1017
Washington, DC 20005

For autistic persons and their families

National Spinal Cord Injury Association
149 California Street
Newton, MA 02158

For paralyzed individuals and their families

National Tay-Sachs and Allied Diseases Association
92 Washington Avenue
Cedarhurst, NY 11516

For persons with Tay-Sachs disease and their families

National Wheelchair Athletic Association
2107 Templeton Gap Road
Suite C
Colorado Springs, CO 80907

For physically handicapped persons

Neurotics Anonymous International Liaison
P.O. Box 4866
Cleveland Park Station
Washington, DC 20008

For neurotics

Orton Dyslexia Society
724 York Road
Baltimore, MD 21204

A clearinghouse for information about dyslexia

Overeaters Anonymous
2190 West 190th Street
Torrance, CA 90504

For overweight persons

Paralyzed Veterans of America
801 18th Street N.W.
Washington, DC 20006

For paralyzed veterans and their families

Parents Anonymous
22330 Hawthorne Boulevard
Suite 208
Torrance, CA 90505

For parents of abused children

Parents Without Partners
7910 Woodmont Avenue
Suite 1000
Bethesda, MD 20814

For single parents

Phobia Clinic
White Plains Hospital
Davis Avenue at East Post Boulevard
White Plains, NY 10601

For persons with phobias

Prison Families Anonymous
353 Fulton Avenue
Hempstead, NY 11550

For families of prisoners

Psoriasis Research Association
107 Vista del Grande
San Carlos, CA 94070

For persons with psoriasis

Reach to Recovery
American Cancer Society
777 Third Avenue
New York, NY 10017

For women who have had mastectomies

Recovery, Inc.
116 South Michigan Avenue
Chicago, IL 60603

For former patients of mental institutions and other persons with emotional problems

Retarded Infants Service
386 Park Avenue South
New York, NY 10016

For parents of retarded infants

Single Mothers By Choice
Box 207
Van Brunt Station
Brooklyn, NY 11215

For single mothers

Society for the Rehabilitation of the Facially Disfigured
550 First Avenue
New York, NY 10016

For facially disfigured persons and their families

Spina Bifida Association of America
343 South Dearborn Avenue
Suite 317
Chicago, IL 60604

For persons with spina bifida and their families

Stroke Clubs International
805 12th Street
Galveston, TX 77550

For persons who have had strokes and their families

Synanon Church
P.O. Box 42
50300 Highway 245
Badger, CA 93603

For drug addicts and other persons who wish to follow the Synanon life-style

Take Off Pounds Sensibly Club
P.O. Box 07489
4575 South 5th Street
Milwaukee, WI 53207

For overweight persons

Theos Foundation
410 Penn Hills Mall
Pittsburgh, PA 15235

For widows

United Cerebral Palsy Association
66 East 34th Street
New York, NY 10016

For persons with cerebral palsy and their families

United Ostomy Association
2001 West Beverly Boulevard
Los Angeles, CA 90057

For persons who have had ostomy surgery

Weight Watchers International
3860 Crenshaw Boulevard
Los Angeles, CA 90008

For overweight persons

Please note: Most of these are nonprofit organizations. In requesting information it would be helpful if you would enclose a self-addressed, stamped envelope.

Chapter Notes

2: THE STAGES OF HEARTBREAK

1. The word *hospice* originated in Europe and refers to a place of lodging for the traveler. In the United States, hospice units are found in most cities and are designed to care for the terminally ill. The basic function of a hospice is to provide nourishment and comfort for those who are in transition.
2. Quoted in Harriet Sarnoff Schiff, *The Bereaved Parent* (New York: Crown Publishers, 1977), p. 1.
3. Quoted in Norris Hansell, *The Person in Distress* (New York: Human Science Press, 1976).
4. Jane E. Brody, "Hyatt Disaster Still Taking Emotional Toll," *Minneapolis Tribune*, July 18, 1982, p. 48.
5. Edgar N. Jackson, *Coping with the Crisis in Your Life* (New York: Hawthorne Books, 1974), pp. 192-194.
6. Virginia Woolf, *Jacob's Room* (New York: Harcourt Brace, 1923), p. 5.
7. Martin E. P. Seligman, *Helplessness* (San Francisco: W. H. Freeman and Co., 1975), pp. 178-184.
8. Paul Tournier, *The Meaning of Persons* (New York: Harper and Brothers, 1957), p. 42.
9. James Agee, *A Death in the Family* (New York: Avon, 1956), p. 33.
10. Seligman, *Helplessness*, p. 185.

11. Clark Moustakas, *Loneliness and Love* (Englewood Cliffs, NJ: Prentice-Hall, 1972), p. 103.
12. Lew Riley, "A Little T.L.C. Goes a Long Way," *Writers Digest*, January 1982, p. 23.
13. Quoted in Robert A. Liston, *Healing the Mind: Eight Views of Human Nature* (New York: Praeger Publishers, 1974), pp. 127-138.
14. Mary Lois Knownack, "Letter to an Experiment with Truth," *Sojourners*, May 28, 1982, p. 27.
15. Kahlil Gibran, *The Prophet* (New York: Knopf, 1923), p. 17.

3: CHARACTERISTICS OF A CRISIS

1. Philip Hilts, "Fouled Up Sleep Habits Probed in Air Crashes," *St. Paul Pioneer Press*, Oct. 5, 1980, p. 15.
2. Bruce Larson, *There's a Lot More to Health Than Not Being Sick* (Waco, TX: Word Publishing Co., 1981), p. 75.

4: HOW PEOPLE SURVIVE ADVERSITY

1. T. N. James and J. W. Keyes, eds., *The Etiology of Myocardial Infarction* (Boston: Little, Brown and Co., 1963), pp. 95-97.
2. Martin E. P. Seligman, *Helplessness* (San Francisco: W. H. Freeman and Co., 1975), pp. 178-184.
3. Ibid.
4. Ibid.
5. Quoted in E. Borman, W. Howell, R. Nichols, and G. Shapiro, *Interpersonal Communication in the Modern Organization* (Englewood Cliffs, NJ: Prentice-Hall, 1969), p. 178.
6. The material on the Vietnam Veterans Memorial is adapted from Paul Weingarten, "Vets' Healing Begins at 'Black Wall,'" *St. Paul Pioneer Press Dispatch*, Apr. 21, 1985, pp. 1, 8A.
7. Ibid., p. 8A.
8. Quoted in Ernest Becker, *The Denial of Death* (New York: The Free Press, 1973), p. 101.
9. Alan Loy McGinnis, *The Friendship Factor* (Minneapolis: Augsburg Press, 1979), p. 109.
10. Quoted in *Leadership* 3, no. 3 (Summer 1982), p. 84.
11. Erich Fromm, *The Revolution of Hope* (New York: Harper and Row, 1968), p. 13.
12. Kay Miller, "After 35 Years Encased in Iron Lung, Doris Nelson's Full Life Comes to End," *Minneapolis Star and Tribune*, Jan. 8, 1983, p. 1.
13. Fromm, *Revolution*, p. 147.
14. Nadine Bruzan, "Doctor Dedicates Good Days to the Horror of Auschwitz," *Minneapolis Star and Tribune*, Nov. 16, 1982, p. 36.
15. Ibid.

5: PRESERVING YOUR HEALTH IN TOUGH TIMES

1. Joseph Carey and David Fink, "I'm Living in Right Time, Right Place," *USA Today*, Mar. 24, 1983, p. 1A.
2. Ibid.
3. Kenneth L. Jones, Louis W. Shainberg, and Curtis O. Byer, *Health Science* (New York: Harper and Row, 1983), p. 55.
4. Eugene C. Walker, *Learn to Relax* (Englewood Cliffs, NJ: Prentice-Hall, 1975), p. 10.
5. Adapted from Gordon Edlin and Eric Golanty, *Health and Wellness* (Boston: Science Books International, 1982), pp. 48-49.
6. Phillip Goldberg, *Executive Health* (New York: McGraw-Hill, 1978), p. 130.
7. Adapted from Marvin Levy, Mark Digman, and Janet H. Shirreffs, *Life and Health* (New York: Random House, 1984), p. 420.
8. Charles T. Kunsleman, *Maximum Personal Energy* (Emmaus, PA: Rodale Press, 1981), pp. 109-110.
9. John M. Gray, "The Safe Sport," *Esquire*, November 1983, p. 28.
10. Adapted from Mary Ellen Pinkham, "The Best Exercise of All—Which You Are Probably Already Doing," *Ms.*, May 1983, pp. 59-61.
11. "High Protein Breakfasts Fuel Learning," *USA Today*, Feb. 2, 1984, p. 1A.
12. Ernst L. Wynder, *The Book of Health: A Complete Guide to Making Health Last a Lifetime* (New York: Franklin Watts, 1981), p. 160.
13. Harry E. Yates, *Managing Stress* (New York: AMACOM, 1979), p. 123.
14. Levy, Digman, and Shirreffs, *Life and Health*, p. 122.
15. The material on amphetamines was adapted from Levy, Digman, and Shirreffs, p. 122.
16. William Fassbender, *You and Your Health* (New York: John Wiley and Sons, 1977), pp. 133-135.
17. Levy, Digman, and Shirreffs, *Life and Health*, p. 63.
18. Nola J. Pender, *Health Promotion in Nursing Practice* (Norwalk, CT: Appleton-Century-Crofts, 1982), p. 89.
19. D. Don Sperling, "Active Mind Is the Key to Healthy Aging," *USA Today*, Feb. 2, 1984, p. 10D.
20. Gene Prigge, "Zest for Life Keeps Woman Young at Heart," *St. Paul Sunday Pioneer Press*, Aug. 7, 1983, p. 4C.
21. D. H. Lawrence, *Lady Chatterley's Lover* (Garden City, NY: Doubleday, 1928), p. 38.

6: WHAT HAPPENS TO THE FAMILY IN A CRISIS

1. Peg Meier, "Parents of Gays Try to Understand," *Minneapolis Star and Tribune*, June 4, 1983, p. 1C.
2. Jim Parsons, "Murder Verdict Reversed: Man Refuses to Be Bitter," *Minneapolis Tribune*, Nov. 29, 1981, p. 1A.
3. Ibid.
4. Quoted in Phillip Goldberg, *Executive Health* (New York: McGraw-Hill, 1978), p. 113.
5. Zev Wanderer and Ericka Fabian, *Making Love Work* (New York: Ballantine Books, 1979), p. 25.
6. Ann Baker, "The Letting Go of Warren Eustis," *St. Paul Pioneer Press*, July 5, 1983, p. 3C.
7. Scott Henderson and Tudor Bostock, "Coping Behavior after Shipwreck," *British Journal of Psychiatry* 131 (1977), pp. 15-20. The authors of this article state that the vessel's name, the *Southern Star*, is a pseudonym used in order to spare the survivors any further distress.
8. Henderson and Bostock, "Coping Behavior," p. 16.
9. Rick Reilly, "Offers Pour In for Herring," *Denver Post*, July 27, 1982, p. 1.
10. Ibid.
11. Nan Robertson, "Victim Who Barely Survived Recalls Terror Toxic Shock," *Minneapolis Tribune*, Oct. 10, 1982, p. 1F.
12. Ibid.

7: GETTING BY WITH A LITTLE HELP FROM YOUR FRIENDS

1. Quoted in Alan McGinnis, *The Friendship Factor* (Minneapolis: Augsburg Press, 1979), p. 35.
2. Philip Caputo, *A Rumor of War* (New York: Holt, 1977), p. 18.
3. Alan Gartner and Frank Riessman, *Self-Help in the Human Services* (San Francisco: Jossey-Bass, 1977), p. 4.
4. Ernest Kurtz, "Why A.A. Works: The Intellectual Significance of Alcoholics Anonymous," *Journal of Studies on Alcohol* 43, no. 1 (1982), pp. 38-60.
5. The twelve traditions of Alcoholics Anonymous are:

   1. Our common welfare should come first; personal recovery depends upon an AA unit.
   2. For our group purpose, there is but one ultimate authority— a loving God as he may express Himself in our group conscience. Our leaders are but trusted servants; they do not govern.

3. The only requirement for AA membership is a desire to stop drinking.

4. Each group should be autonomous except in matters affecting other groups of AA as a whole.

5. Each group has but one primary purpose—to carry its message to the alcoholic who still suffers.

6. An AA group ought never endorse, finance or lend the AA name to any related facility or outside enterprise, lest problems of money, property and prestige divert us from our primary purpose.

7. Every AA group ought to be fully self-supporting, declining outside contributions.

8. Alcoholics Anonymous should remain forever nonprofessional, but our service centers may employ special workers.

9. AA as such, ought never be organized; but we may create service boards or committees directly responsible to those they serve.

10. Alcoholics Anonymous has no opinion on outside issues; hence, the AA name ought never be drawn into public controversy.

11. Our public relations policy is based on attraction rather than promotion; we need always to maintain personal anonymity at the level of press, radio and films.

12. Anonymity is the spiritual foundation of all our traditions, ever reminding us to place principles before personalities.

6. H. I. Marieskind and B. Ehrenreich, "Towards Socialist Medicine: The Women's Self-Help Movement," *Social Policy*, no. 6 (1975), pp. 34-42.

8: FINDING COMPETENT PROFESSIONAL HELP

1. William Fassbender, *You and Your Health* (New York: John Wiley and Sons, 1977), p. 375.
2. I am indebted to Fassbender's *You and Your Health*, pp. 374-381, for some of the ideas expressed on health quackery.
3. Paul Insel and Walton Roth, *Core Concepts in Health* (Palo Alto, CA: Mayfield Publishing Company, 1985), p. 333.
4. Fassbender, *You and Your Health*, p. 385.
5. Ibid.
6. Adapted from Marvin Levy, Mark Digman, and Janet H. Shirreffs, *Life and Health* (New York: Random House, 1984), p. 458.
7. Fassbender, *You and Your Health*, p. 376.
8. Glen R. Elliot and Carl Eisdorfer, eds., *Stress and Human Health: Analysis and Implications for Research* (New York: Springer Publishing Company, 1982), p. ix.

9. Ivan Illich, *Medical Nemesis* (New York: Bantam Books, 1976), p. 63.
10. Steven Findlay, "Our Pill Popping Defies Diagnosis," *USA Today*, Mar. 15, 1983, p. 5D.
11. Lani Luciano, "When and Where to Have Elective Surgery," *Money* 12, no. 5 (October 1983), p. 202.
12. Sidney Wolfe, "Unnecessary Surgery Wastes Lives, Money," *USA Today*, Oct. 31, 1983, p. 10A.
13. These words are an adaption of a quote taken from Carlos Castaneda, *The Teachings of Don Juan* (Berkeley, CA: University of California Press, 1968), p. 63.

9: AFFIRMING A FAITH

1. "Tomorrow," *U.S. News and World Report*, Dec. 6, 1982, p. 16.
2. "Events and People," *The Christian Century*, Jan. 27, 1982, p. 80.
3. "A Search for the Sacred," *U.S. News and World Report*, Apr. 4, 1983, p. 35.
4. Ibid., p. 38.
5. Ibid., p. 36.
6. Dag Hammarskjöld, *Markings* (New York: Knopf, 1964), p. 58.
7. Quoted in John Powell, *Unconditional Love* (Allen, TX: Argus Communications, 1978), p. 8.
8. Quoted in Henri Nouswen, *Reaching Out: The Three Movements of the Spiritual Life* (Garden City, NY: Doubleday, 1966), p. 28.
9. Barry K. Estandt, *Pastoral Counseling* (Englewood Cliffs, NJ: Prentice-Hall, 1983), p. 15.
10. Powell, *Unconditional Love*, pp. 110-114.
11. "Kareem's New Priorities," *Chicago Tribune*, May 26, 1983.
12. Neal Gendler, "Hitting Tree at 50 m.p.h. Brought Skier's Life to Full Stop Only for Time," *Minneapolis Star and Tribune*, Mar. 1, 1984, p. 14.
13. Ibid.
14. I am indebted to the Reverend Roy Phillips, minister of the Unity Church-Unitarian, in St. Paul, Minnesota, for this idea.
15. "The Insanity Plea on Trial," *Newsweek*, May 24, 1982, p. 57.
16. Ibid.
17. Jean-Paul Sartre, *No Exit and Three Other Plays* (New York: Vintage Books, 1955), p. 7.
18. Gordon Slovut, "If Stress Kills, How and Why?" *Minneapolis Star*, Oct. 27, 1980, p. 1C.
19. Jim Klobuchar, "Boy Stands Tall on One Leg, New Attitude," *Minneapolis Star and Tribune*, Apr. 16, 1982, p. 1A.
20. I am indebted to the Reverend Gretchen Fogo, Minister, Centennial United Methodist Church, St. Paul, Minnesota, for this concept.

21. Erik Erikson, *Childhood and Society* (New York: W. W. Norton and Co., 1963), pp. 247-274.

22. Howard R. Burkle, *God, Suffering and Belief* (Nashville, TN: Abingdon Press, 1977, p. 47.

23. Ibid.

24. Romans 8:35-39.

25. Claude A. Frazier, ed., *Healing and Religious Faith* (Philadelphia: Pilgrim Press, 1974), pp. 96-97.

26. Ibid.

27. Mickie Sherman, *The Leukemic Child*, prepared by the Office of Cancer Communications National Cancer Program, National Cancer Institute, Bethesda, MD 20205 (U.S. Department of Health and Human Services, National Institutes of Health Pub. 81-863, February 1981), pp. 73-74.

28. Ibid., pp. 76-77.

10: DEATH WISHES

1. John H. Hewett, *After Suicide* (Philadelphia: Westminster Press, 1980), p. 19.

2. Scott Kraft, "Pregnant at 14 Melissa Putney Found Weight of Life Too Heavy," *St. Paul Dispatch*, May 22, 1983, p. 5A.

3. Earl Grollman, *Suicide: Prevention, Intervention, Postvention* (Boston: Beacon Press, 1971), p.7.

4. A helpful book on teenage suicide is Mary Griffin and Carol Feisenthal, *A Cry for Help: Exploring and Exploding the Myths about Teenage Suicide—A Guide for Parents of Adolescents* (Garden City, NY: Doubleday, 1983). I am indebted to this resource for some of the ideas in this chapter.

5. H. G. Morgan, *Death Wishes? The Understanding and Management of Deliberate Self-Harm* (New York: John Wiley and Sons, 1984), p. 59.

6. Frederick G. Guggenheim and Myron F. Weiner, Eds., *Manual of Psychological Consultation and Emergency Care* (New York: Jason Aronson, 1984), pp. 24-25.

7. Morgan, *Death Wishes?*, pp. 58-59.

8. Griffin and Felsenthal, *Cry for Help*, p. 223.

9. Ibid., p. 218.

10. Judith Guest, *Ordinary People* (New York: Ballantine Books, 1976), p. 2.

11. Griffin and Felsenthal, *Cry for Help*, p. 60.

12. Ibid.

13. Norman Linzer, ed., *Suicide: The Will to Live vs. The Will to Die* (New York: Human Sciences Press, 1984), pp. 201-202.

14. Griffin and Felsenthal, *Cry for Help*, p. 66.

15. Jerry Jacobs, *Adolescent Suicide* (New York: Wiley-Interscience, 1971), p. 16.

16. Griffin and Felsenthal, *Cry for Help*, p. 47.
17. Ibid.
18. Sue V. Petzel and Mary Riddle, "Adolescent Suicide: Psychosocial and Cognitive Aspects," in Sherman C. Feinstein, John G. Looney, Allan Z. Schwartzberg, and Arthur D. Sorosky, *Adolescent Psychiatry: Developmental and Clinical Studies* 9 (Chicago: University of Chicago Press, 1981), pp. 343-398.
19. George Alpert and Ernest Leogrande, *Second Chance to Live: The Suicide Syndrome* (New York: DaCapo Press, 1975), p. 46.
20. Petzel and Riddle, "Adolescent Suicide," p. 346.
21. Griffin and Felsenthal, *Cry for Help*, p. 153.
22. Quoted in Corrine Leoin Hatton, Sharol McBride Valente, and Alice Rink, *Suicide: Assessment and Intervention* (New York: Appleton-Century-Crofts, 1977), p. 113.
23. Quoted in John H. Hewett, *After Suicide* (Philadelphia: Westminster Press, 1980), p. 19.
24. Linzer, *Suicide*, pp. 187-207.
25. Grollman, *Suicide*, p. 113.
26. Ibid., pp. 113-114.
27. Ibid., p. 114
28. Elaine De Figlia, "He Couldn't Live with the Pain," *USA Today*, Feb. 27, 1984, p. 10A.

11: ORDINARY HEROES

1. Marise McDermott, "Rattling Our Sense of Death," *Texas Humanist*, May-June 1984, p. 9.
2. Lance Morrow, "I Spoke as a Brother," *Time*, Jan. 9, 1984, p. 33.
3. Colman McCarthy, "The Rewards of Forgiveness," *Minneapolis Star and Tribune*, June 8, 1984, p. 6A.
4. Clark Morphew, "In Hospice Patients Find Strength to Meet Death," *St. Paul Dispatch*, Apr. 2, 1983, p. 1B.
5. Quoted in Seymour Perlin, ed., *A Handbook for the Study of Suicide* (New York: Oxford University Press, 1975), p. 58.
6. Adapted from Jim Klobuchar, "Even in Losing, the Twins Give us Something to Cheer," *Minneapolis Star and Tribune*, Sept. 30, 1984, p. 1B.
7. The description of Dorothy Peterson's life and death is based on an unpublished Christmas letter written by Linda Peterson Todd, Christmas 1982.
8. Quoted in Alan Loy McGinnis, *The Friendship Factor* (Minneapolis: Augsburg Press, 1979), p. 20.
9. Adapted from Frederick Bailes, *Hidden Power for Human Problems* (Englewood Cliffs, NJ: Prentice-Hall, 1957), p. 57.
10. Adapted from Robert Mills, "An Anatomy of Hope," *Journal of Religion and Health* 18, no. 1 (1979), pp. 49-52.

11. Aldous Huxley, *Brave New World and Brave New World Revisited* (New York: Harper Colophon Books, 1932), pp. 183-184.

12. Barrie Cassileth, Edward Lusk, Thomas Strouse, David Miller, Lorraine Brown, Patricia Cross, and Alan Tenaglia, "Psychological Status in Chronic Illness," *New England Journal of Medicine* 311, no. 8 (Aug. 23, 1984), pp. 13-17.

13. Dan Sperling, "Hope Lives on Among Gravely Ill," *USA Today*, Aug. 23, 1984, p. 1D.

14. Quoted in Father Dennis Geaney, "How to Learn to Live with Death," *U.S. Catholic*, November 1981, p. 28.

15. Adapted from John Ellis Large, *The Ministry of Healing* (New York: Morehouse-Gorhum Co., 1959), p. 21

16. Quoted in McGinnis, *The Friendship Factor*, p. 191.

Further Reading

DEATH

Becker, Ernest. *The Denial of Death*. New York: The Free Press, 1973.
Kübler-Ross, Elisabeth. *On Death and Dying*. New York: The Macmillan Co., 1969.

DEPRESSION

Burns, David D. *Feeling Good: The New Mood Therapy*. New York: Signet Books, published by New American Library, Inc., 1980.

FAITH

Kushner, Harold S. *When Bad Things Happen to Good People*. New York: Avon Press, 1983
Larson, Bruce. *There's a Lot More to Health Than Not Being Sick*. Waco, TX: Word Publishing Co., 1981.
Lewis, C. S. *The Problem of Pain*. New York: The Macmillan Co., 1962.
Peck, M. Scott. *The Road Less Traveled: A New Psychology of Love, Traditional Values and Spiritual Growth*. New York: Simon and Schuster, 1978.

FRIENDSHIP

McGinnis, Alan Loy. *Bringing Out the Best in People*. Minneapolis: Augsburg Press, 1985.

GRIEF

Bozarth-Campbell, Alla. *Life Is Goodbye-Life Is Hello: Grieving Well through All Kinds of Loss*. Minneapolis: CompCare Publications, 1982.

Colgrove, Melba, Harold H. Bloomfield, and Peter McWilliams. *How to Survive the Loss of a Love*. New York: Bantam Books, 1976.

Stearns, Ann Kaiser. *Living Through Personal Crisis*. Chicago: Thomas More Press, 1984.

Stringfellow, William. *A Simplicity of Faith: My Experience in Mourning*. Nashville: Abingdon Press, 1982.

HEALTH

DeBakey, Michael, Antony M. Gotto, Jr., Lynne Scott, and John Foreyt. *The Living Heart Diet*. New York: Raven Press/Simon and Schuster, 1984.

Wynder, Ernst L., ed. *The Book of Health: A Complete Guide to Making Health Last a Lifetime*. New York: Franklin Watts, 1981.

HELPING OTHERS

Hoff, Lee Ann. *People in Crisis*. Menlo Park. CA: Addison-Wesley Publishing Co., 1978.

Kennedy, Eugene. *Crisis Counseling*. New York: Continuum, 1984.

HOPE

Cousins, Norman. *The Healing Heart*. New York: W. W. Norton and Co., 1983.

Simonton, O. Carl, Stephanie Matthews-Simonton, and James L. Creighton. *Getting Well Again*. New York: Bantam Books, 1978.

HOSPICE CARE

Stoddard, Sandol. *The Hospice Movement: A Better Way of Caring for the Dying*. Briarcliff Manor, NY: Stein and Day/Publishers, 1978.

LOVE

Jampolsky, Gerald G. *Love Is Letting Go of Fear*. New York: Bantam Books, 1979.

Powell, John, S.J. *Unconditional Love*. Allen, TX: Argus Communications, 1978.

SUICIDE

Griffin, Mary, and Carol Felsenthal. *A Cry for Help: Exploring and Exploding the Myths about Teenage Suicide—A Guide for Parents of Adolescents*. New York: Doubleday and Co., 1983.

Linzer, Norman, ed. *Suicide: The Will to Live vs. the Will to Die*. New York: Human Sciences Press, Inc., 1984.

Peck, Michael L., Norman L. Faberow, and Robert E. Litman, eds. *Youth Suicide*. New York: Springer Publishing Co., 1985.

About the Author

Robert L. Veninga is a professor in the School of Public Health at the University of Minnesota. He has written extensively in the fields of health education and health administration and is listed in *Who's Who in Health Care*.

Dr. Veninga lives in St. Paul, Minnesota, with his wife, Karen, and their son, Brent Karl.

Learn to live with somebody... *yourself.*

16   G-14